ABI MORGAN: PLAYS ONE

Abi Morgan

PLAYS ONE

OBERON BOOKS
LONDON

WWW.OBERONBOOKS.COM

First published in 2016 by Oberon Books Ltd
521 Caledonian Road, London N7 9RH
Tel: +44 (0) 20 7607 3637 / Fax: +44 (0) 20 7607 3629
e-mail: info@oberonbooks.com
www.oberonbooks.com

A catalogue record for this book is available from the British
Library.

PB ISBN: 9781783191819
E ISBN: 9781783196807

Cover design by James Illman

Visit www.oberonbooks.com to read more about all our books
and to buy them. You will also find features, author interviews and
news of any author events, and you can sign up for e-newsletters
so that you're always first to hear about our new releases.

Contents

Introduction

'The absence is hard,' says Sister Ursula in *27,* before qualifying her statement: 'The absence of nothing is hard.' This middle-aged nun might be talking about God, but she is also giving voice to a common sentiment in this collection of Abi Morgan's plays. Again and again, Morgan constructs her narratives around losses and absences, hollow centres and negative spaces.

In *Splendour,* the earliest work published here, the absence at the heart of the play is immediately apparent. Four women are trapped together in a dictator's palace during a civil war in an unnamed Eastern European country, united only by the missing tyrant himself. Kathryn, a photojournalist, has come to take his portrait; Gilda, the local translator, has driven her there; Micheleine, the dictator's wife, waits for his return; Genevieve, her friend, was married to one of his lieutenants. Oolio - military leader, tyrant and husband - is a black hole in the heart of the drama, a centre of gravity that draws these four different women together.

The next play, *Tiny Dynamite,* is also haunted by a character we never see: the girl who was loved and lost by Lucien and Anthony, and who still binds them together, even though their lives have sharply diverged since childhood. Unlike Micheleine's brittle, forced anecdotes about Oolio, Lucien and Anthony's stories of their missing love spill out in a tumble of words. They cannot help talking about her: it's their way of keeping her alive.

In *Tender,* the half-dozen characters whose lives brush past each other in chance encounters include one of the disappeared – Marvin, who has left his marriage with Gloria to live in hostels, scratching out a living as a domestic cleaner. But where we might expect yearning for the life and loved ones he has abandoned, we don't get one. Like Anthony the drifter in *Tiny Dynamite,* Marvin sees dropping out as a renunciation, rather than a loss: he is free.

And so he resists rejoining conventional society, even when the outwardly successful but desperately lonely Nathan – who has experienced a loss of his own – tries to take him to dinner. He tells Nathan about the other men at the hostel. 'Sometimes one of them will go and cry out in the night. Sometimes I just sit, even lie next to them, hold their hand, great big men holding hands, I never thought I'd see it, not like you think, just giving people company, being almost tender and I stay with them until the morning.' Most times, he tells Nathan, the men wet the bed or wake up shouting for a drink, which jolts him awake.

'Are you happy?' asks Nathan. Marvin thinks only for a second: '...I don't think I've ever been happier in my life.'

These unexpected words exactly echo those of Anthony in *Tiny Dynamite*. 'Don't be sorry,' he tells Madeleine, the fruitseller who has disrupted his friendship with Lucien, just as the unnamed girl did many summers earlier. 'The funniest thing is I'm happy. I don't think I've ever been happier in my life.' Both Anthony and Marvin have learned that clinging on to other people doesn't bring them reassurance, or assuage their loneliness. Freedom is what brings them happiness. (And perhaps Marvin's abandoned wife, Gloria, fears his return as much as she outwardly hopes for it? She has painstakingly rebuilt her life without him, after all.)

Fittingly, the collection has its own gap – a ten-year period between 2001 and 2011, during which Morgan wrote several screenplays, including *Brick Lane* and *The Iron Lady*. The first three plays in this collection – *Splendour*, *Tiny Dynamite*, *Tender* – date from 2000-2001, and the final two, *Lovesong* and *27*, from 2011.

The temptation is, inevitably, to split the work into two distinct periods, or to look for traces of Morgan's screenwriting experience in the later plays. But that is too simplistic an approach, particularly since there is formal innovation and an awareness of the visual in the plays from the start.

Tiny Dynamite crackles with electricity, both metaphorically and literally, through the stage lighting. *Splendour* is even more formally daring: a dynamic, densely woven play. The action regularly freezes and replays from another point of view, and each actor has a soliloquy addressed directly to the audience. When I saw its revival at the Donmar Warehouse in 2015, the staging was minimalist; as directed in the text, with the muffled sound of mortars punctuating the scenes. Against this background, there were vivid, specific objects – a red vase, a Lion King DVD – as well as the unseen painting that preoccupies Kathyrn's artistic eye.

At times, *Splendour* can feel like a high-speed ballet, or perhaps a cuckoo clock with the characters on tracks, moving back and forth on predetermined grooves. Ten years later, *Lovesong* develops this idea further, in a spare text which was accompanied in its first performance by choreography from the physical theatre company Frantic Assembly. The characters – a couple who are shown at the start and end of their lives together – can touch, but not speak, across the years that separate them. As the two timeframes weave past each other, the young Margaret and old Bill and the young William and old Maggie wind around each other in the physical space of the stage. The hollow centre here is the years that pass, unseen by the audience. We see Margaret and William's hopes for the future, and we see what became of those hopes. The juxtaposition is heartbreaking. (The reviews focused heavily on the need to take a hankie to the theatre.)

In the final play in the collection, *27*, the themes of loss and absence are muted, but still present. Sister Ursula fears losing her mind, following her parents in an early decline into dementia. She also feels that the nuns' way of life itself is ebbing away, unsustainable in the modern world. 'My greatest fear is to be left, the last nun standing, remote in hand, shouting quiz answers at the TV screen,' she tells Richard, the scientist who has come to study her sisters' brains.

Love, loss, grief, absence – these are plays which are unafraid to explore emotions which are usually politely hidden. But the pathos never overwhelms you: spots of light and humour break through, even in the darkest moments.

And while the dramas here are often domestic, they are not small or insignificant. They prove the old adage: life is a series of goodbyes. As Gloria tells the pregnant Hen in Tender: 'Kids and love and electric bills aren't really that important. What's holding us together is very fragile indeed.'

Helen Lewis is deputy editor of the *New Statesman,* and writes regularly for the *Guardian*, *Sunday Times* and many other publications. She has hosted Radio 4's Week in Westminster, and is a regular guest on BBC One's *Sunday Politics*. She tweets @helenlewis

TINY DYNAMITE

Tiny Dynamite was first performed at the Traverse Theatre, Edinburgh, on 3 August 2001, with the following cast:

LUCIEN	Scott Graham
ANTHONY	Steven Hoggett
MADELEINE	Jasmine Hyde
Director	Vicky Featherstone
Co-directors	Scott Graham
	and Steven Hoggett
Designer	Julian Crouch
Lighting Designer	Natasha Chivers
Original Music and Sound	Nick Powell

Tiny Dynamite was remounted in February 2003 at the Lyric Theatre Studio, Hammersmith. The cast was as follows:

LUCIEN	Scott Graham
ANTHONY	Steven Hoggett
MADELEINE	Lesley Hart
Production Photography	Manuel Harlan

With thanks to:
Tom Morris, John McGrath and Fiona Gasper, Hetty Shand, Lyric Theatre

Characters

ANTHONY
early/mid 30s

LUCIEN
early/mid 30s

MADELEINE
early 20s

The play is set over one summer.

'I think everything has the potential to be lethal in context. A friend was living in a mobile home in Darwin during the infamous hurricane. He and his wife had to abandon their trailer and run for shelter in a nearby hotel. When they were holed up in the hotel with a lot of other people, they could hear all this thudding on the door, they didn't know if it was others trying to get in – they didn't open the door because the wind was too strong – and the next morning, when they opened the door, it was embedded with splinters and pieces of glass, pieces of straw. These normally benign things, fragile things, would've been lethal, if they had opened the door. That really stuck in my imagination, it was like that story about throwing a sandwich off the Empire State Building and cracking a paving stone – this idea of being killed by a sandwich. These ideas led to those pieces where I shot things through guns that weren't bullets, using things like pearls and money as ammunition.'

Cornelia Parker

A ROADSTOP

LUCIEN is sitting in his car.

LUCIEN: A shy boy is coming home one day through the
city he grew up in when suddenly he gets caught in a
terrible storm. Fearful of lightning and loud noises and
bad things, the shy boy shelters as best he can, forks
of lightning falling down hard around him, burning
out street lights and sparking rain on Tarmac. His best
friend, a small boy, the runt of the litter, scorns his
terror, for nothing scares him.

*ANTHONY runs on stage, carrying a bag of coffees, it's raining, he's
sheltering as he runs towards –*

The runt boy, a quirky child, always the wild card, is
already betraying the early signs of mental disease.
Above him rage the elements, all around him, striking
buildings, and sending local shopkeepers scurrying,
but the runt boy is fearless and taunts the sky. His best
friend, the shy boy of nervous disposition, pleads with
him to come and shelter. He warns if he is not careful
he will lose his life.

*LUCIEN looks up to see ANTHONY standing outside. LUCIEN winds
down the window –*

Suddenly accepting that this is the worst that can
happen to him, the runt boy decides to see if death will
come to him. The shy boy tells him to stop mucking
around it's late. Standing in a central place the runt
boy ignores him, holding out his arms, waiting for the
lightning to strike him down.

*ANTHONY is standing in the rain, looking up. He sees LUCIEN
staring and turns hurrying to the car.*

It does not. The runt boy walks home amazed at his
own good fortune, scoffing the shy boy for his lack of
courage.

As ANTHONY is about to climb into the car he notices:

Still laughing as he arrives outside his front door, the runt boy reaches up for the doorhandle.

ANTHONY slides down next to the LUCIEN, he hands him a coffee, LUCIEN takes drinks, reading the paper oblivious.

A rogue fork of lightning bounces off the letter box, catching the runt boy hard across the chest.

ANTHONY chinks his paper cup of coffee with LUCIEN.

ANTHONY: Kapow!

LUCIEN does not even look up from reading.

LUCIEN: Kapow!

They both drink oblivious.

The runt boy falls down to the ground. He is six years old. A scorch mark visible across his chest.

LUCIEN finally looks up from his paper.

ANTHONY: What you reading?

LUCIEN: Back page.

ANTHONY: Still reading the freak fucking accidents?

LUCIEN: There's no such thing as a *freak* fucking accident.

LUCIEN drinks his coffee. A young girl, MADELEINE stands hitching on the other side of the road. ANTHONY stares as if momentarily recognising her. It is as if for one moment she is there and then she's gone. Beat.

ANTHONY: So are we going?

LUCIEN: Yeah, we're going.

Beat.

ANTHONY: So, let's go.

A car door slams. A crackle of electricity.

A HOUSE

A house, LUCIEN enters carrying a box; sound of bees buzzing, geese somewhere far off.

ANTHONY follows behind him, road map and luggage in hand.

LUCIEN: You don't have to carry –

ANTHONY: I can carry a fucking suitcase.

LUCIEN: ...I can bring the luggage in.

ANTHONY takes in the room.

ANTHONY: It's nice.

LUCIEN: Yeah.

ANTHONY: There's a lake.

LUCIEN: Yeah.

ANTHONY: Where is this?

LUCIEN: It's far away. *(Beat.)* You take whichever room.

ANTHONY: You sure?

LUCIEN: Yeah, you take whichever room.

ANTHONY: This is great. There's a deck. We didn't have a deck last year.

LUCIEN: Glad you like it.

ANTHONY: The rent must be –

LUCIEN: No problem

ANTHONY: Great. Great. Light, it gets good light, makes you feel like you're outside, only inside.

LUCIEN: Anthony.

ANTHONY: *(Beat.)* Talking...talking too much.

Silence.

LUCIEN: I'll just go and get...

ANTHONY nods. LUCIEN goes to get more luggage from the car.

ANTHONY: Thanks for –

LUCIEN: …There's a bathroom. Why don't you go and –

ANTHONY nods.

ANTHONY: Do I stink?

LUCIEN nods. LUCIEN exits.

ANTHONY takes in the room. A bee buzzes around him. He doesn't move. He lets the bee buzz around him, quietly following its journey waiting until it lands in the palm of his hand.

As LUCIEN enters, he sees ANTHONY still hasn't moved.

LUCIEN: There should be towels.

ANTHONY: Right.

LUCIEN: Bathroom's probably through there. There should be a shower…a shower and a bath.

ANTHONY: Both? How clean do you want me? Lucien, this is –

LUCIEN: Good. Go and have a wash now.

ANTHONY nods, exits. LUCIEN waits, then goes to look through ANTHONY's bag. He opens it, looking in to find it empty as ANTHONY comes through, half undressed. LUCIEN stops. ANTHONY doesn't say anything. He opens his hand by the window, the sound of a bee buzzing returns as it flies away.

ANTHONY: Still had the bee in my hand.

LUCIEN nods. ANTHONY nods.

LUCIEN: It's not that I don't trust you.

ANTHONY: It's okay. I don't mind.

LUCIEN: I just thought –

ANTHONY: It's okay.

LUCIEN: We could go out for dinner later if you like.

ANTHONY shrugs. ANTHONY exits. The return of the buzz of the bee. LUCIEN swats the bee away. The buzz carries through.

A RESTAURANT

LUCIEN and ANTHONY sit looking at their menus. Low level muzak. It's pretty empty.

LUCIEN: This is great.

ANTHONY: What you having?

LUCIEN: I don't know. You made up your mind yet?

ANTHONY: I might have the meat loaf.

LUCIEN: You normally –

ANTHONY: Yeah, I'm having the meat loaf.

LUCIEN: …The shellfish is the speciality. You normally have fish.

ANTHONY: Steak, I'll have steak.

LUCIEN: Surf and turf. *(Beat.)* You get fish with that.

ANTHONY: Fish and steak?

LUCIEN: That's what they do here.

ANTHONY: Nah, I won't have that. *(Beat.)* It's pretty empty.

LUCIEN: It's not in season yet, couple of weeks and –

ANTHONY: I know when the summer is. So how's work?

LUCIEN: Good. Busy.

ANTHONY: That's good. You been promoted yet?

LUCIEN: Yeah, February.

ANTHONY: That's great, Luce. *(Beat.)* Wicked.

LUCIEN: Sit in your chair, properly Anthony.

ANTHONY: Sorry… Sorry… Back's not high enough. Nice restaurant.

LUCIEN: It was recommended. In the paper, they do recommendations on the food pages.

ANTHONY: Yeah.

LUCIEN: Reviews and stuff.

ANTHONY: Yeah, I often read the paper. I try and read a paper least once a week.

LUCIEN: That's good. That great.

ANTHONY: Don't give me an Oscar for it.

LUCIEN: I didn't mean –

ANTHONY: *(Beat.)* I read it for the cartoons mainly.

LUCIEN: They're funny.

ANTHONY: I like them.

LUCIEN: Do you read fat dog and his –

ANTHONY: …Mrs…Yeah, yeah. I really like that one.

LUCIEN: I didn't know that. I never knew that. We'll buy you your own paper if you like.

ANTHONY: My *own* paper?

LUCIEN: While we're on holiday.

ANTHONY: *That's great.*

LUCIEN: I didn't mean –

ANTHONY: *(Beat.)* I know how to carry my own suitcase. I can navigate my way out of here.

LUCIEN: I'm not saying.

ANTHONY: Don't talk down to me. Don't creep around me. Don't try and be all smiles to me. I'm not stupid, you know I'm not stupid.

LUCIEN: Anthony

ANTHONY: I know what fucking surf and turf is.

Silence.

LUCIEN: I'm sorry.

ANTHONY: *(Beat.)* I'm sorry. *(Beat.)* Let's have a nice holiday.

ANTHONY nods. LUCIEN holds up his glass. They chink.

Kapow.

ANTHONY chinks glasses with him again.

Kapow, kapow.

THE DECK

ANTHONY sits reading the newspaper on the steps, outside eating an early morning sandwich.

ANTHONY: A man is standing on the top of the Empire State Building. This is his first trip to America, a business trip on behalf of the small pharmaceutical company he works for in London England. The man is eating a sandwich delighted to be standing on top of New York's national monument looking out across a late morning skyline. He has calculated that he can finish eating his sandwich, spend a leisurely ten minutes in the gift shop buying his wife and small son an appropriate souvenir, take the lift down to the eleventh floor, descending the last ten flights of stairs and still have a good fifteen minutes to browse along the top shelf of the down town store next door and be in time for his first meeting of the day. He is proud that already he is using words like *store* instead of *shop*. He is almost a native. He looks at his watch, sees that he ought to be speeding up with his sandwich eating and then remembers that he has failed to alter his watch to cover the important time difference between the two countries; his own and America. Irritated, the man tosses the remainder of his sandwich over the side of the building, returning to his hotel for some extra hours sleep.

ANTHONY throws the tail-end of his sandwich away; a high long shot that sends the sandwich into oblivion.

A woman in the street below en route to her shift cleaning the bedrooms of an uptown hotel fails to see the sandwich falling from above. The sandwich which gathered weight with velocity struck the woman at a hundred and forty-eight mph, and cracked the paving stone below.

Slam of a van door. MADELEINE enters.

A verdict of accidental death was recorded. The sandwich was ham and egg.

Hum of bees, almost electricity.

A box of vegetables fall from above which are caught by the girl. The girl crosses the stage, carrying them.

MADELEINE: Excuse me. *(Silence.)* I brought your vegetables.

The crackle of the electricity above, ANTHONY looks up from reading then freezes on seeing her.

It's the pylon.

ANTHONY stares at her.

It's the sound of the electricity. It makes the lines vibrate. Creates a lot of static, in the atmosphere. People notice it.

ANTHONY stares at her. Silence.

Made you dream yet?

ANTHONY stares at her.

It doesn't effect everyone. *(Beat.)* Apples. You ordered apples and – *(She takes out a list and starts to read from it.)* …bananas. We couldn't get you French beans. It depends what's in season. We've put in broccoli instead.

ANTHONY: My friend does the ordering.

MADELEINE: It's the first time I've delivered to you. You've been here –

ANTHONY: Two weeks.

MADELEINE: Holiday?

ANTHONY: I've seen you –

MADELEINE: You're here on holiday?

ANTHONY: …hitching. You were hitching.

MADELEINE: Yeah. *(Beat.)* Maybe.

ANTHONY: I've seen you. *(Beat.)* I've seen you before.

Silence. ANTHONY keeps staring as MADELEINE slides the box down on the step.

MADELEINE: I need paying. *(Beat.)* Can you pay me?

ANTHONY: I don't have any money.

MADELEINE: Okay, that's fine. You can leave it till next week.

ANTHONY: You work at the restaurant. They do good steak. I didn't do the surf bit. My friend had lobster. It had good mayonnaise.

MADELEINE: Thanks.

ANTHONY: It's difficult to make. *(Beat.)* I hear. Mayonnaise.

MADELEINE: They buy it in big jars.

ANTHONY: Cheats.

MADELEINE: I don't eat there.

ANTHONY: I won't either now I know they're frauds. They really do that? They really really do that? It's disappointing. We're in the country. The land of home-made.

MADELEINE contemplates, makes to go.

My friend's the one who makes the money.

MADELEINE: Tell him he owes me –

ANTHONY: *(Offering apple.)* Do you want one?

MADELEINE: Nah, I can get them when I want. Perk of the job.

ANTHONY: How many jobs you got?

MADELEINE: Four.

ANTHONY: That's too many.

MADELEINE: Kills the time. I need the money.

ANTHONY: Four jobs is too much.

MADELEINE nods her goodbyes and makes to go.

You shouldn't hitch. *(He keeps staring at her.)* A girl shouldn't hitch. It could be dangerous.

MADELEINE: I do it all the time.

ANTHONY: You shouldn't. Anything could happen. Weirdos will pass and spy you and in their guises as friendly looking tourists and local shopkeepers, steal you away and chop you into pieces.

MADELEINE laughs.

MADELEINE: Tourists are never friendly. And the shopkeepers are never local. They come in from the city and sell tasteful shit –

ANTHONY: *(Beat.)* Don't you want the box back? *(Beat.)* What's your name?

MADELEINE takes the box from him, her hand grazes his. A long low hum, like the crackle of electricity, vibrating.

Static.

MADELEINE: Right. *(Beat.)* Must be the pylons.

ANTHONY stands up, goes to say something.

Madeleine.

LUCIEN enters, watching the scene:

ANTHONY: Anthony.

MADELEINE: And your mate's?

ANTHONY: *(Beat.)* The lobster.

MADELEINE laughs, makes to go. ANTHONY throws her an apple, she flicks one arm up, catches it without even looking.

(Calling after.) Madeleine. *(Beat.)* Nice. *(Beat.)* Have one anyway.

MADELEINE bites and exits. ANTHONY watches her as she goes.

THE HOUSE

LUCIEN enters, carrying the bags of vegetables left on the deck.

LUCIEN: You lock the door, it's a simple thing to do. I left the bloody key there, hanging.

ANTHONY: I must have not noticed –

LUCIEN: Yeah.

ANTHONY: …I just got lost walking.

LUCIEN: You have to take some responsibility. You have to pull your weight.

ANTHONY: I will.

LUCIEN: It's a mess in here. You leave the door open, food out and things get in there. They make a mess and stuff. This is outside, this is not like a city –

ANTHONY: No, the fridge would have got mugged.

LUCIEN: Don't be funny. You trying to be funny?

ANTHONY just stares at him.

Don't do that thing… Don't. That stare thing.

ANTHONY: Someone comes in and moves the stuff.

LUCIEN: No Anthony.

ANTHONY: Ants can't move chairs.

LUCIEN: It's knocked over that's all.

ANTHONY: Furniture moves across the room. Tables move right across the room. Big fucking ants that could do that –

LUCIEN: I reckon you do it. I reckon you do it in your sleep.

ANTHONY: And it's not just today. It's not just if I leave the door open.

LUCIEN: There are wild cats, they probably get in –

ANTHONY: No –

LUCIEN: Chairs don't move on their own. There's food gone. Someone's eating the food at night.

ANTHONY: Exactly.

LUCIEN: You're eating the food at night.

ANTHONY: I eat during the day.

LUCIEN: I find stuff. I find jars open, cereal boxes ripped apart.

ANTHONY: It isn't me. It isn't.

Silence.

LUCIEN: I don't care if it is. The way you live your life, the way… You're not in circulation. It's not surprising you forget these things. I leave the key by the door.

ANTHONY: I know how to do these things.

LUCIEN: When was the last time you locked up? When was the last time you even had a front door, Anthony?

ANTHONY: I'm grateful.

LUCIEN: Don't be grateful. Find a method. Find a series of buzzwords in your head that will give a bit of order to your day. Going out. Lock door. Key. By door. Lock. Exit. Enjoy.

ANTHONY: You pick me up. You pick me up and you bring me here and I know that, I appreciate that.

LUCIEN: You don't have to appreciate that. *(Beat.)* You just have to get well.

Silence.

ANTHONY: What's outside, Lucien?

LUCIEN: Trees. Wild cats. They won't harm you. The sound of water, the lake. That hum. Insects, lots of insects.

ANTHONY: I see shadows.

LUCIEN: It's just the trees.

ANTHONY: They cut across me at night, they wake me.

LUCIEN: You have a tree right outside your window.

ANTHONY: Shadows that find me in every corner.

LUCIEN: Sleep on the sofa. I don't mind, we can swap rooms if you like.

ANTHONY: Chairs don't move by themselves, Lucien.

LUCIEN: They're not moving.

ANTHONY: Tables don't fall over.

LUCIEN: They're right in the morning.

ANTHONY: You pick them up. You get up early and you pick them up. Am I right? *(Beat.)* I'm right. *(Silence.)* You know something Lucien, how long have we been doing this?

LUCIEN: What?

ANTHONY: This.

LUCIEN: A while. A long time.

Silence.

ANTHONY: And we never talk about her…

LUCIEN: *(Beat.)* Just get well, Anthony.

ANTHONY: You talk as if you don't want to see her again. As if she isn't –

LUCIEN: She isn't.

ANTHONY: We don't know that.

LUCIEN: If she's alive, Anthony, how does she come to you as a ghost?

ANTHONY: People can haunt you, dead or alive.

MADELEINE enters carrying a bunch of flowers.

Someone's coming for dinner.

LUCIEN does not dare to turn and look. ANTHONY stares at MADELEINE.

LUCIEN: Now you tell me.

ANTHONY: Luce.

LUCIEN: Yes.

ANTHONY: *(Beat.)* I think you'll like her.

MADELEINE holds out the flowers. LUCIEN reaches out to take them from her, as if seeing her for the first time.

THE HOUSE

ANTHONY is laying the table for supper, placing the fork down on the table. LUCIEN is pouring MADELEINE a drink. MADELEINE puts the flowers in a vase.

ANTHONY: I run really fast and then it touches me –
Kapow! Right there on my – There…bounced from

there to there – Kapow! Kapow! Like a fork, like a fork coming out the sky.

From above a fork comes flying down. ANTHONY catches it, without even looking.

MADELEINE: You must have been…

LUCIEN: We were six –

ANTHONY: Nearly seven. And I'm standing there and it's raining. *(To LUCIEN.)* Wasn't it? It was really wet my boots. *(To LUCIEN.)* Weren't they?

LUCIEN: …They were overflowing –

ANTHONY: …overflowing with water. Which is dangerous. Water and electricity you can see its –

MADELEINE: You're bacon. You are potentially bacon.

ANTHONY: Exactly. She gets this. Do you see this girl gets this? I'm standing there and I'm like, *Come on, hit me then.* And nothing, nothing, I don't get hit or nothing so shy boy here says –

LUCIEN: I wanted to, I wanted to get home.

ANTHONY: Shy boy's all moody and I'm running and laughing ahead of him, nothing's going to get me, so we get to my front door and –

MADELEINE: I know what you are going to say. I know what you're going to say.

ANTHONY: It's like the worst –

LUCIEN: It's like the worst place –

ANTHONY: The worst place I could be standing. Lightning, bam! On the front door and then, Kapow – I'm six and it hits me, Kapow on the chest just like that –

MADELEINE: Jesus.

Silence.

ANTHONY: It's funny.

Silence.

MADELEINE: Freaky.

ANTHONY: I had a scorch mark –

LUCIEN: It was a big mother of a scorch mark.

ANTHONY: Right across, didn't I?

LUCIEN: Yep.

ANTHONY: Right across my chest.

Silence. MADELEINE doesn't react.

MADELEINE: Amazing.

ANTHONY: Do you want, do you want some more to drink? *(Scooping up her glass.)* He thinks it was the rubber.

MADELEINE: I'm fine.

ANTHONY: I'll get you a top up. He swears it was the rubber in my boots. *(To LUCIEN.)* We've got another bottle?

LUCIEN nods.

MADELEINE: Must have been –

ANTHONY: A miracle. *(To LUCIEN.)* Wasn't it?

LUCIEN: Definitely touched.

ANTHONY: He's the cynic here.

MADELEINE: I think it's a miracle.

ANTHONY: *(Bowing to MADELEINE.)* Thank you…Thank you…

ANTHONY exits into the kitchen. Silence. The crackle and hum of early evening sounds outside.

LUCIEN: Anthony says you –

MADELEINE: I'm just passing through. I work these places in the summer.

LUCIEN: And in the winter –

MADELEINE: I move on. Wherever. I like to keep on the move. Whatever brings the money in.

Silence.

LUCIEN: I don't want to think what he's doing in there –

MADELEINE: You work? I see you brought your work –

Silence. MADELEINE and LUCIEN look at one another.

LUCIEN: It's boring.

MADELEINE shrugs.

Risk assessment. I assess the risk to small companies. Mainly the young start-ups. I work out what they must look out for, the potential pitfalls professionally and financially.

MADELEINE looks at him. Silence.

It's boring. Desk bound. *(Beat.)* Do you always –

MADELEINE: What?

LUCIEN: …ask so many questions?

MADELEINE: I only asked the one.

Silence.

LUCIEN: He talks a lot. Some people find it difficult. He's always been a live wire. I don't mind it. You get used to it. It's what makes up him.

A crash from the kitchen. Silence. LUCIEN gets up to exit into the kitchen.

MADELEINE: Why do you let him tell that story –

LUCIEN stops midway.

…if you don't believe it?

LUCIEN: It's not that I don't believe it. It's just not freak. There's a logic. If you asses it, the logic. There's always a logic, you can always find logic for accidental events.

MADELEINE: I don't think that's true.

LUCIEN: We are all a kind of semi-conductor. The best place to stand with intense meteorological activity, namely lightning, is a wide open place. The safest place. By confining himself within the width of a metal porch, Anthony placed himself within a perfect circuit – Lightning. Letterbox. Chest. Kapow. The rubber acts as a simple circuit break.

MADELEINE: So where does that leave miracle? Miracles don't have logic, that's what makes them miracles.

Silence.

LUCIEN: We were six, we were only six years old.

MADELEINE: Miracles –

LUCIEN: No.

MADELEINE: …miracles can happen.

LUCIEN: No.

Silence.

MADELEINE: It's a good story.

LUCIEN: It's a good story. He likes telling it. I like hearing it. That's all that matters. *(Beat.)* You weren't there.

MADELEINE shrugs, smiles.

He lost someone. I'm kind to him. Someone he loved very much. I'm perhaps kind to him, kinder than I would be –

Another crash from the kitchen. LUCIEN turns, tenses –

MADELEINE: I got it wrong.

Silence.

I'm sorry.

LUCIEN stares at her. Too long.

LUCIEN: He's an accident waiting to happen.

MADELEINE wets the rim of her glass. A long low hum.

You look ... you look like someone we used to know.

A crackle of electricity. ANTHONY enters.

Sense that the evening has moved on – More relaxed. Laughter. Scene springs back into life. A crackle of electricity. Sense that the evening has moved on further – More relaxed. Laughter. MADELEINE is mid drinking game. LUCIEN is clearly wilting –

ANTHONY: Hello Harry it is Harry...

MADELEINE: Then you've got to say who's Harry?

ANTHONY: He's too pissed. I tell you, I've never seen you so pissed.

LUCIEN: *Hello Harry. It's Harry.* I don't get this game.

MADELEINE: *(Laughing.)* It doesn't matter.

ANTHONY: *Hello Harry. It's Harry. Can you tell Harry, that Harry wants him? (Finishes several drinks with certain aplomb.)*

LUCIEN: I don't get it. I still don't get it.

MADELEINE insists on pouring them another round. A crackle of electricity. Sense that the evening has moved on further – More relaxed. Mellow. They're lying flat on their backs, as if staring up at the stars.

ANTHONY: *Fuck you, you mother fucker.*

MADELEINE: Where?

ANTHONY: *(Pointing up to the stars.)* If you join the three witches with that plough bit.

MADELEINE: I can't see it.

LUCIEN: He's dyslexic.

ANTHONY: *(Pointing up to the stars.)* She's beautiful and we love her.

MADELEINE: Where?

ANTHONY sits up, looking at MADELEINE.

I can't see it.

ANTHONY: Don't you think she is, Lucien?

MADELEINE: You two ... you two are pulling my leg.

LUCIEN: We've drunk too much.

ANTHONY: You've drunk too much.

LUCIEN: Anthony, watch yourself, eh?

ANTHONY: Hear him? We've not drunk near enough.

A crackle of electricity. Sense that the evening has moved on further – Fun. Madness. ANTHONY suddenly pouncing on MADELEINE, a water bottle in his hand, sending shots of water, squirting out of his mouth.

MADELEINE: You've soaked me. You've soaked me.

MADELEINE sinks back down but is up again when – LUCIEN comes through also squirting water.

You're meant to be on my side. Jesus. Jesus.

MADELEINE gulps from her bottle of water and then she drenches both LUCIEN and ANTHONY who run, screaming away. A crackle of electricity. Sense that the evening has moved on further – Fun. More madness. A bee is buzzing around ANTHONY. He stands mouth open until – He closes his mouth. The buzzing grows silent.

MADELEINE: If it stings –

LUCIEN: Yes.

MADELEINE: If it stings, it will make your tongue swell.

LUCIEN: *(Beat.)* Anthony. *(Beat.)* Anthony, please.

A sense of suspended silence until – ANTHONY opens his mouth. The buzzing resumes and flies away.

ANTHONY: He hates it when I do that.

MADELEINE: It's magic.

LUCIEN: It's stupid.

ANTHONY: He's always like this.

LUCIEN: If you get stung –

MADELEINE: Do you put something on your tongue?

ANTHONY ruffles LUCIEN's hair.

ANTHONY: I didn't so we're fine.

LUCIEN: I'm just saying.

MADELEINE: *(To LUCIEN.)* Have another drink. Go on. You're on holiday.

LUCIEN holds up his glass.

ANTHONY: See, see she's good for us.

MADELEINE and LUCIEN are staring up at ANTHONY who is trying to climb the pylon.

LUCIEN: Get down you bloody nutter.

MADELEINE: Anthony, come down.

ANTHONY: I will now prove my theory. That man cannot fly unaided.

ANTHONY jumps and goes crashing to the ground, landing flat on the floor. LUCIEN and MADELEINE run to pick ANTHONY up. ANTHONY lies very still. A growing panic until ANTHONY sits up and plants kisses on both LUCIEN and MADELEINE.

My point indeed proved.

A crackle of electricity. Sense that the evening has moved on further – The early hours of the morning.

MADELEINE: And sometimes I think this will be the place. This will be the place. I stop. I stay.

A crackle of electricity. Sense that the evening has moved on further – Dawn. Mellow. A little dangerous. MADELEINE, LUCIEN and

ANTHONY lie on their backs staring up at the early morning sunrise. Suddenly all the lights go out, distant music goes silent.

It's the cinema screen, they put up a cinema screen, it drains the electricity. You can be half way through cooking your dinner and that's it, stops for the night. Like there's not enough electricity, there's not enough power to go round then suddenly you get that surge. –

Silence.

(Pointing to stars.) Time for bed.

ANTHONY: *(Pointing to stars.)* Not yet.

Silence.

LUCIEN: *(Pointing to stars.)* Stay here if you want to.

MADELEINE stops, about to get up.

MADELEINE: Where does it say that?

ANTHONY: Yeah, where does it say that?

LUCIEN: Sorry. I thought it was a star. Aeroplane.

ANTHONY: That fucks up your whole sentence. *(Beat.)* Stay here if you want to.

Silence.

MADELEINE: *So who do I sleep with?*

Silence. MADELEINE laughs. LUCIEN and ANTHONY get up. They stand awkwardly.

Night.

MADELEINE exits, laughing.

ANTHONY: Night.

Silence. They linger.

(To LUCIEN.) Great girl.

LUCIEN: Great girl.

LUCIEN nods. He scoops up the glasses and heads inside.

Door?

ANTHONY: Lock.

LUCIEN: Progress.

The cross beam of headlights as MADELEINE *hitches a lift home.* ANTHONY *stares as if watching her.*

THE LAKE

MADELEINE *lies on a pontoon, flat on her back, reading from a newspaper.* LUCIEN *dries himself post swim.* ANTHONY *lounges next to them, sunbathing.*

MADELEINE: A woman was out to lunch with her husband celebrating their twenty-fifth wedding anniversary, delighted with the pearl necklace he had just given her. *(To* LUCIEN *and* ANTHONY.*)* Yeah right.

LUCIEN: What's funny about that?

ANTHONY: He's such an innocent.

MADELEINE: You don't know what a pearl necklace is?

ANTHONY: It's like giving a girl a golden shower, without the wee wee.

Silence.

LUCIEN: I still don't get it.

ANTHONY: *(To* MADELEINE.*)* Shall I go on with this?

MADELEINE: Protect him.

ANTHONY: Protect him.

LUCIEN: Tell me.

ANTHONY: Best not.

MADELEINE: However as the lunch progressed, it became clear that this was not a time of celebration, the husband asked his wife for a divorce. The man had fallen in love and planned to marry his very elegant female boss as soon as his rather frumpy wife agreed. A heated argument ensued spilling to outside the restaurant, the wife furious to learn of her husband's infidelity. In a moment's rage the wife clawed at the pearls around her neck, preparing to throw them back in his face. Pulling them with such a velocity, they fired like bullets through the air.

LUCIEN: God, I get it. That's disgusting. Is that what a pearl necklace is?

ANTHONY: It can be pleasurable.

LUCIEN: I don't want to know.

MADELEINE: A young man en route to work, and busy talking on the telephone to his therapist, was momentarily distracted by the site of a pearl flying across his eyeline. The young man walked into a tree and promptly snapped his neck.

The sound of trees, a branch snapping in the woods.

(Turning to LUCIEN.) It's kind of sick.

ANTHONY: It's his porn.

LUCIEN: It's not my porn.

ANTHONY: For the anal and insane. He likes to decode them. He gets bored. He gets bored, very easily.

LUCIEN: It's my job. Some of these are classic.

ANTHONY sinks back onto the pontoon.

Don't you see these are classic?

ANTHONY: Some bored tea boy with fuck all to do all day. *(Beat.)* His grammar's shite.

MADELEINE: The therapist continued talking for a full thirty-two seconds before noticing her client had grown silent. The husband recovered thirty-nine of the forty-seven dropped pearls. Eight are still not accounted for.

ANTHONY: Freaky. *(To MADELEINE.)* Watch and learn, this is how you argue –

LUCIEN: I'm not going to argue.

ANTHONY: *(To MADELEINE.)* You ready? Because it is coming.

MADELEINE: What?

ANTHONY: A full grown woman –

LUCIEN: Here we go again.

ANTHONY: ... can't be killed by a sandwich.

LUCIEN: If she's standing –

ANTHONY: Even if she's standing –

LUCIEN: ... in the wrong place at the right time. A sandwich could hit her. Trigger a heart attack.

ANTHONY: A penny maybe. A penny if dropped could kill you.

LUCIEN: Height plus velocity equals mass... Doesn't matter what size it is, if dropped from a large height, it gathers speed, passes through time, builds momentum, gathers mass and –

MADELEINE: A sandwich is tiny, a sandwich is a soft thing –

LUCIEN: Height plus velocity, it gathers momentum. The softest things can –

MADELEINE: A soft thing can't kill you.

LUCIEN: If dropped from the right height can have an effect. *(Beat.)*

ANTHONY: Okay, you could die but it's pretty fucking freaky. Passing at the exact moment –

LUCIEN: It's science, it's pure science. There's nothing freak about it.

MADELEINE: Being killed by a flying sandwich I think is pretty strange.

LUCIEN: It's the cause that means it's not freak, as long as there is a cause, one can always find the science for the effect. A man is unfaithful – cause. His wife rages breaking her necklace – effect. A pearl goes flying – cause, it distracts a man who breaks his neck – effect.

ANTHONY: A woman with a crooked nose –

Silence. LUCIEN does not stir.

A woman with a crooked nose and funny hair jumps from a bridge.

Silence.

LUCIEN: Which bridge?

Silence.

Height is important.

ANTHONY: *(Cutting in.)* It doesn't really matter.

MADELEINE: Was this in the paper?

ANTHONY: There's water underneath.

LUCIEN: I don't want to play this.

ANTHONY: Where's the cause? *(Beat.)* Where's the cause, Lucien?

Silence.

LUCIEN: The jump.

ANTHONY: That's the effect.

LUCIEN holds ANTHONY's gaze.

LUCIEN: She fell.

ANTHONY: Still has to be a cause. If there's no cause, I'd say that was a freak fucking accident.

LUCIEN: She didn't jump.

ANTHONY: If she jumped it's a fucking tragedy.

Silence.

MADELEINE: Is it in a back copy?

MADELEINE searches through the newspapers –

ANTHONY: No.

MADELEINE: It's an actual true story?

Silence. LUCIEN is clearly struggling. ANTHONY goes to touch him.

ANTHONY: It's a miracle.

MADELEINE: Where's the miracle?

LUCIEN: Yeah, Anthony, where's the miracle?

LUCIEN holds ANTHONY's look.

ANTHONY: The miracle is ... she's still alive.

LUCIEN suddenly gets up, MADELEINE stops searching.

LUCIEN: I might have a swim.

ANTHONY: A boat. A boat sailing underneath breaks her fall. I might come with you.

LUCIEN: No, why don't you stay? Why don't you stay and talk to Madeleine?

ANTHONY stands as if to stop LUCIEN, wanting to reach out and touch him in some way.

I won't be a minute.

ANTHONY continues almost to bar LUCIEN's path.

Stay. I just want to swim. Okay?

LUCIEN swims off.

Silence.

MADELEINE: Is there something I'm missing?

Silence.

ANTHONY: Do you know the San Francisco Golden Gate is not the biggest bridge?

ANTHONY watches LUCIEN swim away.

It's a bridge somewhere in China.

MADELEINE: I didn't know that.

ANTHONY: Yeah, people often make the mistake.

Silence.

The second's somewhere in Asia, one of the Arab states. They've got a lot of money. They can afford the bricks.

Silence.

MADELEINE: What just happened there?

ANTHONY: Lucien? That's just Lucien. He doesn't talk about stuff.

MADELEINE: Not talking –

ANTHONY: That's what I tell him –

MADELEINE: Not talking is bad for you.

Silence.

Do you do this, do you two come away together like this a lot?

ANTHONY shrugs, still looking out for LUCIEN.

ANTHONY: This holiday. This little trip. It's part of a routine. He picks me up, he cleans me up, gets my hair cut, buys me new clothes. I tell him. I say – *I don't care what I wear.* He gives me money. He tells me not to spend it too quick. I say – *I won't.* I always do. I don't mean to let him down. I think he feels I let him down. Last time he found me licking the pavement. He thinks I've lost hope. I just like the taste.

ANTHONY sees MADELEINE looking at him.

We get through it. Normally. He feels better. I look good as new. *(Silence.)* Don't be sorry for me.

ANTHONY looks out as if searching for LUCIEN.

The funniest thing is I'm happy. I don't think I've ever been happier in my life.

Silence.

MADELEINE: She's someone you knew.

ANTHONY holds her look. MADELEINE goes to touch him.

Can I do something? Is there anything I can do to help?

Static. She pulls her hand back –

ANTHONY: I don't know yet. I'm not sure yet. Miracles don't work like that.

Suddenly from under the pontoon, LUCIEN bursts up out of the water, gasping for breath.

LUCIEN: Did you see me? Wow, did you see me?

MADELEINE keeps staring at ANTHONY.

ANTHONY: *(Beat.)* No. You vanished.

MADELEINE keeps staring at ANTHONY.

You completely disappeared.

THE DECK

ANTHONY sitting in the last of the sun, oblivious to bees buzzing around him, reading the newspaper. LUCIEN sits working.

The crackle of the electricity pylon above.

ANTHONY: A farmer and his younger brother decided to remove a bees' nest from a shed on their property with the aid of a pineapple, an illegal firework more appropriately used for large displays, with the explosive equivalent of one half stick of dynamite. They light the fuse and retreat to watch from a window inside their home ten feet away from the hive-stroke-shed. The ricochet of the explosion though successfully destroying the bees nest, shatters the glass, leaving the brother with slight grazes which the farmer decides need medical attention at once. Whilst waiting for the brother in casualty, the farmer is hungry and decides to walk to the local fruit store. Choosing a peach from a large display in the shop window, he purchases and walks back in the midday sun. The farmer takes a bite of his peach en route. A lazy bee is dozing on its skin. The farmer is stung three times by the insect and immediately collapses. An ambulance is called. Unbeknownst to either the farmer or the brother, both are allergic to the venom of the bee. In casualty for the second time that day the farmer dies. The brother, in mourning, asks for the gloves that the farmer once wore. The brother goes home to tell his wife of the farmer's death, unaware that a bee, still alive, is sleeping in the finger of the glove. Bracing himself to go in and tell the news of the farmer's death, the brother slips on the gloves as a tribute to times gone.

ANTHONY pauses, he slowly starts to rip the page. LUCIEN tries to ignore him.

Fortunately the glove has a small hole in the index finger, a hole that he was sure had never been there before. The bee flies away just as the brother is slipping on the glove. The brother is amazed and sees life anew. He begins to throw parties, he invites in the neighbours, gives them free steaks for life and rogers his wife for the first time in ages, a woman who had forgotten what a good shag was.

A long low drone of car horns in the distance, making ANTHONY jump, turn suddenly as –

LUCIEN: They're too noisy with their cars.

ANTHONY: People are celebrating. It's summer, people do that.

LUCIEN: You don't drive. Cars are for driving, not public holidays.

ANTHONY: I'm glad I don't drive.

LUCIEN: You used to.

ANTHONY: Exactly.

LUCIEN: It makes a life a lot easier. You can always get away.

ANTHONY: You never leave the city.

LUCIEN: You always say this.

ANTHONY: ... a few weeks in the summer? Yeah, right, Luce, let your hair down.

LUCIEN: If you drove I wouldn't have to do everything.

ANTHONY: Like what?

LUCIEN: Like the shopping?

ANTHONY: You get it delivered.

LUCIEN: I'm just saying.

ANTHONY: Why?

LUCIEN: It means I have to do it all.

LUCIEN returns to his work. He clocks the box of vegetables.

Did Madeleine –

ANTHONY: *(Shakes head.)* Bloke, her day off. She's great isn't she?

LUCIEN: Who?

ANTHONY: Madeleine.

LUCIEN: You fall in love with –

ANTHONY: No.

LUCIEN: ... women on adverts. Women we passed on the way here.

ANTHONY: No. She's –

LUCIEN: Very attractive. You want to fuck her?

ANTHONY: No. *(Beat.)* Yes but –

LUCIEN: You want to fuck her.

ANTHONY: I don't see ... I really don't see anything wrong in that.

LUCIEN: You wouldn't.

ANTHONY: What you getting at?

Silence.

What you getting at?

Silence.

MADELEINE passes placing a punnet of strawberries in LUCIEN's hands. He looks up, oblivious.

LUCIEN: Did you order strawberries?

ANTHONY shakes his head. The distant toot of horns, a celebration far off –

ANTHONY: I was thinking. I was thinking I might go out tonight.

The crackle of the electricity above moving into a long low hum.

THE WOOD

The glow of a cinema screen down on –

LUCIEN, ANTHONY and MADELEINE sitting looking up. ANTHONY keeps standing up, wanting to move closer to the screen.

LUCIEN: Quit doing that –

ANTHONY: The quality –

LUCIEN: ... the people behind can't see.

ANTHONY: ...is fucking abysmal.

LUCIEN: He's an authority.

MADELEINE laughs.

He is now an authority on the cinema screen.

MADELEINE: They hire it locally. It's normally for Karaoke.

LUCIEN: We're not in the city.

ANTHONY: *(Shouting.)* Everyone has heard of DVD?

Silence. The muffled soundtrack. ANTHONY stands up again.

LUCIEN: You're making it impossible –

ANTHONY: It's impossible to see.

LUCIEN: It's meant to be a bit blurry. It's underwater.

ANTHONY: This film is ancient.

MADELEINE: Anthony sit down. I'm enjoying it.

ANTHONY: *(Sits down.)* Sorry. Okay. Fine.

Silence. The muffle of the soundtrack.

(To MADELEINE.) But I am right aren't I?

MADELEINE tries not to laugh.

LUCIEN: Anthony –

ANTHONY: Sorry, okay. Sorry.

Silence. The muffle of the soundtrack.

(Beat.) I think it's absolutely wonderful. This film is an absolute delight.

LUCIEN: I'm going to hammer you.

ANTHONY: *(To MADELEINE.)* This is the moment I've been waiting for.

LUCIEN: Are you going to shut up? You're being a fucking arse now. People are getting pissed off.

They fight.

MADELEINE: Will you two cut it out?

They stop fighting.

Silence. The muffle of the soundtrack.

ANTHONY lets out a long fart.

They fight.

How old are you two? Will you stop it?

LUCIEN concedes, but ANTHONY is still going. He starts dancing, performing, acting out the movie, it's moving from funny to verging on the weird.

Anthony… Anthony. What you doing what you doing?

LUCIEN: Anthony.

ANTHONY stops. Silence. LUCIEN sinks back to watching the film.

ANTHONY: What?

LUCIEN: You just always take it too far.

ANTHONY: Nobody asked you to come.

ANTHONY sinks back down. MADELEINE shifts to make room for him.

Jesus. Who asked you, eh?

LUCIEN's gaze flicks to MADELEINE, ANTHONY clocks this, realises –

Silence.

ANTHONY leans over and punches LUCIEN in the arm; hard. LUCIEN flinches but doesn't take his eyes off from watching the cinema screen.

Silence.

LUCIEN: I'll get us something to drink.

A long low hum, crickets, sounds of the night through –

A ROADSTOP

LUCIEN is standing, having just bought bottles of beer. He turns and sees MADELEINE standing, facing him. The beam of car headlights, as cars go past.

MADELEINE: I thought you might need a hand –

LUCIEN shrugs –

It's nearly the intermission.

MADELEINE takes her beer. They stand and drink.

LUCIEN: He's sometimes weird like that. People don't always get him. He's harmless. But I can see he could be frightening.

MADELEINE: No.

LUCIEN: Good.

Silence.

MADELEINE: You don't talk much.

LUCIEN: Enough. *(Beat.)* Has Anthony said something. You've probably noticed... He likes you. He doesn't mean to be an idiot. Be careful with him.

MADELEINE: He's not going to break. *(Silence.)* He's a grown man.

LUCIEN: Hardly. Sometimes he frightens people.

MADELEINE: I'm not frightened.

LUCIEN: Good…good…

LUCIEN makes to go.

MADELEINE: Lucien –

LUCIEN stops –

I had a dream last night –

The steady cross beam of passing headlights.

LUCIEN: Yeah?

MADELEINE: Yeah. *(Beat.)* You were in it. You and Anthony. I think we'd been drinking. We were drinking but no I wasn't, I didn't feel, I didn't feel drunk.

LUCIEN: Teetotal dreams. They never work.

MADELEINE half laughs. Silence.

MADELEINE: It's dark, night. I'm walking up this road, it's really busy. Cars are dodging me, it's like they're weaving to miss me –

LUCIEN: They would.

MADELEINE: Yeah… It's this blur of red and white, back and forth. I've no shoes on, I'm laughing – I don't know why I find it so funny. Cars are swaying, like drunks in the road. I feel really cold.

LUCIEN: You don't feel temperature, you can't really feel temperature in your dream.

MADELEINE: I wasn't wearing anything. I don't wear anything in bed –

Silence.

LUCIEN: Right. *(Silence.)* It would be it.

MADELEINE: I was cold. I'm on a bridge. It's a bridge, any moment now, there'll be a flying sandwich eh?

LUCIEN: Yeah.

MADELEINE: And that's when I turn and see you. Looking at me. And I'm not laughing. I'm crying. I wake up and I'm crying. You said something to me. In my dream that – when I wake up I'm crying. I don't know what you say but – I think I jumped. I think I jumped.

LUCIEN puts out his hand as if almost to catch her. She looks at him as he holds both her arms.

The sound of the intermission music kicking in far off –

It's not me who's frightened is it? *(Silence.)* Is it?

Silence.

THE LAKE

Darkness. Laughter far off. The glow of a cinema screen across the lake. ANTHONY *and* LUCIEN *stand dripping wet. Distant sound of* MADELEINE *jumping.* ANTHONY *and* LUCIEN *both watch in suspended silence until* MADELEINE *comes up. They cheer and clap. She enters dripping.*

ANTHONY: Your turn.

LUCIEN: I'm not good at –

ANTHONY pushes him. Sound of LUCIEN falling, suspended silence until –

Sound of LUCIEN coming up.

MADELEINE: *(Calling out.)* You have to swim the whole length.

ANTHONY: *(Calling out.)* The whole length. We're watching you.

Silence. MADELEINE and ANTHONY slump down on the ground.

He's too slow. I like it here.

MADELEINE: I get restless. It's the darkness, the stillness.

They listen.

It's fine in the summer but – Soon they'll have the highest rainfall this side of – Whatever. It gets wet. Summer over. You don't want to get used to it. Get used to it. Then see how you feel. If I get used to it, then I die.

ANTHONY: Drama queen.

They listen.

I like it. I quite like it.

They listen.

There's wild cats. It's never still with wildcats moving around.

MADELEINE: Who told you that?

ANTHONY: Lucien said –

MADELEINE: Cats… There are probably a few cats in the wood. And foxes eating from the bins, getting into people's houses.

Dots of lights above them. ANTHONY bends low.

Fireflies.

ANTHONY and MADELEINE watch as they skim the water. ANTHONY nods.

ANTHONY: Fireflies.

They watch the lake. Distant sounds of the cinema, water, trees.

MADELEINE: Where would you like to be?

ANTHONY: Now?

MADELEINE: In five years' time.

A firefly skims close. MADELEINE moves as if watching it.

ANTHONY: I don't think about that. Wherever.

MADELEINE: Somewhere. It has to be somewhere.

Silence.

ANTHONY: I'd like to love someone. I'd like to love someone I guess. I'd like to be living – I don't know if it will be a house. Maybe somewhere on the…South China sea. We might have children. I'll probably have a job by then.

MADELEINE: With a suit.

ANTHONY: Not a suit.

Silence.

Flip flops and a snorkel.

Silence.

And I'll be… I'll be better by then

A second firefly skims close.

Jesus did you see that one?

MADELEINE keeps watching him. Fireflies gradually start to land on him through the following –

MADELEINE: And where will Lucien be?

ANTHONY: In a tiny box, very high up, screwing his secretary.

MADELEINE: I hope not.

ANTHONY: With a weight problem and a hernia, somewhere painful, from all the stress.

Silence.

MADELEINE: Maybe I should take your seat back.

Silence.

ANTHONY: Sure. I'll deliver vegetables. That sounds great. I'd like that. Only Lucien wouldn't let me go.

Silence.

MADELEINE: You sure it's not the other way around?

Silence.

Does Lucien have someone, does Lucien have anyone back home?

Silence.

ANTHONY: In the city?

MADELEINE nods.

Lucien. No. No. No one would have him.

Silence.

He lost someone.

MADELEINE: He did?

ANTHONY: He thinks I don't appreciate. I do. I do. I know how much she meant to him.

Silence.

You know he has this flat, where everything is very neat?

MADELEINE: You're glowing.

ANTHONY: He's anal. He's really very anal.

ANTHONY is slowly glowing brighter through the following.

He's window boxes, and books, and a really too comfy sofa. He comes home every night on time. He has pictures on his wall. He has toilet cleaner and a loo brush.

MADELEINE: Anthony –

ANTHONY: Sometimes when he's found me I've cacked in my pants. I've been living off liquid. I'm lying in the gutter.

Silence.

I'm fine. I'm doing fine.

In the distance, LUCIEN calling –

He's the one I worry about.

LUCIEN calling, closer now.

LUCIEN: *(Calling out.)* Here I come.

MADELEINE stands astonished, as ANTHONY stands aglow with fireflies. He reaches out to touch her as –

ANTHONY: I'm only telling you –

As LUCIEN heaves himself up on the deck, pausing on seeing.

He's the weirdo.

ANTHONY his head glowing then suddenly – LUCIEN watches amazed as one last firefly hovers around ANTHONY's head. ANTHONY holds LUCIEN's gaze.

THE HOUSE

A beam of headlights, across LUCIEN. He is alone.

LUCIEN: A woman – *(Beat.)* …a woman with a crooked nose – *(Beat.)* …a woman with a crooked nose and a voice, a low, gasping voice met her friends on a bridge for a day out; two boys, now men, she had known for years. The three friends, the three points of the same triangle, spent the day together reminiscing over times gone by and a friendship which had weathered most things in their relatively short lives. The two men laughed at her life, unsuspecting that she had a surprise for them. Returning to the bridge that evening, the woman informed them that she intended to take her life. The woman, who was not drunk at the time and who had in fact matched her friends' many alcoholic beverages with the clarity of water, knew her mind. Stepping into the road, she weaved her way in amongst the speeding traffic, ignoring the childish laughter and drunken grasps of her two friends, who should have known better. *(Beat.)* Should have known. *(Beat.)* Standing with her arms out, ready to take the approaching juggernaut, the two friends were quickly sobered to the idea that this was indeed a woman of her word. They pulled her out of the way. Congratulating themselves as heroes what the two failed to recognise was that the woman was more determined that they thought. Climbing over the railings of the metal bridge, the quieter of the two, the shy boy moved forward to stop her and it was then that she asked the fateful question – *Who loves me? Who loves me the most?* The shy boy knew what was in his heart and that is what she needed to hear. But he also knew the truth would hurt the runt boy – Kapow – kapow. She fell… She fell.

The slam of the door – ANTHONY comes out, his wet costume in his hand which he slings on the side.

ANTHONY: Wild cats got into your beer.

LUCIEN scoops up the wet costume, going to hang it up –

LUCIEN: *(Beat.)* You're drinking too much again.

ANTHONY: Finished the rest of the cornflakes too. You think they'd have more sophisticated tastes.

LUCIEN: Why were you weird tonight?

ANTHONY: She didn't mind –

LUCIEN: You want your towel hung out?

ANTHONY: How old am I, Lucien? *(Beat.)* Don't treat me like I'm ten.

Silence.

LUCIEN: I'm trying to help you. I'm trying to help you get yourself cleaned up.

ANTHONY: What's wrong with being dirty, Luce? What's wrong with me?

Silence.

LUCIEN: You sleep in the gutter.

ANTHONY: I like it. It's the way I feel. I'm living the life the way I feel.

LUCIEN: Something could happen to you. It's dangerous.

ANTHONY: More dangerous than the way you live your life? Keys. Door. Progress. When was the last time you had sex, Lucien?

Silence.

Mine was stood up behind a bar, with some woman I'd met that morning. It was nice. We were drunk. It was something.

LUCIEN: It's fucking sordid.

LUCIEN makes to go in.

ANTHONY: It's living. It's living with it Lucien.

Silence.

Luce –

LUCIEN: Don't be fucked off with me, because you didn't get a shag.

Silence.

ANTHONY: I'm working on it.

LUCIEN: You're only here for the summer.

ANTHONY: So?

LUCIEN: She's a nice girl.

ANTHONY: So?

LUCIEN: You think you can give her a good time? Take her out to nice places?

ANTHONY: Yeah.

LUCIEN: It'll be me paying for it.

ANTHONY: I'm not stopping you.

Silence.

Everyman for himself eh?

Silence.

Christ, it's called taking a risk, Luce.

Silence. A bee buzzes around LUCIEN.

LUCIEN: Risk. What risk do you take? A bee, you catch a bee in your hand, you hold it in your hand and you expect us all to be impressed. When have you ever been stung?

A bee buzzes around LUCIEN.

Never. No danger.

LUCIEN lets it land on his hand. He tentatively clasps it until –

It's called understanding risk.

Suddenly LUCIEN pulls back his hand, stung.

Every time.

LUCIEN sucks on his hand. ANTHONY goes to help him. LUCIEN pulls away.

ANTHONY: Maybe I just don't tell you if I have.

LUCIEN: You? You couldn't keep your mouth shut –

ANTHONY: No.

LUCIEN: Yes.

Silence.

Being crazy is easy.

LUCIEN makes to go inside.

ANTHONY: I want to fit, Lucien. I want to be normal. I just don't know how to be. I don't want to be like this. I want to be quiet, still. I want to not bother you. I want to get my own hair cut. I want to go to sleep not thinking about *her*. Luce – If I could fit. I would. I would try and fit. I would put my money in a bank. I would walk on the pavement. I wouldn't crawl. But this is what I am, this is it, Lucien. It would take a miracle –

LUCIEN wavers, wants to touch him.

LUCIEN: Don't leave that stuff on the line all night.

LUCIEN exits. ANTHONY sits on his own. Suddenly, he reaches up and grasps the light bulb above him, holding it tight, burning himself until – It breaks in his hand, blood.

THE WOOD

The glow of a cinema screen down on – ANTHONY sitting as if watching.

ANTHONY: There was this old blind lady and she lived, I think it was Miami – you know, one of those places with a pool, where everyone else is old, and there's lots of palm trees and those little buggies that you wheel around in if you're playing golf. Her family had farmed her out there, she'd grown up in Vancouver. She liked seasons and changes but in Miami it was always hot. Every year her family would call her, just before Christmas, saying they'd come down and fly her back for the weekend so she could feel the snow, or a cold wind, just what she missed living always with palm trees – every year they would make this promise.
'See you soon, Grandma.'
She'd wait, and she'd wait but they never would turn up. Her grandson was called…it doesn't matter what he was called but he was her favourite, he was her best boy. He'd always send a Christmas card.
'Sorry I can't make it.'
There was a mail guy who delivered letters to the old blind lady every day and after a while he realised that she was waiting for a letter that would never come, a visitor who would never arrive, a special day that would never happen. He felt sorry for her. He liked her. He always made sure he said 'hello' – just chit-chat, nothing much – just the time of day.
Christmas came, it got hotter. The mail guy decided to clean up his flat. A small place – one room. It wasn't as if anyone was going to call. He didn't have many friends. He lived mainly on take-away and those instant meals you heat up. No-one even missed him. His neighbours could never remember his name. It was then he found the letter, a Christmas card to the old lady, lost in the seam of his mail bag, released when shaken out.

49

A Christmas card, glitter, he could feel it through
the envelope, a picture of mountains: Vancouver,
somewhere like that. He would visit her, deliver it. His
job was important to him. And it wasn't as if he had
anything else to do. He knocked on her door.

'Berni.' The grandson was called Berni. 'Berni, is that
you, darling?'

'Mrs Adams, I've got a card for you – '

'Berni, will you come in now?'

She looked him straight in the face. There were flowers
on the table and a turkey slowly roasting. She had a
record on, any old record, the house felt different.

'Where are you?' The old lady cried, feeling his face.

'I'm here,' said the mail guy.

'Sit down, Berni.'

So he sat down, and they ate together, pulling crackers
and he took her for a drive in his mail car and he took
her to the cooling fridge at the postal plant where they
kept all the cold mail, turkeys and stuff that people have
sent for Christmas.

'This is cooler than Vancouver, Berni.'

'It is Grandma. It's even got snow, feel?'

And they danced to her record and he thanked her for
the socks. And when he said goodbye, she said:

'Don't be a stranger now,' in a way that made the mail
guy want to cry. This was the first Christmas in years
he'd not been alone.

'Same time next year.'

'Same time next year,' said the mail guy. As he was
going the old blind lady said:

'You've dropped your card, Berni,' picking it up on the
mantelpiece, where it was left.

'It's for you,' said the mail guy.

'I don't need it.'

Miracle. It would take a miracle.

The flicker of a cinema screen. Surge of music. ANTHONY shoves a
large handful of popcorn in his mouth –

THE DECK

Day; MADELEINE stands with a picnic basket. ANTHONY stands brushing his teeth. LUCIEN reads the morning paper, drinking coffee. It is raining.

MADELEINE: So I was thinking –

LUCIEN: I've a lot of work to do.

MADELEINE: You take a boat, they're just a group of caves, but they're beautiful. Everyone goes…everyone goes at this time of year.

ANTHONY: Sounds great. *(Silence.)* You brought food?

MADELEINE: Leftovers from the restaurant.

ANTHONY: We eat leftovers.

MADELEINE: I was thinking after –

ANTHONY snatches LUCIEN's newspaper off him.

I could cook you dinner here.

ANTHONY: That would be great. *(To LUCIEN.)* Wouldn't that be great?

LUCIEN: We've nothing in.

ANTHONY: We can pick up stuff. *(To MADELEINE.)* Thank you.

Silence.

LUCIEN: How far away is it?

MADELEINE: It's near. It's near the lake.

ANTHONY: Where's your sense of adventure? He'd love to come. We'd both love to come.

MADELEINE looks to LUCIEN.

That's just the way his face falls.

A CAVE

MADELEINE, ANTHONY and LUCIEN standing in a boat in the cave.

ANTHONY: *(Calling out.)* Madeleine.

MADELEINE: *(Calling out.)* Anthony.

ANTHONY: *(Calling out.)* Lucien. *(Silence.)* No echo.

LUCIEN: It swallows you.

> *Silence.*

MADELEINE: The sound, the sound escapes, see, see the light?

> *LUCIEN and ANTHONY look up.*

LUCIEN: It's amazing.

ANTHONY: It's an escape route.

MADELEINE: Where to?

ANTHONY: Anywhere you want to.

> *Silence.*

> Why don't you have my seat back to the city?

> *LUCIEN laughs.*

LUCIEN: Don't be daft.

ANTHONY: I'm serious. I've been thinking. It's quieter here. The people are nicer. They'll need someone to take that cinema screen down in a couple of weeks. Tourists leave a mess. I could get a job clearing up.

LUCIEN: You get a job?

ANTHONY: Yeah. Maybe. It has happened before.

LUCIEN: You wouldn't do a thing here.

ANTHONY: Sometimes Lucien, your faith in me –

LUCIEN: You'd float on your back for weeks –

ANTHONY: Your faith in me is touching.

Silence.

(Calling out.) Touching.

Silence.

I'm hungry.

Silence. LUCIEN won't look at him.

It was only an idea.

A crackle of electricity; ripple of water. Sense of time moving on. Of them finishing off a picnic, sheltering by the side of –

THE LAKE

MADELEINE, LUCIEN and ANTHONY looking up at the rain clouds.

ANTHONY: *(Pointing to clouds.)* Hitler. With not much of a moustache.

LUCIEN: Hitler's not Hitler without his moustache.

ANTHONY: Turning into –

MADELEINE: Roger Rabbit.

ANTHONY: That's right, always go for the bunny.

LUCIEN: Your mum.

ANTHONY: With a hump? You're saying my mother had a hump?

MADELEINE: Does anybody want any more food?

ANTHONY: Stuffed.

LUCIEN: Ditto.

They sit in silence.

MADELEINE: Do you want to –

LUCIEN: No.

ANTHONY: I will.

LUCIEN: We should maybe get back soon.

ANTHONY: Too early.

MADELEINE: Way too early.

> *Silence. Awkward.*

> Okay, okay. We'll swim.

> *Silence. Awkward. The crackle of electricity, a ripple of water; a sense of time moving on to –*

THE LAKE

The splash of water, as MADELEINE comes up from under the pontoon.

Drops of rain. Creak of trees.

LUCIEN sits under a rain coat.

Silence.

MADELEINE slides up next to him. He reads. She looks over his shoulder.

MADELEINE: Why you reading?

> *LUCIEN continues reading.*

LUCIEN: Don't know.

MADELEINE: It's upside down.

> *LUCIEN throws his book high into the water.*

> *MADELEINE laughs incredulous.*

> *LUCIEN laughs.*

> *Silence.*

MADELEINE: You should have a swim, concede defeat. It feels warm.

LUCIEN: Fucking fucking rain.

Silence.

MADELEINE: Why do you tell Anthony there are wild cats? *(Silence.)* He's a grown man.

LUCIEN: He'd get lost.

MADELEINE: You'd find him.

LUCIEN: It's not the point to find him. It's the damage he does along the way.

MADELEINE: To who?

ANTHONY pulls himself up next to MADELEINE, bemused, catching their laughter.

Silence. They sit.

What do you hear?

ANTHONY: Birds. Trees creaking.

MADELEINE: Wild cats?

MADELEINE catches LUCIEN's eye.

ANTHONY: Sometimes. Maybe sometimes.

Trees cracking, sounds of the woods.

LUCIEN: They sound like voices.

MADELEINE: Sometimes.

LUCIEN: Like bits of conversations. Sometimes like whole bits of sentences.

ANTHONY: I can't hear them. What do they say?

Silence.

MADELEINE: It's cold.

ANTHONY and LUCIEN nod.

We should –

ANTHONY: Yeah.

LUCIEN: Yeah.

MADELEINE: Somewhere dry.

ANTHONY: Yeah.

LUCIEN: Yeah.

MADELEINE: Is this okay? *(Long silence.)* Say something. *(Silence.)* You know since I met you two I've never been so happy and never been so lonely in all my life. I don't know what it is but sometimes it's like – You remind me I'm on my own. And suddenly I don't like it. Suddenly it's not familiar. And I don't know where to go. I don't know where to go next.

The crackle of electricity, a ripple of water; a sense of time moving on to –

THE HOUSE

Late; ANTHONY, LUCIEN and MADELEINE sitting in the dark. ANTHONY comes through with a bottle of whisky.

ANTHONY: Okay, okay. A middle-aged dentist was deeply in love with his beautiful fiancée. His only concern was the state of her teeth. As a man who came from a long line of dentists, he knew his mother would be critical of his bride. So he decides to give her a pre-nuptial agreement. High technology latex braces. Sort out her teeth in a sec. Driving her home to meet his mother for the first time, his fiancée decided to give her love a little present of her own. Midway through performing an act of, let's say, oral satisfaction, a small clip from her brace caught around the metal of his flies. The girl starts to choke as the dentist tried to unhook her. Unfortunately

the guy was still driving at the time. The car crashed.
Kapow! They were both found dead in the wreckage.

MADELEINE: Punchline, punchline. You've got to have a
punchline.

ANTHONY: The small latex brace was found hanging from
the dead man's crotch.

LUCIEN: That's pathetic.

ANTHONY: With his fiancée's two front teeth still attached.

LUCIEN: Really lame.

ANTHONY pours them a whisky, LUCIEN shakes his head.

Silence.

They're only stories, Anthony.

ANTHONY: If they're only stories, Luce. I'll tell them how I
want.

Silence.

A woman. A woman with a crooked nose and funny hair…

MADELEINE: I don't think we should do this.

ANTHONY: …a woman with a crooked nose and funny hair
jumps from a bridge.

LUCIEN: I should drive you…I'll drive you home…

MADELEINE: You've drunk too much.

ANTHONY: The woman, a good friend –

LUCIEN: It's fine. You don't need to. We know how it ends.

ANTHONY: – the love of their life had spent the day
reminiscing over times gone by and a friendship which
had weathered most things in their relatively short lives.
The two men laughed at her life, unsuspecting that she
had a surprise for them. Returning to the bridge that
evening, the woman informed them that she intended to
take her life.

57

LUCIEN: She was drunk.

ANTHONY: She drank water all night.

LUCIEN: I don't want to do this now.

ANTHONY: The woman was someone who knew her own mind. The friends laughed. They didn't believe her.

LUCIEN: Why are you doing this?

ANTHONY: Standing with her arms out, ready to take the approaching juggernaut –

LUCIEN: Anthony please. Let's go home, we're going home soon.

ANTHONY: The two friends were quickly sobered to the idea that this was indeed a woman of her word. For what the woman wanted to know was – *Who loves me? Who loves me the most? (Silence.)* There's no such thing as a freak fucking accident. It's cause and effect, Luce. I know the effect. The one friend, a shy boy, was more sober than his drunk friend, he moved a little closer, he offered her words – *Who loves me? Who loves me the most?* You must have said something –

LUCIEN: The wind. The wind carried away my words.

ANTHONY: Who did you say? Luce, I know you said someone –

ANTHONY picks up the chairs and hurls it across the room. An angry, violent outburst, chairs, clothes, beer bottles go flying until –

LUCIEN: *ANTHONY.* I said…*ANTHONY…*

LUCIEN breaks down, pained, crumbling.

Silence. MADELEINE goes to touch LUCIEN, he withdraws.

Silence. ANTHONY watches.

ANTHONY: You stupid fuck.

The creak of trees. Rain.

You stupid, stupid fuck!

Silence.

You just had to say *LUCIEN.*

LUCIEN: We're going home.

ANTHONY: What do you hear, Lucien?

LUCIEN: I don't want to do this.

ANTHONY: You say you hear voices.

LUCIEN: I hear nothing.

ANTHONY: You hear something. It's not difficult. Close your eyes. Hear something. For Christ's sake, hear something! I can't do this all on my own. You stupid fuck. It didn't take much. It really didn't take much. You just had to say it. Luce, please. Tell me what you hear, please.

LUCIEN: 'You two – you two are terrible. But you love us. I love you.'

MADELEINE slowly kisses LUCIEN, first his hands, his back, his face as LUCIEN breaks down. ANTHONY watches; it is almost unbearable.

'I miss you…I love you… Both… You love us both… What's happened to Anthony's hair? It needs a cut. Make sure he gets a cut. You really aren't looking after him. Can't you look after him… Luce…Luce… You never looked after me.'

ANTHONY goes to touch LUCIEN, to try to quieten him but something makes him stop –

'Yes, you say you both love me, but look at you…'

MADELEINE and LUCIEN start to kiss, falling into making love.

MADELEINE: *(Whispered.)* Ssh –

ANTHONY exits.

Ssh –

The creak of the trees.

THE DECK

The rain falls heavier as – A sudden surge of music, lights, every electrical gadget in the house whirring until –

ANTHONY wrapped with every wire and light in the house, a glowing, glittering raging ball, arms outstretched in the rain as if defying lightning to strike.

A power failure, all cuts out –

THE HOUSE

Dawn; LUCIEN, MADELEINE and ANTHONY sit, exhausted, dripping wet. The house is chaos, chairs, tables everywhere.

Silence but for the drip of rain after the storm.

ANTHONY: A woman, once a girl, now a woman with –

LUCIEN: …a crooked nose.

ANTHONY: …with a crooked nose and hair –

LUCIEN: …funny hair –

ANTHONY: …with a crooked nose and funny hair…like a chicken met her friends on a bridge for a day out.

LUCIEN: Two boys, now men, she had known for years. Runt boy and shy boy, she'd given them these names. The three friends, the three points of the same triangle –

ANTHONY: …spent the day together reminiscing over times gone by and a friendship which had weathered most things in their relatively short lives.

LUCIEN: Returning to the bridge that evening, the woman informed them that she intended to take her life.

ANTHONY: Runt boy and shy boy knew they both loved her but at the moment when she should have known this.

LUCIEN: Kapow –

ANTHONY: Kapow – She jumped anyway.

Silence. MADELEINE puts the house in order throughout. Beat.

MADELEINE: However…

Silence. Both turn to look at MADELEINE.

ANTHONY: However – A boat carrying a cargo to –

LUCIEN: China.

ANTHONY: …China? A boat carrying a cargo of the finest flour –

LUCIEN: For dim sum.

ANTHONY: …for dim sum, was sailing underneath, when the captain, Captain –

MADELEINE: Captain Li –

ANTHONY: Okay, Captain Li – was looking up trying to navigate when he saw a young woman falling from the sky. The Captain, who was a clever man –

LUCIEN: And a world expert in calligraphy.

ANTHONY: Calligraphy? Calligraphy – He was a world expert in – anyway. Always useful. Captain Li, at the exact moment when he saw the young woman falling, pulled his boat up just in time for her –

LUCIEN: To land in the flour?

ANTHONY: To land in a mound of flour that left her completely white.

MADELEINE slowly starts to pick up the chairs, and tables, scooping up bottles around them, bringing order out of chaos.

LUCIEN: Captain Li – He had friends

ANTHONY: …who had a summer house off the South China sea –

Through the following, LUCIEN and ANTHONY watch MADELEINE as she tidies up around them.

LUCIEN: A yellow sea… Yellow from the sun and the fish that glinted in it. The Captain had friends, good friends, who heard the amazing story of the girl who jumped –

ANTHONY: And had a miraculous escape into the arms of Captain Li –

LUCIEN: They became lovers –

ANTHONY: They became lovers.

LUCIEN: And had several children. All called Confucius.

MADELEINE: It is believed that she is learning how to dive between China and the Bay of Bengal.

LUCIEN: Captain Li says that she's okay, that she's happy that – She's found a kind of happiness.

LUCIEN watches as a vase of flowers seems to float in front of him. MADELEINE places it on the table.

ANTHONY: *Who loves me? Who loves me the most?*

The sway of the trees outside, a distant creaking.

LUCIEN: Lucien.

ANTHONY puts his hand up. LUCIEN grips it, as if catching it, pulling him up stopping on seeing – A scorch mark, clear on the front of ANTHONY's shirt. MADELEINE goes to touch it.

ANTHONY: Kapow.

ANTHONY puts two fingers like a gun and shoots between his, LUCIEN and MADELEINE's heart.

Kapow. Kapow.

A long low hum, like the crackle of electricity, vibrating above as the lights go back on.

A ROADSTOP

LUCIEN is sitting in the car.

MADELEINE comes running out, with two coffees. She slides in next to him. They sit and drink.

LUCIEN: A rogue fork of lightning caught him hard across the chest. The boy fell down to the ground. He was only six years old.

Cars pass –

In years to come it was said that the boy possessed magic powers. In the darkest hour rumour had it that he shone.

They drive.

A LAKE

ANTHONY swimming. The glow of fireflies.

A MOTEL

LUCIEN sits bolt upright, a sandwich comes flying down from above. LUCIEN catches it. He turns to see – the girl asleep next to him. LUCIEN contemplates. He eats the sandwich.

A car passes, its headlights beam across the stage.

The End.

SPLENDOUR

Splendour was first performed by Paines Plough in association with The Peter Wolff Theatre Trust at the Traverse Theatre on 3 August 2000, with the following cast:

MICHELEINE	Mary Cunningham
KATHRYN	Faith Flint
GENEVIEVE	Myra McFadyen
GILMA	Eileen Walsh
Director	Vicky Featherstone
Designer	Neil Warmington

Splendour was revived at the Donmar Warehouse, London on 30 July 2015, with the following cast:

GILMA	Zawe Ashton
MICHELEINE	Sinéad Cusack
GENEVIEVE	Michelle Fairley
KATHRYN	Genevieve O'Reilly
Director	Robert Hastie
Designer	Peter McKintosh
Lighting Designer	Lee Curran
Sound Designer	Adrienne Quartly
Movement Director	Jack Murphy

Characters

MICHELEINE
the wife, female, late 40s

GILMA
the interpreter, female, early/mid 20s

KATHRYN
the photographer, female, mid/late 30s

GENEVIEVE
the informer, female, early/mid 40s

SETTING:

The play is set in a house, in an affluent neighbourhood on the edge of a large city.

The sound of fireworks/shelling should be abstract.

Evening; A palatial drawing room in the home of a dictator.

MICHELEINE, the wife is our hostess. GENEVIEVE, her best friend, has just entered, her coat on as if she has just come in from outside. She is covered in snow. KATHRYN, a photo-journalist, is standing, her back to us, staring at a large and incongruous abstract painting that hangs on the wall. Her interpretor, GILMA, a local woman has just broken a red Venetian vase. She is sweeping up the broken shards of glass off the floor.

MICHELEINE: Genevieve, your hair it's –

GENEVIEVE: Snow.

KATHRYN: …dripping on her green dress.

GENEVIEVE: I'm fine. The roads are terrible.

GILMA: I'm sorry.

MICHELEINE: It's nothing, just a vase. *(Introducing.)* Gilma.

GENEVIEVE: Gilma.

GILMA: Don't look me up and down like that.

GENEVIEVE: I had to take the back route. Is there anything to drink?

MICHELEINE: Yes. We're onto our third.

(GENEVIEVE walks across the room and pours herself a glass of vodka.)

I am sitting in the garden of friends, good friends a few hours before this moment.

GENEVIEVE: Jesus –

MICHELEINE: …we are having lunch with friends.

GENEVIEVE: *(I.e. drink.)* … Micha, where did you get this?

MICHELEINE: Lunch with Isabella.

KATHRYN: We are drinking chilli vodka.

GENEVIEVE: You saw her?

MICHELEINE: A few hours ago.

KATHRYN: Chilli vodka that is blindingly hot.

MICHELEINE: To my right is a pudgy man I always seem to get stuck with. He laughs too much at a joke my husband makes –

(GILMA hands MICHELEINE back the dustpan and brush.)

GILMA: *(To MICHELEINE.)* I'm sorry.

MICHELEINE: Of course, it's a very funny joke… A nun is walking through a park.

GENEVIEVE: I thought Oolio would be –

MICHELEINE: Coming. You know the office. You're dripping on the carp –

GENEVIEVE: *(To MICHELEINE.)* Micha, there are bells ringing all along the Southside.

(A beat. MICHELEINE takes her coat from her. GENEVIEVE clocks KATHRYN looking at the painting.)

MICHELEINE: A nun is walking through a park when a giant gorilla attacks her. He ravishes her in the bushes and then quickly bounds away. She is clearly distressed and returns to the convent where Mother Superior with some concern takes the young nun aside. 'My dear I can't help but notice, you seem very upset of late.'

GENEVIEVE: The painting –

(GENEVIEVE comes up to look at the painting with KATHRYN.)

I see you've noticed the painting.

KATHRYN: Sorry?

GENEVIEVE: The painting? You like it?

MICHELEINE: We commissioned it. It's not one of his best.

KATHRYN: I'm sorry… *(To GILMA.)* Gilma? Gilma? I'm sorry. I don't understand. *(To GENEVIEVE.)* I'm sorry. I don't understand.

MICHELEINE: *(Introducing.)* Kathryn.

KATHRYN: *(To GENEVIEVE.)* Kathryn.

MICHELEINE: *(To GENEVIEVE.)* She's a very important journalist.

KATHRYN: I've come to take a photograph.

MICHELEINE: This is my best friend, Genevieve. Our husbands have been, were friends for thirty –

GENEVIEVE: …five –

MICHELEINE: …years.

(GENEVIEVE and KATHRYN shake hands.)

KATHRYN: Gilma?

GILMA: The painting. Her husband –

KATHRYN: …painted it? We're discussing fucking painting.

MICHELEINE: *(To KATHRYN.)* Won't you have a little nut?

Moved by the Mother Superior's vigilant concern, the young nun confesses to the recent contretemps with the gorilla in the park. The Mother Superior bestows sympathy but as the weeks pass, a vow of silence is shrouded over the terrible event. But one day the Mother Superior unable to contain herself, betrays a certain curiosity, a certain girlish interest… 'My dear, don't think me indiscreet, but may I ask' – Mid way through the punch-line, the pudgy man who is already laughing, suddenly shoots up and says 'Ssh did you hear that?'

GILMA: *(To GENEVIEVE.)* The bells on the Southside.
I heard them, this afternoon.

MICHELEINE: 'Faint, on a cold breeze.' *(Beat.)* I heard nothing at all.

GILMA: There were people, they were dancing –

MICHELEINE: No.

GILMA: *(To MICHELEINE.)* I saw a soldier being paraded.

GENEVIEVE: Micheleine –

GILMA: That is impossible. You must have been –

MICHELEINE: I must have been –

GILMA: …very far away.

KATHRYN: What did she say?

(GILMA shakes her head.)

MICHELEINE: I sat next to that pudgy man –

GENEVIEVE: Who laughs at almost anything?

MICHELEINE: Oolio did his usual –

GENEVIEVE: Not?

MICHELEINE: The gorilla and the nun.

(MICHELEINE and GENEVIEVE laugh.)

'May I ask, "Did it hurt?"'

'Of course it hurt Mother Superior, I mean imagine this big gorilla, he never rings, he never writes, there's not a bunch of flowers in sight…'

And we're laughing but the truth is –

KATHRYN: Why the hell are they laughing?

MICHELEINE: … I want to but today –

GILMA: *(Touching GENEVIEVE.)* Fuck, you're freezing.

MICHELEINE: … I don't find the joke funny at all.

KATHRYN: I am standing in the foyer of a large hotel a few hours before this moment. In a city that is familiar, a city I have been to several times before. This job that I have come for, this job is particular. I have been travelling since 5 a.m. Greenwich Meantime. I am tired. At the airport there is no one to meet me. It's the usual. I pick up a taxi. The taxi is expensive, too expensive, I argue. I win my case.

MICHELEINE: This portrait of my husband?

GILMA: This photo that you plan to take? You must be important. He rarely courts press.

KATHRYN: It was agreed through your office.

GILMA: A request from his advisors. It was a personal invitation.

MICHELEINE: We're delighted you could come.

(The phone rings.)

GILMA: *(To GENEVIEVE.)* It's snowing.

GENEVIEVE: Only a little now.

GILMA: …You drove along the…

GENEVIEVE: Past the Gymnasium…

GILMA: …I use to swim there as a child…

GENEVIEVE: Since they bombed the bridge last August –

GILMA/GENEVIEVE: …It's the only route to take.

KATHRYN: I arrive at my hotel. There are large lions and a plastic flamingo arrangement in the foyer. The man in the lobby reassures me that they are not real. Reclaimed since the Zoo was bombed. There is frost on the lion's mane.

MICHELEINE: Genie, your hair. I'll get you a towel.

(MICHELEINE picks up the ball of newspaper from the bin and takes it out to throw it away.)

KATHRYN: I ask if there have been any messages for me and a girl standing in the lobby, a girl wearing a coat that is clearly not hers, a girl wearing a coat that is weighed down with shoulder pads, a girl –

GILMA: *(To KATHRYN.)* From the newspaper? Excuse me? You've come to take the photograph?

KATHRYN: …with an accent I can barely understand –

GILMA: I'm an interpreter. The car's… You come? This way.

KATHRYN: *(To GILMA.)* My office?

GILMA: Yes. They contact me.

KATHRYN: They arranged for you to take me?

GILMA: *(To KATHRYN.)* Gilma.

KATHRYN: *(Nodding.)* Gilma. *(Beat.)* She barely understands me. In my mind I am sticking pins in the office PA.

(MICHELEINE comes in, dropping a towel in GENEVIEVE's lap.)

GENEVIEVE: Micha –

MICHELEINE: Genie, what are we to do with you?

GENEVIEVE: Was that Oolio on the telephone?

MICHELEINE: Yes, he's on his way. Gilma? A Northern name.

GILMA: Not always.

MICHELEINE: How's Darius?

GENEVIEVE: He called last week. I think there's a new girlfriend –

MICHELEINE: A girlfriend at last. We had money on it he was –

GENEVIEVE: And Marcus wrote. He's going to bring Gina and the children to stay.

MICHELEINE: *(Eyeing KATHRYN.)* She's watching me. *(Beat.)* That's good. That's lovely, Genie –

GILMA: Stockings –

MICHELEINE: Italian.

GILMA: With underwear I bet to match.

MICHELEINE: Gilma… I wonder I didn't clock that right away.

GILMA: *(To MICHELEINE.)* Nice shot glasses.

MICHELEINE: Siberian. *(Beat.)* Thank you.

GILMA: You're welcome.

MICHELEINE: That sounds very American.

GILMA: Sorry?

MICHELEINE: 'You're welcome'? *(Beat.)* That's very American.

GILMA: The University of California. I studied abroad.

(KATHRYN holds up her bag to MICHELEINE.)

KATHRYN: Is it okay, if I…? Gilma?

GILMA: Is it okay? To unpack her things?

MICHELEINE: Please tell her, of course –

GILMA: *(To KATHRYN.)* It's fine.

MICHELEINE: *(Calling out.)* Marianna… Will she need some help?

KATHRYN: It's fine.

GILMA: It's fine.

GENEVIEVE: The painting is of the city. That is the river and that is the persons… I speak a little of your language…

KATHRYN: Someone should tell her very badly. *(Beat.)* The persons?

GENEVIEVE: Yes. The persons of the town.

KATHRYN: And which bit are the persons?

GENEVIEVE: There are the persons.

KATHRYN: Right.

GENEVIEVE: You see their faces?

KATHRYN: I see. Yes. I see. Right. Is that a cow?

(The phone rings. And rings.)

MICHELEINE: *(Calling out.)* Marianna, Marianna, will you please get the telephone?

(The phone stops ringing.)

No matter. We need more ice.

(MICHELEINE goes out.)

GENEVIEVE: How did you get here?

GILMA/KATHRYN: Taxi.

GILMA: The office said you'd pay it.

KATHRYN: I know this is a lie. A blatant, shameless lie. The office have included it, she has already been paid once today.

GILMA: If there's going to be a problem –

KATHRYN: I reassure her there's not a problem, but I know the tricks they all readily have –

GILMA: It takes on average –

GENEVIEVE: Twenty minutes, fifteen if you're lucky.

GILMA: It's a forty-minute ride. It's better if we pay him. He won't drive us anywhere until he sees there's cash.

KATHRYN: He takes us on the scenic route. The view is one I'm used to, one we've all come to expect. *(Beat.)* She'll ask for forty and I know it will only cost twenty. She splits the extra and the driver gets the ride. *(Beat.)* And he will come back for us? My paper will be waiting? I have to get back to the hotel. I'll need to wire the photos to the paper as soon as they're done.

She nods. *(Beat.)* I don't trust her.

GILMA: *(Nodding.)* She's mean with her money.

KATHRYN: Her shoulder pads crunch as she climbs in the car.

GILMA: The driver is a friend, a friend of my brother's. He's a gambler and a user. I hold back ten. That way he'll come back. That way she won't criticise. Please do not worry. The door?

KATHRYN: Sorry?

GILMA: Not closed.

KATHRYN: *(Beat.)* She leans across me and there is a faint smell of BO.

(MICHELEINE comes through, a bucket of ice in her hand.)

MICHELEINE: Do you know I went out and found the front door wide open? We now have ice both inside and out. *(Holding up ice.)* Genevieve, you said the traffic –

GENEVIEVE: A log-jam all along the North route.

MICHELEINE: *(Beat.)* No one likes the cold nights.
If I didn't know better, I'd say this snow's in to stay. Have you seen outside? Genie lives –

KATHRYN: She lives…?

GENEVIEVE: Only five minutes away –

MICHELEINE: Her husband was –

GILMA: … The nuts are finished.

MICHELEINE: …a marvellous man.

GENEVIEVE: He died…

GILMA: Four years ago…

MICHELEINE: Her husband painted the picture.

GENEVIEVE: She hates it.

MICHELEINE: That painting is very dear to me.

GENEVIEVE: She hates it.

MICHELEINE: Genie, it's still hanging on the wall.

GILMA: Under-wired, most definitely. With stockings and suspenders.

MICHELEINE: La Perla have the ones I normally prefer.

GENEVIEVE: *(To MICHELEINE.)* Have you called Angelica? *(Beat.)* Micheleine? She's at home with the boy?

MICHELEINE: Your accent it's…?

GILMA: Californian. I studied in an American university.

GENEVIEVE: California?

GILMA: Hollywood.

KATHRYN: Hollywood, my arse.

GILMA: It's beautiful.

KATHRYN: She's making chitchat.

GILMA: You've worked in America?

KATHRYN: Elections, a race riot, some bomber in Idaho. The Idaho bomber a few years ago.

GILMA: Idaho?

KATHRYN: In America.

GILMA: Yes, Hollywood.

KATHRYN: A1 wonderful. An interpreter who doesn't actually know how to interp. *(Beat.)* She's not even listening.

GILMA: *(Beat.)* I hear every word.

(GILMA knocks her drink back too hard, coughs.)

MICHELEINE: Careful –

GILMA: It just catches you –

MICHELEINE: …when you're least expecting –
Chilli, chilli vodka.

GILMA: Right at the back of /

MICHELEINE: …the back of the throat.

(MICHELEINE hands her a glass of water.)

(Beat.) Alright now?

GILMA: Thank you.

MICHELEINE: You're welcome.

GILMA: That's quite alright.

GENEVIEVE: *(I.e. drink.)* … Micha, where did you get this?

MICHELEINE: *(Beat.)* Lunch with Isabella. *(Beat.)* She insisted. She insisted I bring a bottle home.
'For the pain. The chilli? To enjoy the pain as you drink it.'

I knock back the last mouthful quickly, gently scalding
my tongue. We won't forget this moment. We want
you to know this. There's an emotion in her voice that
embarrasses me. Embarrasses my husband.

I pray he does not intervene with another joke.

Help me out, sweetheart. We have a little signal –

'Darling, your ulcer? We must get that ulcer home.'

My husband informs us, our car is surely waiting.
It is as we leave I notice the vase.

•

*(GILMA is standing admiring a beautiful Venetian vase, red and
lilac catching in the light, roughly wrapped in newspaper and rolling
on its side.)*

GILMA: It's beautiful.

(MICHELEINE nods.)

MICHELEINE: Venetian.

GILMA: The vase?

MICHELEINE: In Isabella's hallway, resting on a bookshelf.
A wedding present we gave them some years ago.

KATHRYN: She nods so lightly –

GILMA: So carelessly forgotten.

MICHELEINE: Isabella is a woman who guards possessions
carefully. I am therefore surprised when she takes this gift,
this gift that we gave her, she takes this beautiful gift down
from the shelf and offers it to me.

GILMA: A vase which I can see is worth half of what
I earned last month. A vase which, at this moment,
I would dearly like to own. Red. Venetian. She's clearly
distracted… I wonder if she'd notice –

MICHELEINE: *(To GILMA.)* A gift.

(GILMA aware of MICHELEINE watching her, withdraws her hand.)

'Take it – we'd like you to have it.' Is it my imagination or does our hostess shake as she holds it out in her arms?

GILMA: … It would fit in my bag.

MICHELEINE: My smile is a graceful smile but as we stand in her hallway I see there is pity in her husband's eyes.

(The phone starts ringing.)

Marianna, our –

GILMA: *(To KATHRYN.)* …housekeeper –

MICHELEINE: Don't worry, she –

(The phone stops ringing.)

…probably answered it.

(A distant rumble.)

MICHELEINE: There's no breeze. The silence carries everything.

(GENEVIEVE comes in.)

MICHELEINE: Genevieve.

GENEVIEVE: The door was wide open, I didn't think of closing it, I thought she must be outside –

MICHELEINE: I forgot. *(Beat.)* It's her half – day.

Oolio –

He squeezes my hand and leans back to kiss me. Tells me that there are papers at the office that he really must sign. I am to go in alone, he'll be back quite shortly. I clutch the half bottle of vodka and the vase from these strangers that we have known and loved for years.

Something about his manner. Something about his manner…

We pull through the gates and…

KATHRYN: We are here when the wife arrives.

•

(The play begins as before; MICHELEINE our hostess, GENEVIEVE has her coat on as if she has just entered the room. KATHRYN is looking at the painting. GILMA is sweeping up the broken glass off the floor.)

GILMA: I'm sorry.

MICHELEINE: *(Touching hair.)* Your hair, it's –

KATHRYN: …dripping on her green dress.

GENEVIEVE: I'm fine. The roads are terrible.

MICHELEINE: It's nothing, just a bit of glass. *(Introducing.)* Gilma –

GENEVIEVE: Gilma.

GILMA: Don't look me up and down like that.

GENEVIEVE: I had to take the back route. Is there anything to drink?

MICHELEINE: Yes, we're onto our third…

> *(MICHELEINE holds up a pack of cigarettes to KATHRYN.)*

Do you smoke?

(KATHRYN shakes her head.)

I'm giving up.

GENEVIEVE: Jesus, where did you get this?

> *(The phone rings.)*

MICHELEINE: Isabella.

GILMA: Marlboro. A brand new pack.

MICHELEINE: Genie, what are we to do with you?
I'll get you a towel.

•

KATHRYN: She is shorter than I expected and not as beautiful, certainly not as her photos have shown. Her behind is large and there is a thin line of hair bleached on her top lip. Her clothes are too tight and the handbag –

MICHELEINE: Prada. Last season's and shoes to match.

GILMA: Pink with tiny stripy edging. The soles look barely dirty. I pray. Yes indeedy they are my size. *(To MICHELEINE.)* Your shoes, they're very hairy.

KATHRYN: Animal not mineral. Possibly Zebra.

GILMA: She says she thinks you're wearing –

(MICHELEINE laughs.)

KATHRYN: If there's a seam, tell her, it's normally where the anus once was.

GILMA: *(To MICHELEINE.)* She likes them.

MICHELEINE: Please tell her thank you, I have many more.

KATHRYN: Amidst such devastation how do you…

GILMA: Devastation… To cause great destruction…

KATHRYN: *(Beat.)* I barely embarrass her.

GILMA: They're delivered by road.

KATHRYN: How many handbags –

MICHELEINE: …do I actually own? *(Beat.)* A number is not important.

GILMA: I'm glad I've worn my big coat, with very, very deep pockets.

MICHELEINE: A figure is just a crude way to define us all.

I find it rather tasteless… This fascination with quantity.

GILMA: Twelve in each side and one larger pocket just under my arse.

MICHELEINE: Two maybe three…hundred. *(Beat.)*

She asks too many questions. I grace them by –

KATHRYN: …showing us the room where they are stored.

MICHELEINE: How can you quantify something that means nothing to one person and everything to another?

A number is redundant.

•

(KATHRYN's gaze falls to the painting beyond.)

GENEVIEVE: The painting, I see you've noticed –

KATHRYN: On the wall is a painting. An obscene and gross painting. It is modern. In oils. Smeared like shit.

GENEVIEVE: The painting on the wall?

KATHRYN: Gilma, can you tell her, the light, it's fading.

When will her husband –

MICHELEINE: *(Beat.)* My husband… Will you explain to her…

GILMA: At the office…

KATHRYN: Yeah. I got that.

MICHELEINE: He's had to –

KATHRYN: …sign papers. Yeah. She said that before.
(Watching MICHELEINE.) Her nails are aubergine,
the colour of aubergine, and clasped around her bag
even in her house. As if she is under threat, as if she is
under threat or about to go somewhere.

GILMA: *(To GENEVIEVE.)* Fuck, you're freezing?

GENEVIEVE: My heating's jammed –

MICHELEINE: That car –

GENEVIEVE: It's a bit temperamental.

MICHELEINE: Genie, it's time to get rid of that car.

GILMA: … You drove along the…

GENEVIEVE: Past the Gymnasium…

MICHELEINE: The changing rooms are now offices and
the athletic pitch barracks…

GENEVIEVE: Since they bombed the bridge last August –

GILMA: … It's the only route to take.

GENEVIEVE: *(To KATHRYN.)* Your first time here?
Over here?

MICHELEINE: You must visit our coastal towns.

KATHRYN: *(To GILMA.)* I've been mainly…mainly in the
Northern states.

MICHELEINE: *(To GENEVIEVE.)* Gilma's the interpreter,
if you want to talk to –

KATHRYN: *(As if introducing herself.)* Kathryn.

MICHELEINE: … Kathryn, Genie, it's best if we all go through
her.

KATHRYN: The piano?

MICHELEINE: My grandson –

GILMA: *(To KATHRYN.)* …has lessons here.

MICHELEINE: Tuesdays and Thursdays.

What am I doing? Shut up. Stop talking so much.

KATHRYN: I'll have to move it. The piano. Gilma?

MICHELEINE: *(To GILMA.)* Ask her, will you ask her…will I see the photograph first?

GILMA: The photo, she'll get to choose it.

KATHRYN: I wire them direct.

MICHELEINE: He has a little disfigurement to the left of his face –

KATHRYN: The paper trust my choice. I select the best shot.

MICHELEINE: …he's naturally self-conscious. The removal of a mole.

GILMA: Shoot him from the left.

KATHRYN: It will depend on the light.

MICHELEINE: He's a man you admire?

KATHRYN: More fascinated.

GILMA: More fascinated.

MICHELEINE: *(Beat.)* To me he's my husband. The piano…
Be careful. It is a Steinway.

(A sound. Faint. Just audible. In the distance. Bells/shelling/the rumble of guns.)

He squeezes my hand and leans back to kiss me. A small patch of stubble… Back in one hour. Just give them a drink – Oolio… Oolio… He's already gone.

(To GILMA.) Your English. You learnt?

GILMA: In the University of California.

GENEVIEVE: California?

MICHELEINE: *(To GILMA.)* You're very lucky…

KATHRYN: California my arse. *(Watching MICHELEINE.)*
She's nervous.

MICHELEINE: I'm shaking. The hostess' disease. The young girl is sly, her coat is quite terrible –

The older. Tougher. No ring. No man.

Kathryn, it is Kathryn who clocks my hands. God I need a drink.

KATHRYN: We move the piano.

MICHELEINE: Careful –

GILMA: We make a big great scratch as we drag it across the floor. If we're moving pianos I'm asking for more.

KATHRYN: On the stool is an imprint, a perfect crease, a perfect crease of a very tiny child's behind.

GILMA: Her grandson's.

MICHELEINE: He's this tall. A sweetheart. A tiny little sweetheart.

(The ring of a phone. For a long time until –)

Excuse me, a moment –

KATHRYN: She answers the telephone.

MICHELEINE: *(As if on the phone.)* Darling…

GENEVIEVE: She's talking to Oolio.

MICHELEINE: And ruining my floor. *(As if on the phone.)* She seems very nice. She's brought a lot of equipment. *(She laughs.)* I'll tell her… I'll tell her… *(To KATHRYN.)* He's making a joke.

GENEVIEVE: She laughs too much.

MICHELEINE: I laugh too much.

GILMA: Something funny at his office.

MICHELEINE: He says would you mind…

GILMA: Would we mind holding on?

•

(MICHELEINE pours three shots for them. They all chink glasses and knock back in one shot.)

KATHRYN: Wow.

GILMA: Jesu –

KATHRYN: I like it.

GILMA: *(Coughing.)* Jesu –

GENEVIEVE: *(To GILMA.)* Are you okay?

MICHELEINE: I'll get you some water.

GILMA: It catches you –

MICHELEINE: Right at the back of –

GILMA: ...the throat.

MICHELEINE: *(Beat.)* Alright now?

GILMA: Thank you.

MICHELEINE: You're welcome.

GILMA: *(Beat.)* That's quite alright. Nice glasses.

MICHELEINE: Siberian.

KATHRYN: *(Eyeing GILMA.)* I know what you're doing. Put it back.

GILMA: *(Holding up glass.)* M for Micheleine.

MICHELEINE: A whim of my husbands. M on all the silverware.

GILMA: *(Admiring the glass.)* M that's very nice. If I could just get a set.

KATHRYN: Put it back. Put it back.

•

KATHRYN: Her children?

GILMA: They live near.

KATHRYN: The grandson with –

MICHELEINE: My daughter, Angelica.

GENEVIEVE: The girl translates.

MICHELEINE: ...touches everything.

GILMA: *(Beat.)* She's married to an obstetrician.

MICHELEINE: My son is studying –

GILMA: ...at agricultural college –

MICHELEINE: ...in the North. My daughter, Angelica, she lives on the Southside. How's Darius?

GENEVIEVE: Skiing. He's skiing with a new girlfriend.

MICHELEINE: *(Beat.)* A girlfriend. At last. We had money on it he was...

KATHRYN: The woman flinches.

GILMA: *(To KATHRYN.)* A daughter, a son, one grandson and the woman in the green dress –

GENEVIEVE: Two boys. They're all grown up –

GILMA: They don't live at home.

GENEVIEVE: Have you heard from Angelica? Micheleine? She has called today?

MICHELEINE: Don't worry so. Don't worry so.

GILMA: Two glasses, a Zippo lighter, nail varnish and a light thing.

MICHELEINE: Genevieve, you worry too much.

GENEVIEVE: *(To MICHELEINE.)* There were people, they were dancing and soldiers being paraded. If Angelica –

MICHELEINE: There is mud on my carpet.

KATHRYN: … Gilma, your shoes…

GILMA: *(Picking up soles of feet.)* Fuck…

MICHELEINE: Outside…outside…

KATHRYN: Gilma –

(GILMA exits as if going outside.)

GENEVIEVE: There have been bells ringing all day.

KATHRYN: Excuse me…

(KATHRYN holds up her mobile, as if about to make a call.)

MICHELEINE: Genie, you exaggerate.

KATHRYN: Do you mind?

GENEVIEVE: The roads… There's a log-jam.

MICHELEINE: You're always prone to exaggerate.

GENEVIEVE: If Angelica's on the Southside…

(KATHRYN on mobile.)

GILMA: Inside, I can hear them bickering, *she* is on her cellphone.

KATHRYN: Nick, can you hear me? It's Kate.

GILMA: Screeching down the phone. That woman, that woman has a pickle up her arse.

KATHRYN: … Nick… I've arrived… We're here waiting for him…

GILMA: In the taxi, on the way here I take her the long route.

KATHRYN: *(As if on the phone.)* Apparently he's on his way… Nick… It sounds like there's action on the Southside.

GILMA: Down the main street there are fronts of houses, with no rooms only doorways… A boy, too big, too old sleeps in a pram in a hotel front door.

MICHELEINE: I am nervous. I talk.

GENEVIEVE: Too much.

KATHRYN: *(As if on the phone.)* I don't know… Who knows where the fuck he is?

GILMA: At a time like this I think of just leaving them. The wife is rude, the other…wallpaper. And as for camera girl, she can go take a flying-

KATHRYN: *(On phone.)* Shucks and I thought you missed me…

GILMA: It is only a moment and then I remember –

KATHRYN: Yeah, well fuck tomorrow, I need to be over the Southside…

GILMA: The glasses and the knives and spoons engraved with the *M*.

KATHRYN: Nick, you're just not listening… I need to be on the Southside, it's kicking off now… If this is revolution… Yeah well Nick, it's just not happening here. It's Ok?… You sent Makin? You sent fucking Makin?

GILMA comes back in.

GILMA: Who's fucking Makin?

KATHRYN: *(As she loses signal.)* I'm stuck here and fucking Makin's on the fucking South-

(KATHRYN loses her signal.)

Fuck.

GENEVIEVE: Kathryn, my mother's name.

KATHRYN: I'm sorry. I don't understand.

GENEVIEVE: *(Gesturing.)* My mother? Katerina. It's actually the same name.

KATHRYN: Your mother? Right. It's common. I imagine the world over. My mother's was Margaret.

GENEVIEVE: Sorry. I don't understand.

GILMA: In a bin, by the window there's an old MacDonald's bag. Brown with M.

MICHELEINE: My grandson. Yesterday. He just loves MacDonald's.

GILMA: And *Toy Story*. On the table. Now in my bag.

(A sound. A bang. Shelling. Fireworks. Something. Somewhere.)

KATHRYN: The noise –

MICHELEINE: It feels very cold in here. The windows are open.

KATHRYN: Yeah, you hear it this time. Finally –

MICHELEINE: I'll close them.

KATHRYN: Ask her, does she know –

GILMA: Outside. Do you know what is going on outside?

GENEVIEVE: There must be a certain kind of –

GILMA: *(To KATHRYN.)* …professional ambition, she's asking –

GENEVIEVE: *(To KATHRYN.)* … I expect it's dangerous –

KATHRYN: *(Eyeing MICHELEINE.)* She's shaking…

MICHELEINE: I'm shaking. I can hardly close the window.

GENEVIEVE: …especially abroad. To be so eager to get your pictures in the papers.

KATHRYN: Jesus –

MICHELEINE: If there's no wind, even the river sounds… sounds not far away.

KATHRYN: *(To GILMA.)* Tell her, I haven't really ever thought about it before.

MICHELEINE: But you've travelled here, a long way? That shows a certain passion, a certain desire to do, what you do?

KATHRYN: A certain passion… I suppose… Tell her, yes, I guess yes.

MICHELEINE: Gilma. *(Beat.)* You're not married yet?

GILMA: I'm waiting. For someone to come back.

MICHELEINE: A soldier?

GILMA: A soldier.

MICHELEINE: That's marvellous. That's marvellous.

GILMA: Before I was a lecturer, in science, in physical science. Before all this happened…

MICHELEINE: And look at you now.

GILMA: *(Beat.)* She patronises me.

MICHELEINE: I'm getting drunk.

That's clever. You are obviously very clever. You can't quite hear it… Your accent? Am I right?

GILMA: My accent?

MICHELEINE: Its Northern edge. You've softened it. Smoothed it over.

GILMA: I don't think so. I've been here a long time.

MICHELEINE: A long time. *(Beat.)* I mustn't have any more. *(Beat.)* I don't like to tell her but she has my *Toy Story* in her bag.

(KATHRYN holds up her bag to MICHELEINE.)

KATHRYN: Gilma, I'm going to set up.

GILMA: Is it okay? To unpack her things?

(KATHRYN begins to unpack her things.)

MICHELEINE: *(Eyeing GILMA.)* I could possibly negotiate. Appeal to her better nature. It is the favourite film of a very little boy but –

GENEVIEVE: It's the view from our window. Not everyone can see it. It's…

KATHRYN: Black.

GENEVIEVE: Not everyone gets it. It was painted by my husband before he –

MICHELEINE: Excuse me a moment.

GILMA: *(To KATHRYN.)* … When he was still alive. He was found… How do you say? In the water, his body was full of water…

KATHRYN: What?

GILMA: They found him in the swimming pool, floating in the swimming pool.

KATHRYN: *(Beat.)* I get it.

GENEVIEVE: Tell her, he'd been depressed for a very long time.

(MICHELEINE walks across the room, ice bucket in hand in search of some ice.)

•

MICHELEINE: Genevieve?

(She suddenly stands as if she is on the telephone.)

GENEVIEVE: Micheleine?

KATHRYN: Somewhere, in a different house, in a different street not far away, this woman in her green dress is summoned to the phone.

MICHELEINE: Just listen for a moment, listen and I will tell you as best I can.

GENEVIEVE: Micheleine, you've caught me watching the television. That thing where –

MICHELEINE: Of course. Come over right now.

GENEVIEVE: …the man wins a million. *(GILMA touches KATHRYN's camera equipment.)*

MICHELEINE: Don't be silly. That would be fine. Genie.

KATHRYN: It's clear, she's bluffing it…

GENEVIEVE: Micheleine, are you listening? Who are you talking to?

MICHELEINE: There's a lady from the press and we're having a few drinks. He's not back yet… Uh, you know how his work is?

(KATHRYN puts out one hand to stop GILMA picking up a lens.)

KATHRYN: Excuse me…

GILMA: Sorry.

KATHRYN: It's just the grease from your fingers. We all have it and don't know it. It smudges the lens.

GILMA: What's this?

KATHRYN: A light meter.

GILMA: What's it do?

KATHRYN: It measures light. It says the light's fading.

GILMA: She looks at her watch.

MICHELEINE: *(As if on the phone.)* You wouldn't be interrupting. We'd love you to come round…

GENEVIEVE: Micheleine and I have been friends for…

MICHELEINE: Thirty –

GENEVIEVE: …five –

MICHELEINE: …years… We believe in the same things. Our children…

GENEVIEVE: …don't get on.

'Micheleine, I'm in the middle of making supper… Micheleine…'

MICHELEINE: She's very lonely. Her husband…

GENEVIEVE: She's been very good to me. She's been very kind to me.

MICHELEINE: Sometimes I have to fight to get the time on my own. Sometimes she calls and I don't want to talk to her sometimes…but today…she's my very best friend.

•

KATHRYN: Your husband was a painter?

GENEVIEVE: At the local art college…

MICHELEINE: Our husbands were school-friends, that's how we met. Tell them the story of the first time you visited…

GENEVIEVE: Micheleine…

MICHELEINE: A dinner party, the first we ever had…

GENEVIEVE: In that flat…

MICHELEINE: Above the butchers. We were so poor…

GENEVIEVE: Scrag end of lamb…

MICHELEINE: And after someone had brought a bottle of…

GENEVIEVE: Pie-eyed…

MICHELEINE: Pie-eyed…

GENEVIEVE: From some grass…

MICHELEINE: My father's place in the mountain…
    My brother and I used to…

GENEVIEVE: Dry it in their loft… And later… When most of
    the others had gone home…

MICHELEINE: We danced with each other because our…

GENEVIEVE: Preferred to talk…

MICHELEINE: They hated it most when we would giggle…

GENEVIEVE: …while they talked rubbish late into the night.

MICHELEINE: How can you say that?

GENEVIEVE: This is where we differ…

MICHELEINE: My husband never talked an ounce of rubbish
    in his life…

    (A ripple of laughter broken only by the smash of glass.)

•

MICHELEINE: Genevieve –

    *(GILMA bends down and starts to sweep up the broken vase as
    GENEVIEVE stands once more in a familiar pose, pulling the scarf
    off from around her neck. The repetition is faster, now slightly more
    fragmented.)*

GILMA: … Hair dripping –

KATHRYN: … Green dress.

GILMA: I'm sorry.

GENEVIEVE: The roads are –

KATHRYN: … Terrible.

MICHELEINE: Snow –

(GENEVIEVE looks at GILMA sweeping up the glass.)

Just a bit of glass.

GENEVIEVE: Gilma –

(GENEVIEVE waves away MICHELEINE as she goes to take her coat.)

Don't…

GILMA: … Look me up and down like that.

GENEVIEVE: Micha… Micha… Is there anything to drink?

•

(GENEVIEVE walks across the room and pours herself a drink.)

KATHRYN: This man, that I've come to see, to photograph, this man is a tyrant, a man who is now on the edge of civil war. This man is a figure who fascinates, appallingly fascinates, this man, is now, too many hours late.

GENEVIEVE: Well this…

KATHRYN: Yes…

GENEVIEVE: This is… Very exciting…

MICHELEINE: We thought by the window. Sitting at his desk.

KATHRYN: He sends fucking Makin. Scandinavian. Reuters reject. Blonde. Too blonde. Work done to her lips.

(They sit. A silence. Time ticks by.)

GENEVIEVE: She must visit our –

KATHRYN: Northern States. I cover mainly the Northern states.

GENEVIEVE: …coastal towns. It's very exciting to have a visitor from abroad…

MICHELEINE: Genie, don't embarrass yourself. You're gushing.

GENEVIEVE: You're drinking too much.

(GENEVIEVE comes up to look at the painting with KATHRYN.)

(To KATHRYN.) You've noticed the painting.

KATHRYN: Sorry? I can't understand you.

GENEVIEVE: The painting? The painting on the wall?

KATHRYN: When you go to countries where terrible things have happened, things that I cannot mention, things that I prefer to look at through the eye of a lens, when you go to these countries the thing that shocks you is that you are so shocked you are not shocked at all.

(The phone rings.)

GENEVIEVE: Does she understand it? Can you ask her? What does she think of that painting?

MICHELEINE: *(Calling out.)* Marianna…

GENEVIEVE: My husband painted –

MICHELEINE: *(Beat.)* I forgot, today is her half day.

(No one answers it.)

KATHRYN: Then something throws you, some incongruous object, a child's rubber ring or a school book in the mud, or a grown man crying because he can't get a jar open, a jar of honey which he has found in the wreck of his house. You are touched for a moment by the horror of it all and you want to – You want to close the door quickly…

GILMA: What do you think of the painting?

GENEVIEVE: My husband painted.

KATHRYN: *(Beat.)* That painting…that painting is the foot in the door.

(A beat. The phone stops ringing.)

GENEVIEVE: What did she say?

GILMA: Not much at all.

MICHELEINE: Someone will have answered it.

GILMA: *(To KATHRYN.)* Someone will have answered it.

KATHRYN: Gilma, I can't stay here –

MICHELEINE: *(Beat.)* My husband had he not joined the political arena may have been an architect…

GILMA: *(To KATHRYN.)* A builder…

KATHRYN: I'd like to use the phone? Gilma… Gilma… Has she any idea what is happening?

MICHELEINE: *(Beat.)* My daughter. My grandson they live on the Southside.

GILMA: *(Holding up video.)* *A Bug's Life.* Second favourite after *Toy Story.*

KATHRYN: Cartoons. Fuck. Fuck.

GILMA: Could I watch?

MICHELEINE: If you'd like –

KATHRYN: No.

MICHELEINE: She's rude. So sharp. Why are you so rude? They're being rude to me.

Oolio, where are you? Sweetheart, where are you?

KATHRYN: She tells us the story of the first time she met him –

MICHELEINE: I was standing in the library. He kissed me on my neck. Have I told you this story?

GENEVIEVE: No darling, you've not told me.

KATHRYN: She has… Several times… It is clear on the woman's face.

GILMA: *(As if to KATHRYN.)* Her husband made love to her –

MICHELEINE: …around the great buildings of our city…

GILMA: *(As if to KATHRYN.)* Fish markets…and how do you say…the place where you…watch the sharks swim.

KATHRYN: Aquarium.

GILMA: Aquarium.

KATHRYN: How unusual…

GENEVIEVE: Yes…

GILMA: I guess yes.

MICHELEINE: *(To GILMA.)* I'm watching you.

GILMA: Amazing, how they get the bugs to talk like that –

MICHELEINE: She thinks that they're real. Christ –

GILMA: She thinks I think they're real. Christ –

GENEVIEVE: *(To GILMA.)* Kathryn, with your work? You must have travelled?

MICHELEINE: Genie, don't bother her –

KATHRYN: All the time she is talking –

MICHELEINE: ...my husband always says busy people find it boring to discuss work.

KATHRYN: ...her skin is pulling tighter across her mouth, and tiny specks of powder blot the beads of sweat around her nose. The light has now quite gone.

MICHELEINE: We thought by the window.

GENEVIEVE: Micheleine. It's nearly ten o'clock –

MICHELEINE: Please don't ask – Please don't ask again.

KATHRYN: ...and we've been here since four.

•

GENEVIEVE: When Micheleine calls I am not watching the TV programme. The one where the man wins a million.
I am sitting in my kitchen. I have turned all the lights off.
It is dark and outside...the noise is lighting up the sky.
Somewhere there are people smashing shop windows.
And upstairs my neighbour has just hit his wife.

MICHELEINE: Genevieve?

GENEVIEVE: 'You've caught me watching the television.
That thing on the television?'

MICHELEINE: Of course. Why not come over?

GENEVIEVE: 'The one where the man wins a million?'

MICHELEINE: No, that would be fine. That would be absolutely wonderful.

GENEVIEVE: 'Micheleine...'

MICHELEINE: *(Beat.)* There's a lady, she's here from the press.

GENEVIEVE: I put down the phone and sit for several minutes. Upstairs I can already hear someone moving out. They are filling their car with as much as they can carry. Knowing that their Northern neighbours may no longer be their friends. I listen as they bump a washing machine down the stairs. I wonder what I'll take. Certainly not a washing machine and suddenly I realise I'm not going anywhere.

'Micheleine, of course, of course I'll come over.' *(Beat.)* Thirty –

MICHELEINE: …five –

GENEVIEVE: – years is a long time to despise your best friend. *(To KATHRYN.)* Why do you look like that?

KATHRYN: Ask her, ask her how her husband drowned?

GILMA: *(To GENEVIEVE.)* Beautiful colours.

GENEVIEVE: Sorry?

GILMA: *(To GENEVIEVE.)* She thinks beautiful colours.

GENEVIEVE: That's not what she said.

KATHRYN: I'd like to phone my office. It's clear he's not coming.

MICHELEINE: I assure you. I assure you…

GENEVIEVE: Will you calm, Micheleine? Calm.

MICHELEINE: His ulcer is grumbling and he's waiting for some papers. There are some papers he said he has to sign.

GENEVIEVE: *(Beat.)* Feed them. It's suppertime. They're probably hungry.

GILMA: She says that she's starving.

MICHELEINE: *(Eyeing GILMA.)* It is you who is starving.

GILMA: There is fruit and some cheese and some left over cuts.

(The sound of footsteps as though someone is walking down a long silent corridor.)

MICHELEINE: I walk down the corridor to the ground floor kitchen. I notice that the lights have not been turned on in the west wing behind. The darkness is surprising, unfamiliar, unordered. It is ten and by ten, there should be every light on in the house. In the kitchen I still hope to find Marianna. *(Calling out.)* Marianna. *(Beat.)* She normally stays until we are all fed. The oven is off, the larder is empty, she has even taken the flour and sugar from the jars. *(Beat.)* I forget, it's her half day. I scrabble… I scrabble together some kind of supper… Some cheese, some oranges and there is some fat pork at the back of the fridge. I arrange them on a plate, as best I can. I walk back along the corridor. I see fires burning far away, lighting my route back.

(Whispering.) Oolio… Oolio…

KATHRYN: She calls out a pet name.

(KATHRYN is suddenly standing as if in her path, making MICHELEINE jump, almost laugh, her phone in her hand.)

I can't get a signal.

MICHELEINE: Christ… Christ… You made me jump.

GENEVIEVE: How old are you?

GILMA: Twenty-four. I know I look older.

GENEVIEVE: No…

GILMA: Yes, I do. I know this. You don't have to lie.

(KATHRYN and MICHELEINE hover, as if one doesn't know if the other should cross their path.)

KATHRYN: Can I try it in here? *(As if entering a room.)* Wow…

MICHELEINE: For state entertaining. For official visits. You can seat four hundred with relative ease. The marble was mined from a small village in Southern India. You see the awning it was cut from one piece.

KATHRYN: Oolio?

MICHELEINE: A pet name. I thought I heard him come back.

KATHRYN: Micheleine, can you try and understand what I am saying? My office says there are riots building up on the Southside. Soldiers being shot. Probably looting. Micheleine are you aware of any of this?

(MICHELEINE turns and heads back as if with the others.)

MICHELEINE: I am aware of the young Northern girl, Gilma, as she wipes her plate with the skin of an orange, eating the peel to get the last of the grease.

GILMA: Jackie Collins? My God, I love Jackie Collins.

MICHELEINE: I am aware of my best friend, my dearest friend, Genevieve who is trying to make conversation, trying to make everything alright…

GILMA: Second shelf. Lady Boss… American Star is her best.

MICHELEINE: I am aware of something happening outside of here, I can hear the noise, I just chose to lie. My husband, he finds them relaxing. I prefer…

GILMA: Shakespeare. The complete works…

KATHRYN: Lady Boss. Sometimes there are pockets of insight that one can't help but try and shoot.

(As GILMA licks the last of the food off the plate with her fingers.)

MICHELEINE: Please mind the china. The plates are a set.

GILMA: *(Holding glass.)* Nice glasses.

MICHELEINE: Siberian.

KATHRYN: I'm not an idiot. I know what you are doing.

MICHELEINE: Gilma has a boyfriend. A soldier.

GENEVIEVE: That's very nice. A soldier?

GILMA: The State Military.

GENEVIEVE: That's admirable. A soldier –

MICHELEINE: Gilma's from the North.

(Silence.)

KATHRYN: I need to use the phone now.

GILMA: Where is your telephone please?

KATHRYN: Mine can't get a signal.

MICHELEINE: Just to your right.

(KATHRYN goes to use the phone.)

GILMA: The woman in the green dress watches me while I finish my food up. It is obvious what she is thinking. 'Her manners? Of course she's from the North.' I eat the orange peel not because I have to, not because I am in poverty but because I like the taste.

KATHRYN: At last he picks up the line is faint.

GENEVIEVE: Your accent?

GILMA: It's been five years.

GENEVIEVE: You've visited your family?

GILMA: No. Not often.

GENEVIEVE: That's a pity. I couldn't live, I really couldn't without mine.

MICHELEINE: Liar.

> They've never actually visited her. I love Genevieve. She's my very, very best friend but sometimes… I won't say this. I'd hate to embarass her.

GENEVIEVE: I'm sorry.

GILMA: Sorry? What is there to be sorry about?

KATHRYN: *(As if on the phone.)* You sent fucking Makin? I'm stuck here…

> Nick… I've been here since four o'clock. There's not a taxi for miles… I can't walk… It's freezing… Would you stick around for this?

> Well maybe he's got the right idea… The joke's on us… Fuck, the fucking photo, the light has gone.

GILMA: I visit my family, one day last summer. They ask me how I am. I can't bear the way they eat. I show them the clothes and the things that I have brought them. A jacket from Marks and Spencer's. A video – a hip and thigh diet for my mother. 'Hip and thigh…hip and thigh…where is the food for me to get fat?' This is said, so that I send more money for them each month. 'Even in a war you must make the effort… Even in a war, mother…' Even in a war, I polish my shoes.

MICHELEINE: Gilma has a boyfriend. A soldier.

GENEVIEVE: That's very nice. A soldier? I hope you love him very, very much.

MICHELEINE: You –

GILMA: …plan to get married when he gets home.

> As soon as I say this, I wish that I hadn't. Not because I am lying but because it was never true.

KATHRYN: *(As if on the phone.)* … I don't know what's going on here. I don't know why I'm here. Nick, don't piss around. I don't know what to do now. You sent Makin.

GILMA: Fucking, fucking Makin.

KATHRYN: *(As if on the phone.)* Fuck you. Fuck you. Yeah fuck her too.

GILMA: She swears a lot. *(Beat.)* Her office is telling her to stay where she is.

KATHRYN: *(As if on the phone.)* He may have asked for me but he's not fucking here.

(KATHRYN, as if slamming down the phone.)

Gilma, the taxi. We can we get the taxi?

GILMA: We said not until later. We have to wait.

MICHELEINE: My husband has a driver. Perhaps I could call him.

GILMA: She makes gestures to find her diary and call her husband at work.

GENEVIEVE: Your work must be fascinating you take photos for a living?

MICHELEINE: Genie, don't bother her. Oolio says busy people don't like talking about work.

KATHRYN: In places of crisis –

MICHELEINE: My favourite photo of us is at Christmas…

KATHRYN: …places of war.

GENEVIEVE: And you are not moved by the things that you see?

KATHRYN: I'm sorry?

GENEVIEVE: You don't understand at all.

MICHELEINE: It was taken last Christmas. With all of us. The family.

GENEVIEVE: Micha, have you called Angelica? Is she at home with the boy?

(MICHELEINE goes and pours herself another drink.)

KATHRYN: On the desk is a photo. Of her husband with his family. He is wearing a paper hat, he is flushed, the hat's awry, like a comical drunkard or a man with one eye. There is a smile on his face and clasped around wrinkled fingers are those of his grandchild hugging the skin… He's very…

MICHELEINE: Like his grandfather... Do you have children?

KATHRYN: No. Not at all.

MICHELEINE: *(To KATHRYN.)* Are you married?

GILMA: She's asking if you are...

KATHRYN: No.

GENEVIEVE: I imagine there is no time...no time with your work...

KATHRYN: Sometimes it is easier if I say I am married. Sometimes it is easier...

MICHELEINE: *Bug's Life.* Now also stolen. Slipped in her jacket. *Toy Story* in her bag. *Bug's Life* most probably wedged under her bra.

This photograph of my husband? This photograph that you plan to take? You must be important. He rarely courts press.

KATHRYN: It was agreed through my office. A request from his advisors.

MICHELEINE: He's a man you admire?

KATHRYN: More fascinated.

GILMA: More fascinated.

MICHELEINE: To me he's my husband.

KATHRYN: And to the rest of the world?

(The phone rings. And rings until – it stops.)

GILMA: ... You drove along the...

GENEVIEVE: Past the Gymnasium...

GILMA: I was there the day they filled in the pool. The day they poured in the concrete.

MICHELEINE: The changing rooms are now offices and the athletic pitch barracks... There were no headquarters. *(Beat.)* I suggested it one evening after supper in bed.

GENEVIEVE: She wants us to admire her.

KATHRYN: In this light she is almost bearable.

MICHELEINE: By morning there were engineers knocking down walls.

GILMA: Your husband used to swim there?

MICHELEINE: He'd been depressed a long time.

GENEVIEVE: With my children.

MICHELEINE: Don't upset her.

GENEVIEVE: Marcus is twenty-one. Darius our youngest is almost eighteen.

MICHELEINE: You've heard from him?

GENEVIEVE: Last week. A painter like his father. He's been skiing for the winter.

MICHELEINE: She is lying.

KATHRYN: She is lying.

GENEVIEVE: He's met a new girl. He doesn't say exactly but as a mother you know.

MICHELEINE: Genevieve.

KATHRYN: The look on her face says she is desperate for us to believe her. The look on her face knows we suspect it's not true.

MICHELEINE: *(Beat.)* A girlfriend. At last. We had money on it he was…

GENEVIEVE: My husband used to tease him. He is gentle like his father. *(To GILMA.)* You don't have children?

GILMA: No. Not yet…

GENEVIEVE: And you?

KATHRYN: No, not at all.

MICHELEINE: *(To GENEVIEVE.)* It's a joke. Don't look so serious. You take me far too seriously.

(MICHELEINE offers GILMA an orange. She takes it.)

KATHRYN: *(Watching GILMA and GENEVIEVE.)* She offers her an orange.

(The phone rings. Eventually MICHELEINE gets up to answer it.)

KATHRYN: She goes to the phone.

MICHELEINE: Hello. *(Long silence.)* Don't do that darling. *(Breaking into a long broad smile.)* He's teasing me on the telephone… We're eating… Only cold cuts… *(Calling out.)* We'll leave some for you.

GENEVIEVE: As we drink the last of the vodka, her comment still burns me. You may have had money on it Micha, but I know my son is not gay.

MICHELEINE: All the time that I am talking they shell oranges on my floor.

KATHRYN: All the time that the wife is talking, the lady in the green dress is pulling a thread from her hem.

GILMA: It's lovely… It's lovely… That green is a lovely colour…

GENEVIEVE: You think so?

GILMA: I think so…

(Eyeing GENEVIEVE.) She has five notes in her purse. A bus ticket and a library card. And a photo of a man, he is eating a hunk of sausage and standing with a watering can, squinting in the sun.

GENEVIEVE: My husband was fascinated with light and how it fell on life… His paintings were always the balance of dark and light… It seems very black but the more you look, there is… You see in that corner, that tiny chink of –

KATHRYN: She's crying.

(GENEVIEVE gets up to pour herself another drink.)

She's crying. She's trying not to show us. But as she pours herself a drink, there are tears in her eyes.

(GILMA touching KATHRYN's camera equipment.)

KATHRYN: *(To GILMA.)* Don't do that… Please don't do that… You keep on touching…

GILMA: Sorry…

KATHRYN: If you keep on touching you'll get grease on the lens.

(MICHELEINE enters as if off the phone.)

MICHELEINE: He asks that you leave him some of the ham, please. It's his favourite, his sister sends it from her own farm.

She stares at me. I turn and catch her eye, aware she's always watching me.

KATHRYN: You don't look…

MICHELEINE: 54-55 next month.

KATHRYN: She's a vain woman. This flatters her.

GILMA: She says you don't look it… She says…

KATHRYN: Tell her she has beautiful skin.

MICHELEINE: That's really very nice of you… That's really very kind of you…

GILMA: I take the five notes and a photograph.

I slip the purse of the green lady back in her bag.

GENEVIEVE: In my house I have several photos.
Of Micheleine with my family. Micheleine and him and my husband and me. On boating trips and birthdays and there is even one at my husband's memorial. Micheleine sitting, head bent down at her husband's side.

KATHRYN: She has this way of turning her head, as if trained, as if knowing that this is captivating…

GENEVIEVE: The photo was commented upon, noted, that they both visibly cried.

(To anyone.) I have the most marvellous photo of Micheleine at my home.

MICHELEINE: There's an edge in her voice.

GILMA: She says she has a photograph of Micheleine at her husband's funeral.

KATHRYN: The friend barely can look at us. She can barely believe she's said it.

MICHELEINE: Have you, Genie? I don't think I've seen that one.

GENEVIEVE: I always admired the coat you wore.

MICHELEINE: You can borrow it…any time at all.

•

(GILMA holding the broken bits of vase. A silence broken only by the ring of the phone. MICHELEINE lets it ring for some time until –)

GILMA: I'm so sorry. It was just… In my hand.

MICHELEINE: *(Calling out.)* Marianna… Marianna… I'll get you. *(Calling out.)* Marianna… I get you… I'll one minute… *(Going.)* We need more ice.

(MICHELEINE scoops up the ice bucket to go and get more ice. The phone stops ringing.)

GENEVIEVE: I bolt the gate behind me. I climb into the car. My neighbour has many possessions littered across the grass. A washing machine, a wheelbarrow, a bed, a table… *'You should think of leaving. They won't want you staying here.'* I choose to ignore him. I'm not ungracious. I'm not unfriendly. As I pass in the car, I see his dog sleeping in the machine's metal drum. I drive along the North route and past the Gymnasium.

I stop. I lie in the snow. Wet, seeping through my coat, as if I am floating, as if I could just drown, just drown. I think of going to sleep.

After, the streets are already littered and there are several broken panes of glass. Someone has set off a burglar alarm and there is a crowd near the crossroads. I lean forward and lock my doors. I take the back route here. I drive through the gates and already I know it is over. Maybe now my sons will come back.

(MICHELEINE enters, back with a fresh ice bucket of ice, passing the dustpan and brush to GILMA.)

•

MICHELEINE: Genevieve –

(MICHELEINE stands. GILMA is once more on the floor sweeping up some glass with a dustpan and brush. KATHRYN is standing looking at the painting. GENEVIEVE now has her coat on, her hair still wet, pulling off her scarf as if she has just arrived. The repetition is faster, fragmented into a ricochet of words.)

Hair…

GENEVIEVE: Snow.

(GILMA sweeps up on the floor.)

MICHELEINE: Venetian… Special vase –

GENEVIEVE: The roads…

KATHRYN: Green dress.

GENEVIEVE: Oolio –

(MICHELEINE offers KATHRYN a cigarette. KATHRYN declines. GENEVIEVE pours herself a glass of vodka.)

MICHELEINE: Onto our third.

Genevieve. Kathryn… Gilma… Best to go through her.

KATHRYN: You're freezing…

GENEVIEVE: The heater on my car packed up…

KATHRYN: You have a car?

GENEVIEVE: Very old. Very battered.

MICHELEINE: I am shaking. I am frightened. I want to tell them I am very, very frightened. I had not planned for this. What happens next?

GENEVIEVE: Micheleine, there is trouble –

MICHELEINE: I was showing them my handbags.

GENEVIEVE: As far as the North route.

MICHELEINE: The military?

GENEVIEVE: Are not around.

MICHELEINE: Hair…

GENEVIEVE: …dripping.

MICHELEINE: Towel…

(MICHELEINE goes to get GENEVIEVE a towel. GENEVIEVE watches KATHRYN looking at the painting. The phone stops ringing.)

GENEVIEVE: *(To KATHRYN.)* The view from our window… From our house… You see? That is the river and that is the persons…

KATHRYN: And which bit are people?

GENEVIEVE: You see their faces?

KATHRYN: Your husband painted?

Your husband painted it?

For them?

(GENEVIEVE nods.)

GENEVIEVE: *(To GILMA.)* Tell her, will you tell her, I find it frightening too.

(MICHELEINE enters and drops the towel into GENEVIEVE's lap.)

GILMA: They are talking about the painting. All three standing in front of it. That is when I take *Toy Story*. That is when. When their backs are all turned. Earlier Kathryn has asked her –

(A sound. A bang. Shelling. Fireworks. Something. Somewhere.)

KATHRYN: The noise? It's getting nearer.

MICHELEINE: It's much louder if you have the windows open.

GILMA: She closes them. Ignores our gaze. I translate of course.

MICHELEINE: On a clear day…

GILMA: When there's no wind…

MICHELEINE: You can hear almost everything. The silence carries everything.

GENEVIEVE: When the children were younger you could sometimes hear them splashing no matter how far you were from the swimming pool.

MICHELEINE: Genevieve. Don't gush now. What are we to do with you?

(GENEVIEVE hands back the towel to MICHELEINE.)

Help me, Genie, help me. I don't know what to do.

GILMA: *(Watching MICHELEINE.)* She's frightened. You can see this. She smiles but she is frightened. Her mind is elsewhere. She won't notice what I take.

MICHELEINE: When I pick up the phone, the first time there is no one. The silence is empty but there is definitely someone there… The second time I can hear them talking in the other room…

GENEVIEVE: My husband was fascinated with light and how it fell on life…

MICHELEINE: She's trying to impress them, flailing around in artist talk…

'Hello.' *(Long silence.)* 'Don't do that darling.'

Someone is sending insults down the line… Terrible words cutting through the silence –

'Bitch. Whore. Say goodbye now.'

A northern accent. And then – Mama… Mama *(Breaking into a long broad smile.)* He's teasing me on the telephone.

KATHRYN: Terrible things happen, you shoot what you can. You do your job.

(A sound. A bang. Shelling. Fireworks. Something. Somewhere.)

GILMA: Bang.

(A ripple of laughter as GILMA makes them laugh.)

MICHELEINE: A noise. Like gun fire.

I am worried because I think I hear my grandson crying. I am worried because…

(Beat.)

My daughter… Angelica…lives on the Southside.

KATHRYN: If you keep on touching you'll get grease on the lens.

(MICHELEINE as if slamming down the phone.)

(MICHELEINE as if re-entering the room.)

MICHELEINE: He asks that you leave him some of the ham, please. It's his favourite, his sister sends it from her own farm.

GENEVIEVE: Micheleine…

MICHELEINE: It wasn't him… It was someone… I don't know who it was… It was someone…

GENEVIEVE: How did they get your number?

MICHELEINE: I don't know… I don't know…

GILMA: If I hadn't been a lecturer, I might have been a photographer…

KATHRYN: People always say this…

GILMA: Do they? I wonder why.

GENEVIEVE: Call him.

MICHELEINE: I have tried. I don't even get his secretary.

GENEVIEVE: Do you think?

MICHELEINE: No.

GENEVIEVE: Do you think maybe…

MICHELEINE: No.

GILMA: Buzz Lightyear is not real, he's an electronic space man and the cowboy…he's the hero. He doesn't like it when he moves in on his patch.

MICHELEINE: What are they talking about?

GENEVIEVE: They're making conversation.

GILMA: The cowboy is in love with… I can't remember who the girl is.

KATHRYN: Barbie?

GILMA: Of course, Barbie, but she is the fantasy, the cowboy has a real love that the space man steals.

KATHRYN: This is a ridiculous conversation… This is a fucking ridiculous conversation…

MICHELEINE: Bo Peep. It's Bo Peep. I've watched it with my grandson.

GILMA: Of course it all turns out alright in the end. *(Long beat.)* You've not had sex, it's clear –

KATHRYN: Piss off.

GILMA: …in a very, very long time.

KATHRYN: Fuck you.

GILMA: Desperate.

KATHRYN: Is that nice and clear?

GILMA: When? One year…two…

KATHRYN: Three… Three weeks ago… Actually.

GILMA: Not bad. And you enjoyed it?

KATHRYN: Brief. Necessary. Uncomplicated. Yes I enjoyed it.

GILMA: I sometimes get it wrong.

KATHRYN: The wife is upset. She is being hushed by the woman in the green dress. *(To GENEVIEVE.)* You're freezing…

GENEVIEVE: The heater on my…

KATHRYN: Could you drive me, if I paid you, over to the Southside?

GILMA: On the Southside is the flat where I live with my boyfriend's mother. She is poor and I work to make sure there is money coming in –

GENEVIEVE: The North route is log jammed…

KATHRYN: But there's a road, we drove past it…

GENEVIEVE: I can't.

KATHRYN: Please –

GENEVIEVE: Don't ask me. I can't.

MICHELEINE: She can't. Alright? Alright.

(Beat.)

GILMA: This morning I receive a call from my agency. There is one phone in the hall, which you can only use at certain times in the day. I am told I am to come to interpret for the wife of a diplomat and a journalist, a photographer who is coming into town. Giving the taxi driver instructions which I have picked up from the agency, it is only then I realise where it is we are to go. He is not just a diplomat, he is more than a diplomat.

MICHELEINE: Gilma's from the North.

GENEVIEVE: Your accent?

GILMA: It's been five years.

GENEVIEVE: You've visited your family?

GILMA: Sometimes.

GENEVIEVE: *(To KATHRYN.)* I'm sorry. I can't. The roads are too icy.

KATHRYN: Snow.

GILMA: Snow, slowly falling outside.

(The four women stand as if looking out of the window, watching the snow fall as it floats by outside.)

GENEVIEVE: The night my husband died –

MICHELEINE: You were having supper with us…

GENEVIEVE: He had gone to take the children to the Gym –

MICHELEINE: And left her all alone. I persuaded you to come and eat with us… Our husbands were school friends, that's how we met. Tell them the story of the first time you visited…

GENEVIEVE: Micheleine…

MICHELEINE: A dinner party, the first we ever had…

GENEVIEVE: In that flat…

MICHELEINE: Above the butchers…

GENEVIEVE: Pie-eyed…

MICHELEINE: Preferred to dance…

GENEVIEVE: …while they talked rubbish late into the night…

MICHELEINE: This is where we differ… My husband never talked an ounce of rubbish in his life…

KATHRYN: Maybe if I could take the car.

MICHELEINE: You have the right kind of insurance? I didn't think so. That would be dangerous.

(KATHRYN laughs.)

Have you not family? Someone you should think of. Have you no-one who may be worried about you back home.

GENEVIEVE: I don't think it would get you there.

KATHRYN: It is no more dangerous than what is going on in here. Translate it… Gilma will you please tell her what I said?

GILMA: The car's fucked. Don't keep asking. I've paid for the taxi. To take us back to the Southside.

(KATHRYN looks to GILMA who remains silent until –)

She says that is fine. She will wait for the taxi ride.

(MICHELEINE nods, offers KATHRYN another orange from the bowl… KATHRYN hesitates then takes it and starts to peel, she walks as if going outside.)

GENEVIEVE: Fireworks.

(KATHRYN nods. They look up as if above the sky has just lit up. The sound of shelling.)

KATHRYN: Fireworks. And not even November…

GENEVIEVE: Sorry…

KATHRYN: It doesn't matter.

GENEVIEVE: I'm sorry. I don't understand.

KATHRYN: Sometimes, tonight, I wonder why I do this.

GENEVIEVE: I loved my husband.

KATHRYN: Yes.

GENEVIEVE: Love. I loved my husband.

KATHRYN: Sorry.

GENEVIEVE: I want you to know that.

(GILMA peels an orange.)

MICHELEINE: There's a bowl…

GILMA: She is watching even when I peel an orange.

MICHELEINE: Why don't you put your peel in the bowl?

GILMA: Sorry. Sorry.

MICHELEINE: There's no need to be sorry… *(Beat.)* Your boyfriend, the soldier, is he from the North?

GILMA: His family live here, here in the city.

MICHELEINE: I thought not. I thought not in the army. If he was from the North, they wouldn't let him in.

(GILMA pauses in peeling her orange, letting the peel drop to the floor.)

KATHRYN: How far away? *(Beat.)* How far away do you think they are? You know they'll come here.

GENEVIEVE: *(Looking at KATHRYN.)* I wonder, looking at this woman, if this was a different time, if we spoke the same language, if this hadn't happened, if I wasn't me and this all hadn't happened, would we be friends?

KATHRYN: The light. It doesn't matter…

GENEVIEVE: She carries a kind of melancholia… Your family?

KATHRYN: Family. Just me. Not really any family.

GILMA: What are you fucking looking at?

GENEVIEVE: A kind of melancholia that is familiar to me.

GILMA: *Bug's Life* in my pocket.

MICHELEINE: Don't think I haven't noticed…

GILMA: Shit she's going to say it.

MICHELEINE: Gilma *(Long silence.)* you've some orange in your teeth.

(GILMA picks, nods. Silence.)

GILMA: Your husband is a great man.

MICHELEINE: To me he is my husband.

GILMA: My boyfriend has his picture above our bed.

MICHELEINE: He's a soldier. As it should be.

GILMA: Yes of course, as it should be –

(MICHELEINE holds out her hand. GILMA disposes the peel into her hand.)

Thank you.

MICHELEINE: You're welcome. Gilma.

GILMA: Gilma. Micheleine… Are you not worried about your husband?

MICHELEINE: Are you not worried about your soldier?

KATHRYN: The woman in the green dress is shivering… Genevieve? I'm going inside.

(MICHELEINE rolls back laughing as if GILMA has just told her the funniest joke.)

MICHELEINE: *(As if bursting into conversation.)* That is the rudest joke that I ever heard.

GILMA: He learned it in the army.

MICHELEINE: And it best stay there. We thought that you had gone…

GENEVIEVE: I was showing her the car.

KATHRYN: She's right, I can't drive it.

GILMA: The car is fucked.

KATHRYN: That's not what I said.

GILMA: She says you're right, she can't drive it. But thanks very much.

KATHRYN: If you are going to talk for me can you try and get it right.

GILMA: If you don't speak it how do you know what I am saying?

(The phone rings. MICHELEINE does not move.)

If you don't speak it how do you know what I am saying?

KATHRYN: I know.

GILMA: Pardon. *(Beat.)* You don't speak a word.

GENEVIEVE: I'll get it, Micha.

(The phone rings some more. GENEVIEVE goes and answers it.)

GENEVIEVE: *(As if on the phone.)* Hello… I'll tell her but she won't like it. I hear you… I hear you… That kind of talk doesn't wash with me…

(GENEVIEVE, as if coming back off the phone.)

MICHELEINE: You spoke to him. He's on his way, Genie.

(GENEVIEVE is silent.)

Did he give you a message? Did he not want to speak to me?

GENEVIEVE: No.

MICHELEINE: No?

GENEVIEVE: No.

Is there any more to drink?

MICHELEINE: See. He's on his way.

GENEVIEVE: The photograph. Where did you find it? In your hand? The photograph?

GILMA: Under your chair. It must have slipped…

GENEVIEVE: Out of my purse. Marcus is twenty-one. Darius almost eighteen. There's a new girl. He doesn't say exactly but I know –

MICHELEINE: *(Beat.)* A girlfriend. At last. We had money on it he was…

GENEVIEVE: No. You always say that, but no you are wrong.

MICHELEINE: What do I say? Genevieve, if I have upset you…

GENEVIEVE: You haven't but let us now at last set the record straight. My son is not gay. My son is gentle. My son is like his father, but for you it is easier to say…

MICHELEINE: Genie –

GENEVIEVE: Easier to say…

(GILMA stands up and moves across the room, placing back the video of 'Bug's Life' onto the table.)

GILMA: My favourite is *Toy Story* –

KATHRYN: She places it on the table. She is totally unashamed. The wife and the friend, Genevieve, stop their arguing, the wife is momentarily bemused…

MICHELEINE: My grandson's.

GILMA: And there it is back. *(To MICHELEINE.)* Your husband is a man I admire, Miss. Your husband is a man who I believe is doing good. Your husband, I am grateful to your husband for all he has done –

MICHELEINE: For your people? For your family?

GILMA: My family is not my family. My family is my soldier. My family, like your husband, despises people from the North.

My mother says 'A soldier? You are sleeping with a soldier?' 'Yes, mother. Yes, mother. What is wrong with that?'

One day through her door my mother gets a tongue, cut out from the throat of my brother, her youngest son.

MICHELEINE: That's most surprising. I'll tell my husband. He will be surprised to find that…you…feel the same way. Well done.

GILMA: Bloody and dirty and staining the newspaper it's
wrapped in. A dirty Northern tongue. A warning to us all.

You're welcome.

MICHELEINE: That's quite alright.

KATHRYN: In a Northern town not far away, an old man
brings me a baby, a baby that the soldiers have gouged the
eyes out from.

GILMA: What?

KATHRYN: The old man is holding the baby up to me to
witness, holding it up, asking me to take it, to take it in
some way.

GILMA: What?

KATHRYN: I feel sick. I feel sick, not because I have not seen
this before, because I have just used the last of my film.
I pretend to this man. I shoot anyway.

You're from the North.

GILMA: I'm whatever I want to be. In my pocket, is your
licence. International. *(As if reading.)* Kathryn Margaret
Foxton. Kate Foxton.

KATHRYN: Give that back.

GILMA: It fell out in the taxi. You might need it when you get
home.

KATHRYN: I'm going to tell the agency. Not to use you again.

GILMA: That is fine. That is fine. I can always find work elsewhere.

KATHRYN: And after. Where will you go then? When your
soldier is back? What happens then?

*(A sound. A bang. Shelling. Fireworks. Something. Faint. Yet closer
than before.)*

MICHELEINE: When I first met my husband, my father did
not want us to marry, it was all a secret, I used to meet him
at an old school hall outside of the town.

KATHRYN: *(Watching MICHELEINE.)* Lamplight. A window. She
kneels on a chair. Her feet hang. Her nose pressed against
the glass. The sound of… The snow keeps falling.

MICHELEINE: One winter, when the snow was so thick that for days we would never leave the house, only my father would be picked up and driven to work. The days were very boring and my sister was so irritating and all I wanted to do was see him, this boy, who I did not yet know whether I loved, when there was a tap at the window and I looked down and it was him and I say… *'Ssh my little sister will give us away.' 'Don't worry my darling, no-one will know that you have been with me, walk in my shoe steps, follow behind me and then there will be only one set of footprints in the snow.'* So I followed him through the dark of a very, very short day and that afternoon, while my sister played house with my mother, we made love for the first time until I was sore –

He leans back to kiss me. A small patch of stubble. Something about his manner. Back in one hour.

I feel sick.

Genie, I'm rambling –

GENEVIEVE: It's late…

MICHELEINE: Did someone win a million – ?

GENEVIEVE: No, a fat lady had trouble with a question on the Pope.

MICHELEINE: Did you know the answer?

GENEVIEVE: No.

MICHELEINE: You must read more, Genie, you really must read more.

GENEVIEVE: New handbag.

MICHELEINE: Last season's.

GENEVIEVE: It doesn't look it.

MICHELEINE: You're sniping…

GENEVIEVE: I'm not, Sweetheart.

MICHELEINE: You're picking a fight.

GENEVIEVE: Micha, when I drove over, I saw they had firebombed the Southside.

MICHELEINE: Along the Terra –

GENEVIEVE: Yes –

MICHELEINE: Oh my God… My God…

Coffee –

(*MICHELEINE goes as if to make coffee.*)

GILMA: Is Micheleine alright?

GENEVIEVE: Her daughter she lives –

KATHRYN: With the boy?

GILMA: With the boy…

KATHRYN: Your family?

GENEVIEVE: …moved away when their father –

MICHELEINE: I ring the office.

The woman who finally answers it is my husband's secretary. She spent last Christmas here when her house was burgled and she had nowhere to go.

'Where's Oolio…? He's not there… But he was coming to sign papers. He was coming to you to sign papers. But he's taken the car.' There's noise. A lot of noise.

Hello… Hello –

(*The woman hangs up on MICHELEINE or is cut off.*)

See, he's on his way.

(*Aside to GENEVIEVE.*) He didn't call. You didn't talk to him –

GENEVIEVE: Micha –

MICHELEINE: Why did you lie?

GENEVIEVE: Did you want me to tell you that some man with a thick Northern voice, a thick Northern gruff voice, a thick angry Northern gruff voice thinks you're a whore?

I thought not. (*Beat.*) I thought not.

MICHELEINE: It's the waiting.

GENEVIEVE: Yes… I know… I understand that.

(*MICHELEINE suddenly breaks into a low, wailing, engulfing outpouring that shocks and silences those around her, for several seconds until, regaining composure –*)

MICHELEINE: No milk? The milk is on the sill. I put it there this morning. Excuse me…

KATHRYN: No one says anything until –

(The clitter-clatter of heels as if disappearing down a long corridor.)

MICHELEINE: I have never noticed until this day what a clitter-clatter my tiny mules make along this corridor. I have never noticed the way my husband winces every time I run to greet him, fuss around him, scoop the work papers out of his arms and ask him to tell me about his day. 'Darling, your shoes.' I thought it was just him…just his grumbling ulcer… I thought that my conversation… my concern…my direction when yet another problem fell in his lap, yet another blot on the landscape threatened to disrupt some important advance, soothed this noise. That my advice, taken, relied upon, needed, often acted upon, was enough to disguise the clitter-clatter of heels I have observed in other women.

'Where's Oolio?'

'He's not here.'

'But he was coming to sign papers. He was coming to you to sign papers.'

'Micheleine, you must get out of the house. Micheleine you must get a car and get out of the house and get out of the city as soon as you can.'

'But he's taken the car…'

There's noise. A lot of noise…

'Micheleine. I can't talk to you now. He has left you. He has left us.'

(The footsteps stop. MICHELEINE takes the milk and pours it into a jug.)

KATHRYN: He wasn't on the phone, was he?

GENEVIEVE: No.

KATHRYN: He's gone.

GILMA: At that moment I see my mother-in-law…

My non-mother-in-law, my boyfriend's mother, where I live until my boyfriend comes home…

I kiss him with my dirty Northern tongue.

At that moment I see my mother-in-law screaming at others to get out. They have stolen her television and are writing things on the wall… The Northern invasion… It is from my mother-in-law that I have learnt to speak. She turns a blind out to the odd clumsy vowel, I assure her that this is a throwback to some distant relative a long time ago who came from the North side… I know she doesn't believe me but the money I bring in is more important to her. It is I who stole the trainers that she wears on her feet. Nike Air, size seven. Men's. Too big. Uncomfortable. Taken from a journalist who was careless with his bag. If this is it…if this has not been for anything better than this –

GENEVIEVE: You have walked into this mess…

KATHRYN: This is what I do.

GILMA: Where's he gone?

GENEVIEVE: I don't know.

•

(GILMA smashes the vase in her hand.)

GILMA: I'm sorry –

MICHELEINE: Gen…

GILMA: It was just in my hand.

(GILMA bends down and starts to sweep up the broken vase as GENEVIEVE stands once more in familiar pose, pulling the scarf off from around her neck. Language is almost obliterated, the physical actions more important than what is said.)

Hair…

GENEVIEVE: Kathryn…

(GENEVIEVE and KATHRYN go to shake hands but stop.)

KATHRYN: Gilma, outside, ask her does she know that outside, the crowd, they'll be seeking a revenge.

(GILMA does not respond.)

KATHRYN: Gilma?

GILMA: I can't translate that.

KATHRYN: You won't translate that?

GILMA: I won't translate that.

GENEVIEVE: I think she is questioning whether it is right to stay.

MICHELEINE: *(To GENEVIEVE.)* Did you go? You did not. Even when your husband died. You did not leave. Did you? Did you? Look at your hair.

GENEVIEVE: Why have you stopped crying? I could feel sympathy for you when you were crying. I can remember the warmth of that night when we ate scrag end of lamb and our husbands danced with us and mocked us and laughed at us. And thirty-five years on here we are now.

I think she is right. I think you should go.

MICHELEINE: I'm not listening.

GENEVIEVE: You can hear me.

MICHELEINE: I'm just not listening.

GENEVIEVE: Oolio has left you…

MICHELEINE: *(Eyeing KATHRYN.)* You've been listening too much to her.

GENEVIEVE: On the way here, on the North route I passed the Terra Strata, the road is firebombed, my neighbours were cheering…

GILMA: The Terra Strata. My boyfriend and I live near.

MICHELEINE: How long have I known you? How long have I known you?

GENEVIEVE: Thirty –

MICHELEINE: – five…

GENEVIEVE: …years.

MICHELEINE: And you give up now… He will not be pleased with you… Don't blame me if Oolio's angry with you…

(GENEVIEVE gathers together her coat and bag, as if preparing to go.)

(MICHELEINE picks up a towel and rubs GENEVIEVE's hair.)

GENEVIEVE: I want to be with my children. If I drive around the back road I might make it to the Strata –

MICHELEINE: And you think they'll want to see you? They don't want to know you. I know, Genie, don't make us laugh any more, everyone has always known. You let them down. Children don't forget that.

KATHRYN: Woman in the green dress. Almost bent double. Mouth slightly gaping as if she is going to laugh or as if she is trying not to lose the sweet out of her mouth.

Genevieve, are you alright?

(GENEVIEVE nods.)

(To GILMA.) What did she say?

GILMA: She says –

MICHELEINE: Your sons don't love you. They've lost where they've come from –

GILMA: She says –

MICHELEINE: When was the last time they even sent a card?

GILMA: She says –

GENEVIEVE: You make it hard for me to like you.

GILMA: When did you last see –

MICHELEINE: …your own grandchild.

I understand why you're angry. I understand that there is jealousy – Your husband is dead while mine is still alive. *(To KATHRYN.)* Suicide is painful.

GENEVIEVE: It wasn't suicide.

MICHELEINE: Suicide is surprising, but we weren't surprised. *(To GILMA.)* Translate it.

He was a very unhappy man. *(To GENEVIEVE.)* When the inquest was called you were happy to admit this, you were happy to acknowledge that he had not been as well as before.

He had a certain darkness, a way of not seeing the world... It was irritating, destructive to say the least. I've kept the painting as a tribute to him. A reminder, that on every life some rain must fall.

(To GILMA.) Translate it.

GILMA: *(To KATHRYN.)* Do you understand?

KATHRYN: Yes, I understand.

MICHELEINE: He'd been depressed. It was clear he'd been depressed for a long time.

(GENEVIEVE sinks into her chair. MICHELEINE comes over and takes her hand.)

KATHRYN: The wife, head to head with the lady in the green dress. The loll of a scuffed sandal next to the wife's thin zebra mule.

MICHELEINE: I'm sorry. I'm sorry. Genevieve, I'm sorry, but there was nothing, nothing anyone could do.

GENEVIEVE: She calls me up, and says –

MICHELEINE: Genevieve, get your self up here –

GENEVIEVE: We have oysters to eat. There's far too many, so won't you join us. Bring...

MICHELEINE: *(To KATHRYN.)* Her husband. Her husband was a very good man.

GENEVIEVE: I leave him a note. Say come on later.
He's taken our youngest son to the swimming pool. Fourteen. Darius is just fourteen.

GENEVIEVE: I arrive at this house and drink oysters and a liqueur. It goes to my head. I'm almost a flirt. Somebody mentions... 'Your husband is a long time.' I'm happy. Not worried. He'll be at home with the boys. And when I get home, the house is empty. The police have called. I'm to go at once. I arrive at the station to find my youngest sitting in a waiting room, holding his father's swimming towel.

He drowned. He'd been depressed. He'd taken too many… I know what pills he takes. No, you're wrong, who kills himself in view of their child? Takes and swims and drowns in view of their child. Without me even ringing them, I look up and see Micheleine and him, and I know, I see through my youngest's eyes.

MICHELEINE: If we hadn't have kidnapped you. I'm so sorry, Genie…

GENEVIEVE: My youngest wants to speak, to say something but I squeeze his hand hard –

No… I was with my friends all night long. I tell the officers. I see Oolio laughing in a back room with some officers, some brusque aside, some inside joke, about nothing, about some man who drank some magic beer and thought he was Superman, a stupid nervous joke, inappropriate yet needed, badly timed yet delivered with the telling of a raconteur, funny, making her laugh. And I know… I know you killed my husband.

MICHELEINE: He painted the picture, a commission for my husband. It was meant to be the most glorious view. Instead he gave me polemic, instead he gave me mind numbing politics, lies. That painting lies.

GENVIEVE: I know the way these things are done.

GILMA: I was there the day they filled in the pool.

MICHELEINE: There were no headquarters. *(Beat.)*

I suggested it one evening after supper in bed. It seemed the only tribute to a very dear friend.

GENEVIEVE: She thinks that we admire her.

KATHRYN: In this light she is almost bearable.

MICHELEINE: By morning there were engineers knocking down walls.

Genevieve, we're not going anywhere. We're here for the duration.

You and I have nothing to be ashamed of.

125

KATHRYN: Your daughter? She lives on the Southside.

MICHELEINE: No matter.

KATHRYN: But your grandson?

(A beat.)

(MICHELEINE smoothing across the piano stool, as if ironing out a crease, she takes a seat.)

MICHELEINE: Yes, I hear what you say.

GENEVIEVE: The morning after my husband's funeral, I sit in his studio and I look at the painting and suddenly I see what the rest of the world can see. A frightening view, a view of the outside. Unsettling, mocking, outspoken, outside of what one is allowed to say and I hear Micheleine.

But darling, where's the glorious view?

GENEVIEVE: The next day I drive the painting over to Micheleine. 'You must have it. Please take it. He painted it for you.' And I let them comfort me. Let them joke about his outspokenness. Because that painting frightens me, it frightens me like it did them. And from that day I am lost to my sons who see me fawn, and smile, and listen and console with these people so that they can survive. So that I…

(In the distance. Shelling. Fireworks. Something. Somewhere. Very distant. Muffled by the snow and the wind and the distance.)

GILMA: I look at this woman. I have her bus pass in my bag. And a lip pencil and some tweezers and a small St Christopher.

KATHRYN: Taxi?

Cunt bastard's way too late.

(GILMA knocks back her coffee, slipping the cup and saucer into her bag. GILMA exits as if waiting for the taxi. MICHELEINE sits on the piano stool watching as KATHRYN packs up her equipment.)

MICHELEINE: Where do you live? At home. Where is your home?

KATHRYN: I'm sorry… I don't understand what you say…

MICHELEINE: It's nice? Your home.

KATHRYN: Gilma…

MICHELEINE: And when you walk in, what do you see?

KATHRYN: I'm sorry… *(Calling out.)* Gilma? Translation please…

MICHELEINE: There is a mirror, and a table, with a key on the table and a vase of flowers, normally fresh, next to a rack of shoes –

KATHRYN: *(Calling out.)* Gilma –

(GILMA smokes a cigarette, which she has only just lit, admiring the lighter, in her hand.)

MICHELEINE: When you walk into my house you walked along the corridor and there are several prints, cartoons, political, mocking, which my husband likes…

KATHRYN: I don't understand you…

MICHELEINE: A bicycle is always against the door, always waiting for my complaint to Marianna who should have moved it. It is not mine. Turning left is the drawing room and to the right is reception –

KATHRYN: Gilma –

MICHELEINE: I have chosen everything in this house. Everything in this house has a place, has been chosen for a reason, everything I have formed an attachment to.

(The sound of distant violence. Getting closer. GILMA as if standing in the snow, watching the distant violence coming near.)

GILMA: Kathryn, I call out. No one hears me. The city burns now brightly. Kathryn… *(Calling out.)* Kathryn we have to go soon…

KATHRYN: They will come in this house and they will ransack it and take your things and you know what they will do to you then –

MICHELEINE: You've never looked have you? When you walk in your house, you've hardly noticed what is around, have you?

GENEVIEVE: Micheleine…

MICHELEINE: Have you?

(GILMA enters.)

Ask her?

There's mud on my carpet. Your shoes.

KATHRYN: What is she saying?

GILMA: She is asking about your house. The rooms.

MICHELEINE: I want to know what her house is like, she has
come into mine… Ask her. Ask her.

GILMA: She says –

(A beat.)

KATHRYN: Hallway… Lampshade… I don't know…
(To GILMA.) Will you tell her, I think she should leave now?

MICHELEINE: In the bedroom there's a –

KATHRYN: A bed –

MICHELEINE: *(Beat.)* That is it?

GILMA: *(To KATHRYN.)* That is it?

KATHRYN: There's a lamp and some proofs of photos that I
am always about to check.

MICHELEINE: And what is on these photographs?

GILMA: The photos? By your bed?

KATHRYN: I don't want to… The massacres in the Northern
states. There are several pictures of children with their
wounded mothers. There's a boy with his father. They've
cut off his hands… There are pictures of soldiers they're
taunting a local man. They're making him kill his dog.
There's a small shot looks like nothing… Just like a puddle,
it's iced over but through the water… There's a face…
A child still grubby from the sandwich he was eating,
the morning the soldiers came and burnt his house.

MICHELEINE: Tell her I want her to take a photograph.

GENEVIEVE: Micheleine, I'm leaving –

MICHELEINE: Tell her.

GILMA: You've to take the photo.

MICHELEINE: Tell her I want her to take the photograph of
me before and after they come –

GILMA: Before and after they come…

(A ricochet of noise. Muffled but nearer…)

MICHELEINE: Tell her, a woman who describes her subject better than her own home, a woman with such attention to detail for her subjects, such an eye for detail, this is a woman after my own heart…

Tell her what does she have left if she doesn't have history? Tell her I'm a piece of history right under her nose.

Tell her I want her to shoot my right side, even after… My right side is the side I want the world to see…

Tell her outside of history she is nothing… A parasite… I am history… I know what I leave behind…

Tell her I want to be seated in front of the painting… Tell her I take back nothing…

(From somewhere the phone rings. And rings. And rings. And stops. Silence. GENEVIEVE picks up her coat and bag and makes to go.)

Genie. Don't drip, sweetheart, you're leaving a trail of water. *(Calling after.)* Be careful. The roads are icy.

(GENEVIEVE pauses, then walks over to MICHELEINE and slaps her hard across the face. A silence. GENEVIEVE turns and exits.)

GENEVIEVE: *(Calling back to GILMA.)* You can have a lift if you want.

MICHELEINE: Kathryn's staying. *(To KATHRYN.)* How can you not?

(GILMA walks across the room before taking off her shoes and dumping them in the bin.)

GILMA: Your shoes… A Northerner needs your shoes.

MICHELEINE: Gilma –

GILMA: A Northern name. Did I not say before?

(MICHELEINE looks down at the mules on her feet, then slipping them off she holds them out to GILMA.)

MICHELEINE: I think they're your size.

(GILMA hesitates, then takes them, nods her thanks and exits.)

KATHRYN: I am sitting in the lobby of my hotel. After.
The taxi driver is arguing. He did turn up last night…
He haggled about the money even when all around him…

In my wardrobe there are several packets of linen
unopened. This is not some fetish just always the thing
I buy. When I find myself walking aimlessly around a
department store, normally en route back from some job
somewhere, I always buy sheets, or pillowcases, whatever.
I always buy clean white sheets. I suppose that's my whim.
I take them home and am about to unpack but instead I
leave them in the wrapper, for next time. I don't know
why. I don't know why. Some kind of comfort I suppose.
To know that somewhere they are there.

As we drive to the airport, the taxi driver curses. An old
lady dances while a young soldier is shot. He is dragged
through the street by a rope by his neighbours, who this
week are the ones seeking revenge.

On the plane, they serve pineapple and chicken with thin chips,
and for once, I am not hungry. For once I want to go…home.

(A ricochet of noise. Louder. Nearer.)

A window. Lamplight. The peel of an orange. The turn of
the face as she stands looking out.

MICHELEINE: My face against the light. His book collection in
the background. My skin. I have good skin.

The world is white…

KATHRYN: The hallway. The darkness. The door open outside.
Outside –

MICHELEINE: The snow. Everything is…

KATHRYN: …everything is…

MICHELEINE: …stay and take your photograph

What else is there to do?

(The rhythmic ricochet of noise the silent undercurrent.)

I am seventeen, it is snowing, I am walking back with…
he's ahead of me… I tease him to hurry up, bored with his
pace. He is lumbering and frightened of the ice and won't

go any faster so I step across him and this time it is he who has to tiptoe behind to match my boot. And he does, laughing. It is snowing, and we are laughing. And that is when I know I have found the love of my life.

Oolio… Keep up.

KATHRYN: I'm sorry. I don't know what you're saying.

(MICHELEINE turning slightly to the right.)

MICHELEINE: My right side…

(The ricochet of noise grows louder, carrying the ripples of violence, of shelling as KATHRYN hovers with the camera in her hand, as if holding a gun.)

Shoot… Shoot…

(KATHRYN hesitates then slowly aims her camera –)

The End.

TENDER

for Jacob

Tender was first produced by Birmingham Repertory Theatre Company with Hampstead Theatre and Theatre Royal Plymouth, at Hampstead Theatre on 6 September 2001 with the following cast:

SQUEAL	Nick Bagnall
HEN	Caroline Faber
TASH	Kate Fleetwood
AL	David Kennedy
NATHAN	Sean O'Callaghan
GLORIA	Nicola Redmond
MARVIN	Benny Young
Director	Anthony Clark
Designer	Niki Turner

Characters

TASH
late 20s/early 30s

SQUEAL
late 20s/early mid 30s

HEN
early 30s

GLORIA
mid/late 40s

MARVIN
late 40s/early 50s

NATHAN
mid/late 30s

AL
mid/late 30s

The play is set in a city.

There are several locations.

SCENE 1

Flat, London. Dawn light. SQUEAL in lady's dressing gown, late 20s, peering into a fridge. A wall. A window. Nothing else. TASH, late 20s, enters in towel and shower cap.

TASH: Back. Second shelf.

SQUEAL: (*Sniffing carton.*) It's off.

TASH: I'm making cheese.

SQUEAL: It doesn't matter.

TASH: It was a joke. (*Beat.*) I don't eat breakfast…

SQUEAL: Squeal…

TASH: Right… Squeal?

SQUEAL: Yeah.

TASH: Weird.

SQUEAL: As in pig.

TASH: Let's try and keep the magic shall we… (*Beat.*) How did you…?

SQUEAL: I was just in the pub and someone said party at…

TASH: (*Pointing to self.*) Veronica's.

SQUEAL: Veronica's.

TASH: My name.

SQUEAL: Liar.

TASH: You been reading my post?

SQUEAL: Only the junk mail, *Veronica.*

TASH: Keep your snout out, *SQUEAL.*

(*TASH lights a fag. Opens the window and perches on the sill. He stares at her. Too long.*)

SQUEAL: (*Gesturing to fridge.*) Some of the stuff in here…

TASH: Don't tell me…

SQUEAL: What do you live on…

TASH: High finance.

SQUEAL: Yeah?

TASH: I'm actually a broker. There's only two women on our board of directors and you're looking at one of them.

SQUEAL: You never would have –

TASH: I don't look the type do I? I hate the way people make assumptions. Air Nike trainers, you must be Soho in media; suit, shirt and matching metallic tie, you're something stylish in high finance. It's all a load of…

SQUEAL: …guessed –

TASH: …bollocks. You know what I mean. And then everyone thinks why then has she never got any money –

SQUEAL: …considering everything that you said last –

TASH: …but it costs a fortune to buy anywhere in London even if it is in some rundown Kosher ghetto with no tube line and a hiding to –

SQUEAL: …last night…Tash –

(*TASH is finally silenced.*)

We didn't do anything.

(*Silence.*)

TASH: You can go home now.

SQUEAL: Nothing last night. Alright? Okay?

(*A long silence. SQUEAL stares at her. Too long.*)

Fine.

(*SQUEAL exits. TASH stubs her fag out on the window sill, thinking on this.*)

TASH: (*Calling out to him.*) You take it too seriously.

(*SQUEAL comes back, dressed and putting his shoes on.*)

You need to work at the pump 'em and dump 'em bit.

(*SQUEAL continues to ignore her.*)

(*A long beat.*) Nothing?

SQUEAL: Nothing.

TASH: (*Beat.*) I'm glad. (*Seeing his face.*) I don't mean to…

SQUEAL: It's nice to meet someone so –

TASH: Honest.

SQUEAL: It's not as if we're – fourteen –

TASH: I wish.

SQUEAL: You're making me feel –

TASH: Say it.

SQUEAL: (*Beat.*) …like not asking you for that second date.

(*As SQUEAL reaches for his coat, zipping it up and getting ready to go.*)

TASH: Yuri Gagarin. First man on the moon. I remember.

(*SQUEAL continues to get ready, reaching for a motorbike helmet.*)

And then we talked about oceans of water in the space between stars, the kind of soppy bollocks you talk. Squeal is that really your name?

SQUEAL: Yes. Most people call me –

TASH: (*Cutting in.*) And –

SQUEAL: And?

TASH: And you told me about trying to get in the RAF as a fighter pilot at seventeen only they found out you were colour blind and green and red are pretty bloody important if you're going to stop or go and miss a mountain. The joke about the mountain, it was funny. And you cried for a week and I said… 'Great pull line, get the girl everytime…' See. I don't forget. Then after the party… which was wild…you came on to me…
I fought you off… You said when are we going to fuck. I burst into tears. My mate, Hen said… I looked like white trailer trash but it was a fucking fantastic party… Wasn't it?

SQUEAL: I was in the pub and someone said, 'Party at Veronica's.' But you weren't going. So I hung about and we came back and we talked and you drank and…

TASH: And?

SQUEAL: That's it. No fucking fantastic party. (*Beat.*)
Do you want to go out with me again?

TASH: No.

SQUEAL: Right.

TASH: I'll make some tea.

SQUEAL: Milk's off.

(*TASH goes over and opens the fridge.*)

TASH: Have a drink.

SQUEAL: No thanks.

TASH: Have something. You don't have to go.

SQUEAL: What else is there?

TASH: Stay.

SQUEAL: Is this what you do? I stay, you want me to leave. I leave, you try to keep conversation going.

TASH: Hey, we've just met.

SQUEAL: And you think I'm a mug.

TASH: I don't.

SQUEAL: Yeah you do. That's fine. A one night stand is fine but –

TASH: But?

SQUEAL: I liked last night. Why don't we –

TASH: No. I like it like this. Have breakfast?

SQUEAL: You don't eat it.

TASH: I could make an exception.

SQUEAL: You started this.

TASH: Where?

SQUEAL: On a train.

TASH: Tube.

SQUEAL: It's dangerous, I could have been…

TASH: I started this on a tube…

SQUEAL: On a tube giving me the eye…

TASH: That is a matter of opinion.

SQUEAL: Giving me the eye…

TASH: A matter of…

SQUEAL: …and wanting me to follow you.

(*A long beat.*)

It was a long walk to that pub. I didn't just go for a drink.

TASH: You enjoyed. I thought you enjoyed…

SQUEAL: The intimacy of strangers?

TASH: Stay and we'll have some tea and –

SQUEAL: We'll talk about planets and things we care about and I'll make you laugh and some time very probably as we're really sobering up, you'll cry and I might get a feel and for a moment I'll be everything you want –

(*SQUEAL stops himself saying something.*)

TASH: (*Beat.*) You've done this before?

(*Silence.*)

SQUEAL: Look at yourself.

(*He exits.*)

TASH: Thanks for nothing… (*Calling after him.*) And then what?

(*TASH watches him go; goes to the fridge, takes out the milk, sniffs it.*)

SCENE 2

Office, London. Morning. A table, two chairs. The sounds of the street outside. HEN, early 30s and pregnant, is sitting patiently in front of a word processor as GLORIA, late 40s, stares into space. A long pause.

GLORIA: I've done this –

HEN: Yes –

GLORIA: I've had to do this several times before.

HEN: Yeah, I know. I bet it's –

GLORIA: Frustrating?

HEN: It would drive me –

GLORIA: It does. It is.

HEN: It's just that going through it all again, might jog something else and gives me a chance to get to know your case.

GLORIA: You're new?

(*HEN nods. Silence.*)

HEN: Take your time.

GLORIA: Tall. Six feet two. Thinning hair, probably greyer now. Blue eyes. Grey suit. With navy mac and briefcase. Obviously things will have changed by now but –

HEN: Obviously.

GLORIA: Date of birth. Fifteenth November '50. Scorpio. Managed own dry cleaning firm. Parents both dead. No family except one cousin, he never really saw. Liked walking, bird watching, odd bit of football. One scar. Thumb. Bread knife. Nearly cut his finger off. Should have got a stitch.

HEN: That's significant.

GLORIA: It's the insignificance of it all actually.

HEN: Right –

GLORIA: I've had eleven months already of this.

(*Silence.*)

HEN: It was a normal day?

GLORIA: Sorry.

HEN: Nothing out of the usual? The insignificance of it all?

(*Silence.*)

I don't mean to offend you, Mrs…

GLORIA: Gloria.

HEN: Gloria… I just meant Mr Tate, Marvin, hadn't said anything out of the ordinary? Nothing alerted you to your husband's disappearance…

GLORIA: That doesn't mean it was as a normal day…

HEN: Of course.

GLORIA: It could never be a normal day. The colour is too bright, the sound turned up too loud and every smell and taste of that day is –

(*GLORIA stops herself, it's still physical this pain.*)

HEN: Imprinted in your mind.

(*Silence.*)

GLORIA: Re-lived.

(*GLORIA looks to HEN. Silence.*)

HEN: I see. Of course.

GLORIA: Do you get training for this job?

HEN: Yes. I'm training at the moment. They need volunteers.

(*Silence.*)

Over ten thousand people go missing every year… fifty-seven per cent of them come back within the first twenty-four hours.

GLORIA: And the other four thousand and…?

(*GLORIA looks at her, looks away, resumes her stare out of the window.*)

One month more and it will be a year.

(*Silence.*)

I don't want to start counting the anniversaries.

(*Silence.*)

I'd like to see the other woman. I normally see the one with glass –

HEN: I'm her cover.

GLORIA: You know I go through this every month? You should have the same people. It's very distressing. It isn't exactly a good advertisement is it? Missing persons and every time you show up the staff have disappeared.

HEN: We're dependent on volunteers. We tend to find people move on if they…

GLORIA: Don't have a vocation?

HEN: Feel they're unable to work within the strictures of the job. Our funds are quite low. There's only so much we can do without…

GLORIA: Any visible signs of a crime, misadventure or injury.

(*HEN stops, takes GLORIA in.*)

HEN: We're happy to co-operate with the police but we don't actually receive any financial support…

GLORIA: Without a full scale investigation.

(*HEN looks up from typing.*)

You've got to do something to kill the time.

(*A long beat.*)

HEN: Children?

GLORIA: Not really.

HEN: Sorry?

GLORIA: That's a blessing.

HEN: I didn't mean –

GLORIA: Why have any more people in pain?

HEN: Mrs…

GLORIA: Gloria.

HEN: Gloria… Are you having counselling?

(*Silence. GLORIA almost laughs.*)

GLORIA: I find swimming helps…

HEN: That sounds good.

GLORIA: He didn't like chlorine. I never went but now… Something good has come out of something bad.

HEN: Exactly.

GLORIA: Are you going to put that down? About the swimming…

HEN: I don't think it's…

GLORIA: Because perhaps if you could release that sort of information… I've also decorated the hallway. Citrus colours. He liked blues... It might encourage him to come home...

HEN: Gloria...

GLORIA: If he knows the full extent I am going to make my life tick over. Move on. Keep going. That I'm not a responsibility then maybe he'd want to come back...

HEN: A lot of people...

GLORIA: Blame themselves and ask whether there is something they could have done?

HEN: Exactly... They feel that...

GLORIA: I was a fantastic wife...

HEN: I'm sure...

GLORIA: The house was always clean, I ironed shirts. I used to even run him a bath. It's old fashioned but it's what I did...

HEN: It must be impossible to make sense of why he would just go like that...

GLORIA: I try to make sense of it every day. Saturday was our shopping day and Sundays we'd often go to the neighbours... People don't often get on with their neighbours... I get on with mine... We got...get on with ours...

HEN: Being on your own is very daunting –

GLORIA: You know that?

HEN: If you were married for... (*Reading screen.*) ...twenty-two years...

GLORIA: Twenty-three Monday...

HEN: Partners often find in the period of readjustment that...

GLORIA: Please. Don't talk to me like that.

(*Silence.*)

I'm actually starting to enjoy it, that's the fear... I'm actually finding that it is becoming normal and that's what I find frightening... That's what worries me most... That if he did come back, maybe I wouldn't want... That's why I think it's so important that you release that kind of information… Like I've done the garden and the back wall was coming down but John from next door has helped me fix it and that you just get on. I'm not helpless. If he knows that. That I'm stopping needing him… I think he'll come back…

HEN: I don't think I can help you here.

GLORIA: There's a slot on TV. With music and they show pictures of people missing. People in Christmas hats, slightly pissed people or tired people with rucksacks, at parties or hugging their mum, and it's the ones who are left who they should show pictures of. Photos of them smiling and on holiday and waving a flag. Photos that say they don't need them. That might jog some memory in the mind of those who have gone. That they had a family and responsibilities…

HEN: Gloria…

GLORIA: That they don't go to bed at night anymore wondering where they are. That at last they have found peace…

HEN: If that were true you wouldn't be here.

GLORIA: Have you ever been left?

HEN: Gloria, I understand how you must be…

GLORIA: Have you?

(*HEN's silence says it all.*)

Then how do you know…

(*A long silence.*)

HEN: If I could just take down some more details.

(*Silence.*)

GLORIA: How many weeks…until your baby?

HEN: A few yet.

GLORIA: That's good. That's lovely. A new life. Congratulations.

HEN: Thanks very much.

GLORIA: That's quite alright.

(*GLORIA looks to HEN. Holds her stare. HEN returns to typing.*)

SCENE 3

Loud bar. London. TASH is standing, suit on, glass in hand. Bright lights. Abstract painting. HEN sits gripped, orange juice in hand.

TASH: And I'm in this bar and I see him and because at that exact moment I am the most interesting woman in the place who understands him. Then I have to go over and say, 'Wotcha' and then I see who he's with and she's really bloody famous and you'd know her…you know that woman who's in that…we saw it…with the…

HEN: Fuck –

TASH: 'Superb' I say… 'You were so gorgeous in that… It made me and my friend cry.' And she's all fluffy and preening herself at this and I say, 'I love you…' And him, fucking famous arty tough looking fart who I will not repeat…

HEN: Get on with it –

TASH: For fear, he'll stuff me in a tank and pickle me as 'Fucking Pissed Cow dribbling all over my bit of squeeze.' He looks at me, so fucking mean he was and he says, 'Go Away' – in a monotone bloody Babylon 5 android sort of way and I…

HEN: Because you're pissed…

TASH: Because I'm pissed and because I've powdered my nose far too many times for me to truly justify any intellectual conversation, proceed to tell him just how boring I would find myself and what is he doing here? Because shouldn't he be at home with his wife and child. And I've really hit a nerve now…

HEN: Tash… What made you say? What made you say –

TASH: 'Go away.' And he pushes me on the shoulder so I push him…

HEN: You stupid fucking…

TASH: And we end up playing this pat a cake, pat a cake, melarky and I'm getting more embarrassing and will not leave them alone. I'm like a limpet, clinging…and I'm not a clingy person…am I?

HEN: No. You? No.

TASH: So they get up to go and of course I have to follow because I'm with Magda –

HEN: Bad girl.

TASH: Great girl. Very good for me. I'm with Magda and she's saying 'Who?' And I say… Fart art who puts things in pickle stuff and she's reeling now because she's copped off with Ben behind the bar who's feeding her Sea Breezes through a drip and cutting up her own lines on the till and so we have to find him…

HEN: Tash…

TASH: Don't get like that… So she's dragging me around but I've forgotten him by then and I'm just praying he's forgotten me so I sit myself down with this tall guy and I keep saying 'So what's your name?' 'Paul…' 'And what do you do?' 'I'm a popstar.' 'So what's your name?' 'Paul…' 'And what do you do?' 'So what's your name…?' 'Paul and I'm a fucking famous pop star,' and he tells me who, that band, fucking elevator music, what is that band, anyway he tells me the name of the band and I say, 'Aren't you meant to be black?' which pisses him off something chronic and I say, 'Look I'm sorry' and I can't seem to leave him alone and I tell him I'd be bored with him if he was me and then I say…

HEN: You didn't…

TASH: I pull out my trump card, the one that normally always gets them… Because I'm off my rocks the way I was at…

HEN: Diane's wedding…

TASH: …And by this time I am almost dribbling all over the carpet… I say to him… 'Look I'm off my tits. I've been tied up and drugged and made to take copious amounts of alcohol I didn't really want…don't be rude to me…

Imagine if I was your mother… Imagine if I was your sister.' And this is it… This is the big whammy, Hen… Are you ready for it? Look like it then… 'Imagine I was your sister…' And he looks at me, this super big pop star and for the first time I see him, I recognise him and I look around and the place is crawling with Jack shit celebs and me and he says…

'My sister wouldn't degrade herself like you.'

HEN: (*Beat.*) Oow…

(*TASH knocks back her drink. A pained silence.*)

TASH: You know…It happens. You get over it but I tell you I still can't listen to their music without feeling physically sick.

HEN: I'm sorry.

TASH: See that's why I wasn't going to tell you. Because I knew you'd get upset.

HEN: I'm only saying.

TASH: It's a story. It's designed to amuse.

HEN: It still must have hurt.

TASH: You see that's when I really question our friendship. When you try to do that 'let's tap into the soft underbelly of her mind,' time. It was a laugh. I told you to make you laugh.

HEN: It is funny.

TASH: Then why aren't you laughing? Fat cow.

HEN: Pickled cow.

TASH: It was the drugs…I'd hardly touched a drop.

HEN: That makes it better? Jesus Tash – So?

TASH: What? What are you drinking?

HEN: I'm alright. The other night?

TASH: You're not fucking drinking.

HEN: I'm alright. It's so fucking loud here. Why do you always want to meet where it's so bloody loud?

TASH: I can't wait for you to shit that watermelon. You're boring without a drink in you.

HEN: I'll be up all night. Tash –

TASH: Al keeping you busy.

HEN: Hah, yeah. Al's knackered, he's working on that site, you know that big site –

TASH: How would I know a big fuck off building site?

HEN: Funny. Very funny. We need the money.

TASH: Is that why you're slaving over a hot computer?

HEN: I enjoy my job. I'm doing something worthwhile.

TASH: And I'm not?

HEN: I didn't mean that… But while we're talking about it –

TASH: Fuck off –

HEN: You never settle –

TASH: I'm a late developer.

HEN: You never settle anywhere for more than a few weeks.

TASH: Who would…who would serve deep fried Mars Bars –

HEN: You got yourself into that job –

TASH: …stay longer than a few weeks…days… I do do…I can do skilled work. I just challenge, getting into the job then –

HEN: Shagging your way out.

TASH: (*Beat.*) What is the crime, I don't see the crime in that?

HEN: What is it… Today… You're so defensive. (*Beat.*) You copped off the other night.

TASH: I'm always copping off the other night. Have a little one? Go on… Why not?

HEN: It stunts the growth.

TASH: Mental growth of the mother if she can't knock back the odd glass of…

HEN: Will you please… Red wine. One glass.

TASH: That a girl!

(*TASH nods to a waiter. Silence.*)

I could kill him. I could honestly kill him. This wasn't meant to happen.

HEN: Will you get over it? I've been with him six years.

TASH: And you were not meant to get pregnant. It's such a cliché.

HEN: You're avoiding the subject.

TASH: I had a fuck. Doctor. Bit lame with his hands. Which is disappointing in a man of medicine. Haven't seen him since the deed. Nothing much to add.

HEN: And I was hoping.

TASH: No please. Shall we go on?

HEN: No. I don't want to get too tired. I promised Al. He worries.

TASH: You promised Al. (*Beat.*) I like Al. I love Al. He's like a brother to me.

HEN: You just get like that. More protectful. More aware… There was a time I would just step out on a zebra crossing even if…especially if I saw a car. I figured the insurance policy would pay for the new leg and the holiday of a life time. It would be worth it but now…

TASH: When you get like this it leaves me cold. I'm sorry.

HEN: You're getting worse.

TASH: I'm definitely getting worse.

HEN: You should have got use to it by now.

TASH: It's a shock.

HEN: What?

TASH: That you're settling… You're choosing to settle. You're having your future now.

(*Silence.*)

It's gorgeous. It's lovely…

HEN: It's normal. Women of our age have children. It's a good age.

TASH: For doing something with your life.

HEN: I don't remember that being single was so great.

TASH: Oow.

HEN: (*Beat.*) Sorry.

TASH: Point deserved. If I could be like you. I don't choose this –

HEN: Yes you do. You could if you wanted.

TASH: Could I? How do you do it? You know I watch people on tubes and in the street, couples together, and I think how do they do it… Ring each other, keep seeing each other, keep wanting to be together, eat enough meals, and share enough Christmases to justify that they are no longer single.

HEN: You're too –

TASH: Don't say choosy. People always say choosy when what they really think is –

HEN: Perhaps they didn't browse long enough?

TASH: I like Al.

HEN: I like Al.

TASH: *Like?*

HEN: I *love* Al.

(*They drink.*)

This woman was in work today. Typical case. Husband had just walked out, nearly a year ago now. Paid up the mortgage, fed the cat, dry-cleaned his suit, saw she was alright, discussed with her what he'd like for his tea, left the house and just didn't bother coming back. Maybe that's what happens. Maybe you just pick something up, wear it for a while and then put it down. For most of us death or some other woman gets there before that decision is made but for some people…

TASH: You never know someone. You think you do but one day you look up and – I'm just not romantic.

HEN: Yes you are. You could have whoever you want.

TASH: Yeah, yeah, yeah… The pick up is the easy part. It's the staying with, I can't get a taste for.

HEN: What's his name?

TASH: The service is shite here.

HEN: Don't tell me…you didn't even get his name… Tash…

TASH: Squeal… His name's Squeal.

HEN: As in pig?

TASH: Yeah.

HEN: Sounds good.

TASH: Sounds nothing.

HEN: You just don't trust men.

TASH: Please. Cliché.

(*Silence.*)

I'm sorry it's just – children aren't everything.
(*Silence.*)

You alright?

HEN: (*Beat.*) Laughing.

TASH: (*Long beat.*) Do you know there are oceans of water between the stars and the moon?

SCENE 4

Outdoor pool. London. GLORIA sitting on the side of a swimming pool, in costume, goggles and hat as SQUEAL stands in trunks, drying himself with a towel. GLORIA suddenly flinches.

GLORIA: Christ.

SQUEAL: Are you okay?

GLORIA: I've been… (*She cranes around, trying to see over her shoulder, feeling her back.*) …stung.

SQUEAL: It's the start of the lazy wasps. They get lazy waking up –

GLORIA: And I'm dinner. Oow.

SQUEAL: You need vinegar.

GLORIA: Serves me right for just sitting.

(*SQUEAL makes to go.*)

You're a very good swimmer.

SQUEAL: It's a bit cold today to be honest.

GLORIA: I used to come here as a girl.

SQUEAL: Yeah?

GLORIA: Hasn't been decorated since. They're all very colourful here aren't they? All the people.

SQUEAL: I guess.

GLORIA: It's my daily ritual. I sit here.

SQUEAL: You don't swim…

GLORIA: Not really… If it's hot I might have a dip but… I just enjoy the sunshine and the people. You get to remembering faces.

SQUEAL: Uh huh.

GLORIA: (*Beat.*) That's how I remember yours.

(*SQUEAL nods, smiles, turns to go.*)

You're a lawyer.

SQUEAL: Sorry?

GLORIA: In the city. You look like a lawyer.

SQUEAL: No –

GLORIA: I sometimes get it wrong. I sit and try and work out what people do.

(*GLORIA rubs her shoulder.*)

SQUEAL: It'll pass soon.

GLORIA: Little buggers.

(*SQUEAL nods, makes to go.*)

Teaching then?

SQUEAL: Doctor.

GLORIA: Of course. You've got the hands of a doctor.

SQUEAL: People always say –

GLORIA: It's true.

SQUEAL: People always say that.

GLORIA: My husband has the hands of a dry cleaner. They're soft but very red from all the fluid –

SQUEAL: He should wear –

GLORIA: I tell him.

SQUEAL: He should wear gloves. You tell him.

GLORIA: Doctor's orders. He says it keeps them soft. For wetting the ring of pint glasses. He wets them and rings them… He always knows it makes me laugh.

SQUEAL: (*Beat.*) Still –

GLORIA: Still –

(*SQUEAL makes to go.*)

What kind of doctor?

SQUEAL: Casualty. I'm a houseman. I'm just in casualty at the moment.

GLORIA: But you're helping people. That means something.

SQUEAL: Yeah, sewing up knife wounds and mopping up drunks.

GLORIA: Your family must be very –

SQUEAL: Just my dad. Yeah, he thinks it's alright.

GLORIA: He must be very proud. A doctor.

SQUEAL: No –

GLORIA: A doctor is what every one wants in the family.

SQUEAL: He doesn't say much. I never know.

GLORIA: He will be.

SQUEAL: You think? (*Beat.*) He has a bad heart.

GLORIA: That's no excuse. Make sure he tells you.

SQUEAL: Okay…

GLORIA: Gloria.

SQUEAL: I'll tell him, Gloria.

GLORIA: You tell him. People don't appreciate each other enough.

(*Silence. SQUEAL picks up his wet towel, turns to go.*)

SQUEAL: You should have a swim. It's great once you get in.

GLORIA: Too chilly for me today…

SQUEAL: You always just sit?

GLORIA: You been watching me?

SQUEAL: It's a waste of a ticket.

GLORIA: Giving me the eye.

SQUEAL: It must be a couple of quid a day. You'd be as good sitting by the pond than…

GLORIA: (*Sharp.*) It's company.

(*Silence. SQUEAL hovers.*)

Sometimes conversation. I fall into conversation. I met a woman last week who'd lost an eye.

SQUEAL: That was careless.

GLORIA: Cricket bat in the eye. She said it gave her a whole different perspective.

SQUEAL: It would.

GLORIA: Losing an eye like that. (*Beat.*) You probably see that all the time.

SQUEAL: It's still a shock.

GLORIA: Yeah.

SQUEAL: Still would take some getting used to.

GLORIA: Yeah. (*Beat.*) How would you put your mascara on?

(*A half ripple of laughter. SQUEAL hovers.*)

SQUEAL: Right… Okay… Vinegar on that wasp sting.

GLORIA: I can't even feel it.

SQUEAL: Bye then…

(*As SQUEAL turns to go.*)

GLORIA: I can't swim… I can doggy paddle a bit but –

SQUEAL: That's a start.

GLORIA: Marvin was fantastic swimmer. I wonder now why I never… I just sit at the side.

SQUEAL: You should give it a go.

GLORIA: I don't like to get my ears wet.

SQUEAL: They do classes.

GLORIA: I'd hold everyone back.

SQUEAL: I saw a big man must have been about eighteen stone and he was learning the other week…

GLORIA: I'd be their first drowning.

SQUEAL: You'd float.

GLORIA: Not me. I'd sink to the bottom.

SQUEAL: No you wouldn't.

GLORIA: How do you know?

SQUEAL: Well whatever.

GLORIA: Yeah whatever.

SQUEAL: Breast stroke's easy.

GLORIA: I'm sure…

SQUEAL: Dead easy… I could…

GLORIA: What?

(*SQUEAL hovers.*)

SQUEAL: I better get off. Careful you don't roast. Your shoulders look…

GLORIA: Yes…

SQUEAL: They're's nothing to be frightened of. Lifeguards all round the edge and people everywhere to save you.

GLORIA: (*Almost to herself.*) A doctor.

SQUEAL: Bye, Gloria.

(*SQUEAL makes to go.*)

GLORIA: He should look at you and say I'm proud you're my son.

SQUEAL: Squeal.

GLORIA: The runt of the litter.

SQUEAL: Yeah. (*He hesitates and turns back.*) Gloria…

GLORIA: Yeah.

SQUEAL: If you want…

GLORIA: Yes.

SQUEAL: If you'd let me…

GLORIA: Please.

SQUEAL: Breast stroke's the easiest one to get.

(*GLORIA turns, smiles. Holds his stare. Too long. She tentatively nods her head.*)

SCENE 5

Supermarket, South London. AL is wheeling a shopping trolley. HEN is ahead, contemplating the cereals.

HEN: So you never wonder?

AL: Nah?

HEN: You never imagine for one moment what it might have been like if it had been someone else?

AL: It wasn't. It was you.

HEN: So you think it's fate.

AL: It's choice. You have a choice as to how you live your life. Some are good at it, some are crap.

HEN: So you chose me.

AL: Not exactly. There are random moments and moments of decision. You were a moment of decision following a random event.

HEN: We've been together for the last six years. What's random about that?

AL: It wasn't planned. Getting pregnant was a random event.

HEN: And you think that's what makes up life?

AL: We came to buy some cereal. You said you were hungry and it had to be cereal.

HEN: We were drunk.

AL: Random moment.

HEN: Choice to keep it?

AL: Moment of decision.

HEN: And you think that's what makes up life?

AL: I don't know. I'm a builder.

HEN: So.

AL: We got peanut butter?

HEN: It's a lifetime. We are talking about a lifetime.

AL: Have you been talking to Tash again?

HEN: I always talk to Tash.

AL: She's single –

HEN: So.

AL: And thirty –

HEN: Just. And that makes her bitter?

AL: It makes her stir it with her mates who have people.

HEN: You don't have me.

AL: Cheers.

HEN: Don't you ever think you have me.

AL: Alright…alright… Keep your wig on.

HEN: Sometimes you make me nervous.

AL: Right.

HEN: You can react a bit.

AL: Alright. (*Beat.*) Right.

HEN: Is that it?

AL: Hen, where you from?

HEN: Southall.

AL: Where am I from?

HEN: Southall.

AL: So what does that say?

HEN: What?

AL: What does that say?

HEN: We both know where to go to get a good curry?

AL: It says you know me. And I know you. And your dad knows where I live so if I did anything to make you nervous he doesn't have to walk far to do me one.

HEN: 'Til death us do part?

(*AL avoids this conversation concentrating on the cereal choice.*)

AL: Crunchy? (*Holding up jar.*) I'm getting crunchy.

HEN: A baby's a lifetime.

AL: Only swans mate for life.

HEN: You're cynical.

AL: Couldn't even spell it. I'm not cynical, I'm pulling your leg. I said yes. I said yes, didn't I?

HEN: This isn't just you and me. It isn't like a quickie and a phone number scribbled down on the back of your hand.

AL: It's hardly a teen cock up. We've been going six years, Hen.

HEN: I don't want to end up like Tash. I don't want to wake up and find myself on my own with a kid.

AL: She hasn't got one.

HEN: But she's on her own.

AL: There are worse things.

HEN: What are you saying?

AL: People do it. Bring up kids on their own.

HEN: Is that what you're suggesting?

AL: No. No.

HEN: You're winding me up now.

AL: We're having a baby.

HEN: And that's alright with you?

AL: I said yes.

HEN: But you've hardly thought about it.

AL: What's there to think about?

HEN: Like where we're going to live, if I'm going to give up my job, whose name he's going to have.

AL: So we've decided it's a boy then.

HEN: It's not funny. Like if you want it.

AL: Yeah, I want it.

HEN: You wouldn't have wanted to wait?

AL: Maybe a year or so but –

HEN: See –

AL: But only 'til the house was finished. I wanted us to be able to live in the house.

HEN: What are you saying? What are you saying?

AL: I'm saying if we were working to Railtrack Guidelines then maybe we might have kicked around waiting a bit longer but… Hen… We only came out to buy cereal.

HEN: Do you love me?

AL: They've got an offer on Pampers.

HEN: Do you love me?

AL: (*Beat.*) With all my heart. (*He moves off with the trolley.*) I'll get this.

HEN: (*Beat.*) I don't want to be like Tash. I don't want to be like Tash living in a shit heap, no one to love, moving from one naff job to another –

AL: Maybe she finds happiness in other ways.

SCENE 6

Loft apartment, Soho, London. NATHAN is sitting in his loft apartment; modernist, Conranesque, slick in Joseph sweats, dressing gown and Nike. He butters a bagel. TASH stands videoing him.

TASH: And what exactly are you doing now?

NATHAN: I'm buttering a bagel. Then…depending on my mood, I will place a small square leaf of smoked salmon on the top, sometimes I might slice a pickle but mostly, it's a nub of black pepper and my dark coffee which I get at Grodinski's, the FT if I feel in the mood.

TASH: And you always put the salmon on after?

NATHAN: The bagel, then the cheese, then the salmon, then the pepper.

TASH: Or the pickle.

NATHAN: The pickle if I'm in the mood or even a lemon.

TASH: Now what would I do?

NATHAN: Well you could say something like – 'Would you find it useful if perhaps, you could buy it all in one pack, cheese, bagel, salmon, pepper…?'

TASH: Lemon?

NATHAN: And the lemon. Say in one pack?

TASH: You want me to kind of think along those sort of lines?

NATHAN: The company is paid to see where the gap is in the market. To see the way people live, eat, consume. So if you can come up with any observations along the way, that's great. That's dandy.

TASH: Okay…

NATHAN: I hope you don't mind this. Doing this meeting in my flat? It's just Sundays –

TASH: Sundays. I know Sundays are sacred.

NATHAN: Most of my employees hot desk anyway. We're rarely ever in the same room at the same time. Tash. Natasha. Russian?

TASH: Croydon.

NATHAN: Try and hold the camera level if you can. It's just the clients get pissed off –

TASH: Sure –

NATHAN: Fuck it. I'm the boss. You wobble if you like. (*Beat.*) So?

TASH: So… Would you find it useful if perhaps you could buy it all in one pack, cheese, bagel, salmon, pepper, lemon?

NATHAN: It's an idea. Maybe a gimmick but I can do it myself. The enjoyment is doing it yourself. They might say something like that. You often find people initiate the opposite response if you present them with a specific idea. Remember to get them to hold up the packet of whatever they're buying to the camera. We need to show the client, to let them see their branding.

TASH: Okay… Could you hold up the lid of the cheese packet? I've just got to logo register.

(*NATHAN holds up the lid for the camera. TASH films it zooming in.*)

We're very grateful.

NATHAN: I'm happy to oblige.

TASH: We're finding logos very important at the moment. Red's always a good colour. See a red logo on the cheese lid. It's probably what made you buy it.

NATHAN: That's great. That shows initiative, it's just a little more than you need.

TASH: Right, sorry.

NATHAN: I think you're great at this, Tash. You're spot on.

TASH: Yeah?

NATHAN: Really…really great.

(*NATHAN reads his paper, aware he is being filmed. He pours himself another cup of coffee, adding sugar, then pouring in a little more coffee.*)

TASH: Coffee…then sugar…then coffee?

NATHAN: It melts it quicker. It's a habit. Nothing else.

TASH: It's interesting.

(*NATHAN pours another cup and places it opposite him.*)

And you're pouring another cup?

NATHAN: For you.

TASH: Thanks.

(*NATHAN flicks through a CV as he eats and drinks.*)

NATHAN: You've done a lot of jobs. Your CV shows a lot of jobs.

TASH: Yeah.

(*NATHAN is buttering a second bagel and placing it on a plate opposite.*)

NATHAN: Eat.

(*TASH puts down the camera.*)

TASH: Cheers.

NATHAN: There's no harm in that. Taking your time to find what you really want to do.

TASH: Would I be doing this in people's houses?

NATHAN: Sometimes but... Mainly supermarkets, the large food chains. I go out and do it myself sometimes. That's unusual in the agency but I like to keep in touch. It makes the client feel like I really know their product.

(*Silence.*)

I spend a lot of time with housewives. They tend to be our biggest resource. I think you'll be good with them. (*Beat.*) It's quick money.

TASH: That's what I always want. I've been doing up a flat... Talking about doing up my flat. (*Beat.*) I never do. (*Beat.*) Earning money...earning money can be a motivation. (*She sniffs the coffee.*) Real.

(*NATHAN shrugs.*)

You don't look like an instant man.

(*TASH rests her camera on the side and sits down to take the coffee.*)

NATHAN: Good. Good observational skills –

(*Silence. NATHAN pours her another cup of coffee. TASH smiles, a little embarrassed. NATHAN smiles a little embarrassed.*)

TASH: You live on your own? It feels as if...

(*Silence.*)

NATHAN: (*Beat.*) It takes getting used to, living on your own. So you're interested?

TASH: Yeah...

NATHAN: Good...that's great. Well, let's get you rocking and rolling. How about starting –

TASH: Today. I could start today.

NATHAN: Tomorrow's fine just I'll walk you down just…let me take a shower.

(*TASH nods, flicking the camera up.*)

TASH: Of course. We want you just to do everything as you would normally do.

(*NATHAN gets up to shower.*)

NATHAN: You can put down the camera now.

TASH: I was just getting into it.

(*NATHAN eats a tangerine. TASH flicks the camera back on him.*)

(*Beat.*) Fruit. You always end with fruit?

(*NATHAN holds up the tangerine bag label up to the camera; smiling.*)

NATHAN: It aids digestion. See, I logo registered, Natasha.

TASH: …you do seem to have picked up the technique, Nathan.

(*NATHAN eats. TASH sits, stealing a bagel from his plate.*)

I'll walk you down.

SCENE 7

A park, South London. GLORIA is sitting on a park bench with SQUEAL. They are eating sandwiches and take-away drinks enjoying the sunshine. Their hair is wet. They've just been for a swim.

SQUEAL: You breathe out as you pull.

GLORIA: I drown if I breathe and I pull. I open my mouth and I drown.

SQUEAL: So you close your mouth, then you breath out through your nose.

GLORIA: That's unhealthy. That's bad for you. In through your nose, out through your mouth. Germs pass that way.

SQUEAL: You're swimming in a thousand gallons of chlorine, anything would be zapped. (*Beat.*) You're funny. You're pulling my leg.

(*GLORIA laughs to herself.*)

GLORIA: Gullible.

SQUEAL: Not in the dictionary.

GLORIA: It's so nice with the sun.

SQUEAL: Yes.

GLORIA: I feel so nice. (*Beat.*) I walked past your flat the other day.

SQUEAL: Yeah…

GLORIA: The one with the bins outside.

SQUEAL: It's good for the hospital.

GLORIA: I couldn't live without my garden.

SQUEAL: Gloria –

GLORIA: I did live with my husband but he's not there anymore.

SQUEAL: You still wear your wedding ring?

GLORIA: Can't get it off.

SQUEAL: My dad still wears his.

(*Silence.*)

A garden must be great in this weather.

GLORIA: It is now. Was a state but… I've almost finished it now. Patio and a little pond near the shed. With fish. I wanted Koi carp but they're expensive. £200. Imagine paying that for a bag of fish and chips? (*Beat.*) Frogs and goldfish are just as nice. (*Beat.*) He liked fish and chips.

SQUEAL: You never had –

GLORIA: No. Marvin was always handful enough… I was never the mothering kind.

(*GLORIA watches something in the distance.*)

There are girls who take men down here and do things behind those trees, aren't there? I'm not stupid. If you sit here long enough. (*Beat.*) Good job it's summer. Maybe that's what my husband did. Maybe he used to come down here and pick up a girl and stand up against a tree and... They would have sex. And maybe one day he couldn't come back and face me with it. Maybe he knew I'd smell it on him or just know. A wife's instinct.

SQUEAL: I don't think...

GLORIA: You didn't know him. Maybe that's what he did. And maybe afterwards she would hand him her knickers and fold them into a little square and let him slip them in his pocket. And maybe he would come home and for his tea, and sit down and eat whatever I've put in front of him and all the time he'd be thinking I've got some girl's pants in my pocket. (*Beat.*) Could you never see yourself doing that if you were married?

SQUEAL: No, Gloria.

GLORIA: You say that.

SQUEAL: No.

GLORIA: Just a thought. There's a bench as well. By the pond. And John next door is going to help me build a Gazebo.

SQUEAL: Is that edible?

GLORIA: For flowers. For sitting. For sitting in and thinking. He won't recognise the place when he gets back, will he Squeal?

SQUEAL: I don't know.

GLORIA: That man...

(*GLORIA has not taken her eyes off someone in the distance.*)

...with the cap on... That man. Can you see that man? Go over. Will you... Just... Squeal... Will you... He's wearing... That cap... Like my... Please will you just look for me... Just go over and ask him...

SQUEAL: I don't know him, Gloria. I never...

GLORIA: (*With realisation.*) It's not him. (*Beat.*) It's alright. It's not him.

SQUEAL: I'm sorry.

GLORIA: I drive everyone mad. I always think…

(*SQUEAL puts out his hand and rests it on GLORIA's. She tentatively tightens her grip around it, stroking it.*)

I'm always wrong…

SQUEAL: Gloria…

GLORIA: Have you ever been in love?

SQUEAL: Gloria…

GLORIA: I don't mean married love. I mean love with no responsibility. Love with no expectation. Love without the cleaning and the washing shirts.

SQUEAL: Sometimes…

(*GLORIA loosens her grip on his hand.*)

GLORIA: Yes.

SQUEAL: (*Beat.*) Maybe sometimes I think I could be… I could fall…become in love with someone.

GLORIA: And her?

SQUEAL: (*Beat.*) She's a bit slower on the uptake.

(*A long silence as GLORIA sits clearly upset, clearly not willing to speak.*)

You should try backstroke. Backstroke's the easiest. Next week I'll show you backstroke.

(*GLORIA turns and looks at him. She nods. She smiles.*)

GLORIA: And after I could cook your tea.

(*SQUEAL does not know what to say.*)

SQUEAL: If you want.

GLORIA: I bet you like…

SQUEAL: Everything.

(*The squawk of birds as SQUEAL and GLORIA both instinctively look up. The slow beat of wings as if in a flock on migration.*)

GLORIA: I wonder where they're going to.

SCENE 8

Bar, Soho, London. TASH and HEN. Same bar. Same drinks. Same routine. Loud.

TASH: So I'm sitting there thinking this is weird, I'm sitting there seriously wondering how I'm going to get myself out of this one because I don't know if you remember but when I lived with Itkin.

HEN: The Jewish boy from hell.

TASH: I was writing the name in all the mirrors if you remember and something which I, now, as a reformed character…

HEN: Since the pickled cow incident.

TASH: Since I spilt my emotional innards out all over the carpet of that coke trodden single cracked orchid shit hole in the heart of metropolis, do not and for full velocity of that concept, do not let grace my nostrils or gums. I am not looking to get drawn into flagrante delicto with some twisted sister, battered childhood, anal retentive and other sexual deviant practising tosser, even if he does have a white peace pad in Soho. I am not looking for a shag with an emotional timebomb just waiting to explode all over my life, probably into my bank account and certainly an experience which will entail several short sharp trips to the Woman's centre, your legs up in stirrups trying to deny any knowledge of that large scaly pustule adorning your feminine minge.

HEN: You slept with him.

TASH: Excuse me. I don't spend all day listening to the rejected. He was nice… He walked me down… It's going well. The job. I'm not interested… I'm really not interested. He's obviously the kind of guy who gets dumped.

HEN: When did you get so bitter, Tash?

TASH: Sorry?

HEN: You slept with him.

(*AL walks in.*)

TASH: Alright. You coming to the –

HEN: Sorry I meant to –

TASH: No that's fine, that's great…

(*AL kisses HEN hello as he gestures to the waiter for a drink. TASH kisses AL.*)

AL: Alright Tash.

TASH: Hello gorgeous.

AL: What time's the – ?

HEN: Eight.

TASH: (*To AL.*) You won't like it. It's that thing with –

HEN: The girl who's in –

TASH: It's romantic…

HEN: Playing the monkey?

TASH: She wasn't a monkey.

HEN: They were all bloody monkeys. She was in love with –

AL: I like romantic films.

TASH: Great.

(*Silence.*)

How's the house?

AL: Put the windows in at the weekend.

HEN: Sash. They're reclaimed sash.

TASH: Nice one. I've not even stripped a wall yet.

HEN: Al could –

AL: Yeah, I could –

TASH: No, I'm alright –

HEN: We've got a steamer.

AL: It's like butter with a steamer.

TASH: I like the walls.

HEN: They're bloody awful.

TASH: They're *my* bloody awful. (*Beat.*) I like them. Cheers but –

AL: You're fine.

HEN: Sorry I should have –

TASH: It's fine. I guess we got the –

AL: Booby prize.

TASH: …night your mates didn't need you to sit on their sofas like lard, drink beer and watch football.

HEN: Nasty. Why are you two so nasty to each other?

TASH: We are lovely to each other.

AL: I didn't say a word.

HEN: We should –

TASH: We're fine.

HEN: The trailers. Al likes to watch the trailers.

AL: That's not true. It's fine.

HEN: Three's a very bad number. Three is notoriously difficult. Someone is always left out.

TASH: Which book are you reading now?

HEN: It's not a book. I'm just saying.

TASH: How do you live with her?

AL: Take the pills and buy in Sky Sport.

TASH: You're looking very toned.

AL: I've been working a lot –

TASH: So are you going to let this one finally stop and give herself a rest?

HEN: We can go and see a film together. We can go and see a bloody film together.

TASH: You didn't mention he was coming.

HEN: It was last minute.

TASH: You should have said if you wanted to spend the evening with Al.

HEN: I wanted to spend an evening with you both. This isn't a competition.

TASH: What you talking about? (*To AL.*) Do you know what she is talking about?

HEN: You don't help yourself Tash. You don't make yourself easy.

TASH: What? I don't discuss window frames and what colour carpets and what wallpaper I need to put up on my walls and –

HEN: I don't mean that. You make it hard for people to like you.

(*Silence. TASH laughs. HEN laughs.*)

It's a bloody film. We can go and see a bloody film without it turning into full combat.

AL: Sorry.

TASH: You don't have to be sorry.

AL: I wasn't talking to you.

HEN: Al.

(*Silence.*)

Get over it you two, eh?

TASH: You want to do my decorating?

AL: If you like. With the steamer I've got, I tell you it's like cutting through –

TASH: Yeah. Okay. Thanks.

(*TASH thinks of offering some gesture of affection; instead she chinks her glass with HEN, leans forward and kisses AL on the cheek.*)

AL: Hen says you've got a new job.

HEN: Market research.

AL: That's probably good money.

TASH: It's sitting looking at people's sad lives.

AL: I guess it depends how you're feeling. Everyone looks sad if you're feeling –

TASH: A bit blue? Don't say a bit blue. (*Looking to AL.*) I saw you the other week.

AL: Yeah?

TASH: Lunch hour. You were with –

AL: My boss' daughter's doing work placement.

HEN: What's her name? She's got a lovely name.

AL: If it's a girl, we're going to call her Natasha.

(*AL holds TASH's stare.*)

Like butter. I'll come over next week.

TASH: Great.

HEN: (*Beat.*) He hasn't done the job yet.

(*HEN breaks into a smile, pushing him affectionately as a ripple of laughter finally breaks between the three. HEN wets her finger and absently rings the top of her glass. It makes a low long hum.*)

SCENE 9

Street, London. TASH in a hurry, dressed up. Rain. Traffic. SQUEAL running past showering under a wadge of documents, in a hurry, not slowing down.

TASH: So I was thinking –

SQUEAL: Sorry?

TASH: These oceans. Do they have fish in? Do they have whales and if that is the case, that is officially a mammal and where there are mammals there are humans, so are therefore the stars planets, with people living on them and those oceans of water are like our Atlantic?

SQUEAL: I don't know what you're –

TASH: I knew you were a bullshitter –

SQUEAL: Sorry.

TASH: If you were telling the truth, you would be pleased that I have remembered your late night ramblings and be willing to defend your theory –

SQUEAL: It's raining –

TASH: This precludes thought.

SQUEAL: (*Beat.*) Hello Tash –

TASH: I'm past that bit. I'm mid-sentence with you now –

SQUEAL: I'm on call.

TASH: Yeah, me too. Consultancy, it's the direction most people in marketing are going now –

SQUEAL: What?

TASH: So your theory is flunked.

SQUEAL: Right.

TASH: Doesn't matter.

SQUEAL: We're getting –

TASH: I hate umbrellas. I think people who carry umbrellas look too –

SQUEAL: Prepared.

TASH: – anal. I find that a big turn off.

SQUEAL: I don't carry one. Do you?

TASH: Do you? Sorry. You go.

SQUEAL: Coffee. Do you want a get a coffee?

TASH: No.

SQUEAL: Okay.

TASH: I'm –

SQUEAL: Sure. Definitely.

TASH: Decorating. Got a mate decorating. A mate's bloke. She's pregnant. Very nearly due.

SQUEAL: Great.

TASH: They were planning but they weren't planning then bam –

SQUEAL: It's not as hard as it looks.

TASH: No. (*Going.*) I'm decorating. I've got a mate decorating. My mate's bloke. He's –

SQUEAL: Great.

TASH: That's your favourite word.

SQUEAL: A man of few.

TASH: Okay then. Bye.

(*TASH makes to go.*)

SQUEAL: Is that it? 'Okay then. Bye.'

TASH: I'm going for mauve on the kitchen walls and yellow in the bedroom. I know purple's a bit ecclesiastical but fuck it, it's a nice colour, it's a calming colour.

SQUEAL: What are you talking about Tash?

TASH: I thought you wanted to talk a bit longer.

SQUEAL: Why are you so weird? Why can't you just do simple things normal?

TASH: I'm talking.

SQUEAL: You're being all weird.

TASH: Weird like what?

SQUEAL: Weird like this. I only asked you for a cup of coffee. It's okay, you don't have to say yes. I'm not breaking my heart over it.

TASH: Fine. Okay. Nice seeing you then.

SQUEAL: Tash.

TASH: Do you know that a woman was standing on a golf course in Berkshire and it was raining so hard that a small koi carp with an ID tag clipped on its fin fell from the sky? It had got vacummed up in the big weather cycle in Tokyo. I read that in the paper this morning.

SQUEAL: (*Laughing.*) You're amazing.

TASH: At least I'm making conversation. I'm talking, saying something instead of 'Yeah great'.

SQUEAL: Okay.

TASH: It's hardly fighting the chemistry. You could hardly say that you and I talk and we're fighting the chemistry.

SQUEAL: Slow down, slow down.

TASH: You get good value for money with me.

SQUEAL: I never said –

TASH: If you want to talk to one of those daft bitches who simper at your every word, then go fling around your 'greats' and 'yeah okay' somewhere else.

SQUEAL: Fine, cheers, enough said. Have a nice day.

TASH: Don't look injured.

SQUEAL: Look what?

TASH: If you can't do it, don't stop me in the street and say hello. I've passed you twice this week –

SQUEAL: I didn't see you –

TASH: – on the bus and you've said fuck all.

(*Silence.*)

SQUEAL: On the bus?

(*Silence. TASH and SQUEAL start to laugh.*)

How was I meant to see you if you were sitting on a bloody bus?

(*Silence.*)

TASH: Goodbye then.

SQUEAL: We could go and have a coffee.

TASH: No thanks.

SQUEAL: (*Calling after.*) Tash… Tash… Can I have your phone number?

TASH: What? And never fucking call?

(*TASH exits. SQUEAL looks on. Rain.*)

SCENE 10

Flat, London. AL scraping paper off the walls with long smooth moves. TASH standing, eating back of the fridge food.

AL: China and Malaysia. There's a few left in India, but to be honest the indigenous Tiger, I reckon there's probably not more than 100 – 150 left in the world.

TASH: Right.

AL: That doesn't include breeds in captivity. There's a small ratio of the rarer breeds that are surviving solely on the fact that there are a quantity of them still bred in captivity. Like the Siberian White Tiger which I reckon there aren't more than 30 – 35 alive in the wild.

TASH: Yeah.

AL: Remember I adopted one for Hen's brother last Christmas. Whipsnade do them.

TASH: Yeah. I remember her saying.

AL: You'll get indigestion eating like that.

TASH: It's the way I always eat.

AL: If you folded out that table you could move my brushes over a bit and sit down.

TASH: I like standing up. I'm going out later.

AL: My dad got a hernia always eating standing up on the job – Conductor.

TASH: Yeah, Al. I know. You say it everytime you come around and I'm standing eating like this.

AL: Mind my own. Sorry. These are good walls underneath here.

TASH: Yeah, what's Hen doing tonight?

AL: Watching telly. I'll get us a takeway later.

TASH: Friday night and you're staying in?

AL: Yeah.

TASH: Friday night and you're staying in?

AL: We got a parrot in here? We can't do much at the moment. Hen's knackered.

TASH: She shouldn't be working.

AL: I keep telling her.

TASH: Do you?

AL: Yeah. What you looking at me like that for?

TASH: How long have you been with Hen?

AL: '94, '95 – Six years.

TASH: Long time.

AL: Life time. For me. I couldn't get a girlfriend before her.

TASH: Really?

AL: Ha ha. (*Pointing to ceiling.*) You want me to do that bit as well?

(*TASH nods.*)

Hen keeps saying, when are you going to settle?

TASH: No. You all have a perverse interest in understanding why I'm not doing what you're all doing. I think you're worried I know something you don't. I don't mind. My family have long stopped minding. This is it. This is me.

AL: Nice cornicing.

TASH: I love you.

AL: I don't make her work. I'd prefer it if she didn't work.

TASH: You need the money, she says.

AL: We'd manage.

TASH: Doing up your house is like haemorrhaging money.

AL: It's a good investment.

TASH: You've been stung.

AL: Bollocks, you don't know what you're talking about.

TASH: I saw you.

AL: What? I can scrape off the paint around the moulding that will clean it up a bit.

TASH: I saw you. How old is she? Sixteen? Seventeen?

AL: I don't know what you're talking about.

TASH: Boss' daughter? Work placement?

AL: (*Laughing.*) You can't be serious. I'm not taking it serious. You are being serious. How long have I been with Hen? How long have you known me?

TASH: You're still a bloke.

(*AL stops work, laughing.*)

AL: You're serious.

(*TASH makes to go.*)

TASH: You're insulted.

AL: Too fucking right I'm insulted. A sixteen year old temp. Not finished her A levels. You don't get it do you? You sad, silly cow, you don't get it.

TASH: I'm just saying. I know. I'm just saying I know. So do something about it.

AL: (*Beat.*) What were we doing? On this hot date? What were we doing?

TASH: You were buying sandwiches. You were having a sandwich.

AL: Bloody hell. Ham or egg?

TASH: Don't piss around.

AL: You don't piss around. You don't fucking piss around. Tash. Are you honestly serious?

TASH: You touched her arm. You were holding her by the arm. Sort it out or I'm telling Hen.

AL: Telling her what? (*Beat.*) Telling her what?

TASH: Don't make me say it.

AL: You don't know what you're fucking talking about.

(*Silence.*)

When was the last time you were touched eh? Can you remember? And I don't mean some drunk grope in the back of a cab. When was the last time? I'll tell you when I was. This morning, just as I was going out, I reached for my keys and Hen brushed the back of my neck. She leant back, from reading her visa bill and she stroked the back of my neck. I've had six years of that and I still like it. And you think I'd give that up for some tossy little feel over a mozzarella and avocado ciabatta.

(*Silence.*)

You should get out more.

TASH: (*Beat.*) Too much keeping me up at night.

AL: Like you're proud of it. Like picking men up in the way you do is something to brag about…

TASH: I hinted. There was no bragging involved.

AL: So why tell Hen all about it all the time? (*Beat.*) It hurts her.

TASH: Maybe I'm having a better time.

AL: She loves you.

(*TASH holds AL's stare.*)

TASH: You haven't got the monopoly on that. (*Beat.*) Do something.

AL: Six years? You think I'm about to throw away six years?

(*AL returns to scraping the walls. TASH carries on eating, watching him.*)

I don't know what you're talking about.

SCENE 11

Supermarket, South London. SQUEAL is standing talking to NATHAN who is videoing him as he takes things off shelves and puts them into his basket.

NATHAN: And coffee is how you start your day?

SQUEAL: Yeah. I suppose so. Yeah, coffee is what I normally have. Does the shop pay you to do this?

NATHAN: It's client based. If you could just turn the lid a little, so I could catch the label. Logo registering.

SQUEAL: I don't really believe in this.

NATHAN: It's helping people. It's helping us help people decide what they need to buy.

SQUEAL: What they *need* to buy? What you want them to buy?

NATHAN: And after the coffee?

SQUEAL: I'm sure you have to do your job but I've just come in for a jar of coffee maybe some biscuits for later not to help your fat cat boss shove us more junk we don't need, okay?

NATHAN: Yeah, I completely understand it's just your input would be invaluable. I just have two more people to do and then I can finish for the day.

SQUEAL: It's only half past eight.

NATHAN: I started early. I was let down.

SQUEAL: And I do night shifts so if you wouldn't mind.

(*A man, MARVIN, shuffles past, a pint of milk in hand, browsing over tea bags. SQUEAL resumes his search for the biscuits.*)

NATHAN: (*To MARVIN.*) This is the tea and coffee section, don't let me disturb your normal pattern of behaviour but was that actually the teabags you were looking for?

MARVIN: It's whatever's the cheapest.

NATHAN: Interesting. Very interesting. You work?

MARVIN: Sorry.

NATHAN: You do something in the service industry.

MARVIN: Sorry.

NATHAN: We find a high percentage of the technical professions or even service industry tend to favour that brand of particular beverage.

SQUEAL: The guy is just buying tea. Could you not go and do this somewhere else?

NATHAN: You see I'd like to be able to say yes but this is highly important, highly sensitive information.

MARVIN: I work in the cleaning industry. I like to bring my own tea.

NATHAN: Right. So I wasn't that far left of field. Very interesting. Very kind of you to divulge. Share.

(*SQUEAL shakes his head as he makes to go.*)

You will be having milk with that coffee?

SQUEAL: Possibly.

NATHAN: Natural or freeze dried? (*Beat.*) Coffee mate or cow's own?

SQUEAL: Are you taking the piss?

MARVIN: Excuse me, do you know where they've moved the detergents?

SQUEAL: Sorry?

(*MARVIN moves off. SQUEAL continues with his shopping. NATHAN films throughout.*)

Could you stop that now please? Please? (*To checkout girl.*) Could you tell him to stop or I'll call the manager? Please. It's been a long night. I've been on the night shift. Please.

(*NATHAN refuses to stop as he films the contents of the shopping bag.*)

NATHAN: Almost finished.

MARVIN: I think you should perhaps leave the gentleman alone.

NATHAN: It's important for the advertising…

SQUEAL: You should know better. You should know better not to tell people to drink more, to eat more, to live more, to buy more. Do you know what people like you do? The damage that people like you do. I see the damage that people like you create. The stress in people's lives to buy more, to keep up the mortgage repayments, to have another drink to eleviate that stress, to eat another fat filled pile of crap which clogs up the heart and makes it difficult to live, to even breathe. I've just spent last night working on the heart of a very fat man, opening it up and discovering the consequences of what you sell. The pain that you deliver. The hope that you give people, to make their lives better, for more, more, more.

(*SQUEAL, through his tirade, has managed to push the man up against the wall of the supermarket as MARVIN looks on.*)

What happened to love and care and not thinking that *you* know what people *need*? When they don't even know themselves.

MARVIN: Alright, son. Calm down? Okay?

(*SQUEAL slowly eases his grip, nodding. Then holding up the bottle of coffee he shows the label to the camera.*)

NATHAN: I'm sorry. I'm really very sorry.

(*SQUEAL turns and puts down his coffee and exits. MARVIN takes in the scene.*)

MARVIN: You alright?

(*NATHAN nods.*)

If he'd thumped, you could have sued.

(*NATHAN nods, clearly shaken as MARVIN resumes his shopping.*)

NATHAN: Would you mind if I filmed you doing that?

(*MARVIN shakes his head and shuffles away, with NATHAN following him.*)

It would help if we start with your name.

MARVIN: (*Long beat.*) Marvin.

(*MARVIN turns and hesitates, staring at first NATHAN and then the camera.*)

I know you. I clean in your block.

NATHAN: Do you?

MARVIN: I do all the blocks around there.

NATHAN: Marvin.

MARVIN: (*Beat.*) I'm looking for the polish but they've moved it all around so – I'm lost.

NATHAN: (*Without looking up from camera.*) And now you are found.

INTERVAL

SCENE 12

Surburban garden, East London. GLORIA is hanging out washing. HEN is standing talking to her. GLORIA keeps coming to a man's shirt at the bottom of the pile and stopping herself, shuffling through the wet washing for anything but –

GLORIA: You don't normally. It's not normal for you to visit at home.

(*Silence.*)

HEN: We had an anonymous call last week. A possible sighting. It's the normal feedback when we've done any recent press release. People want to help but this time, I have to say the description was surprisingly accurate.

(*GLORIA stands frozen to the spot.*)

It's several hundred miles from here but it could be…

GLORIA: Do you know the American backstroke is different from the English?

(*HEN shakes her head. GLORIA puts down her washing and demonstrates, kicking with one arm and a leg.*)

It's a sharp straight down movement, so you slice the water. I've been learning them both and it definitely improves your speed, not that I am concerned about speed but it is nice to know one has the option.

(*HEN nods. GLORIA smiles. She takes the washing inside. HEN shifts her hand suddenly across her bump. She felt something kick.*)

HEN: I'm sure he doesn't think that.

GLORIA: How do you know?

HEN: Those who are left often blame themselves.

GLORIA: And those who leave should stop and think what they're bloody doing. (*Beat.*) Shouldn't they?

HEN: Do you want to follow up that sighting. It is quite a way away but –

GLORIA: How far?

HEN: Skye. Just off the coast of Skye.

(*Silence.*)

I've an address. If you'll take it. Or I can arrange for someone to perhaps go with you if you don't want to go on your own.

(*Silence.*)

No one is forcing you.

(*Silence.*)

There's no guarantee. I don't want to raise your hopes.

GLORIA: But anything is better than nothing?

(*GLORIA pauses, looking down into the washing basket. She is down to the last shirt.*)

I don't miss his nail clippings in the bath, coat never hung up, channel flicking, he always was channel flicking just when you were settling down, enjoying something. The way he ate, he was a noisy eater, a little click, his jaw clicked, clicked so I knew he was sat at the table before I'd even put the plates down. I don't miss his silence and his little observations, the birds, we've got a lot of birds in the garden… 'Look, Gloria, isn't that a…' I don't know. I don't know. 'The blue one, the little blue one with the yellow tip, look it up in the book…' Always reading too late at night, reading me bits, letting me fall asleep while he was reading me bits. And always being too hot, always too hot in bed, getting up to get water in the night and waking me… 'Sweetheart, have a sip. You don't drink enough.' I don't. He's right, I don't.

HEN: If it is him?

GLORIA: You ever sit in silence with someone so long…that only the fart behind his newspaper breaks it…makes you laugh. The way he used to do that. Always used to do that. All those little things.

(*Silence.*)

I guess that's married life for you.

HEN: (*Beat.*) I'm not married.

GLORIA: Who is now? Kids, and love and electric bills aren't really that important. What's holding us together is very fragile indeed.

HEN: Kids, and love and electric bills *are* everything.

(*GLORIA laughs.*)

GLORIA: Everything and nothing.

HEN: What else are you doing with someone? If that's not it –

(*Silence.*)

GLORIA: You're having a baby. We never had children. How can I say – We never had children. I'm sorry.

HEN: It's fine.

GLORIA: What would I know?

(*Silence.*)

HEN: This wasn't planned.

(*Silence.*)

Al, my boyfriend…he calls it a random event. He hates the idea of any kind of destiny. I find it hurtful. It wakes me in the night the thought that if this is random it could have been anybody's but for that one night it was me. That this could be someone else. He thinks I'm talking about destiny but I'm not. I'm talking about the fact that in meeting me there was nobody else. In meeting me I was the only mother possible for his child.

GLORIA: There's always somebody else.

(*Silence.*)

HEN: I don't want to hear that. I'm sorry. I hear you now but I don't want to. I'm sorry. I'm sorry.

(*GLORIA finally pins up the man's shirt. HEN clocks it.*)

GLORIA: There's always one that sneaks into the washing somehow.

(*Silence.*)

HEN: Let's talk about…

GLORIA: Scotland.

(*Silence.*)

HEN: Good. (*Beat.*) It should be beautiful this time of the year.

SCENE 13

Flat, London. MARVIN cleaning NATHAN's flat; bin bag, duster, polish. An oil lamp. MARVIN flicks it on and waits. The bubble of oil doesn't move. NATHAN comes through reading some papers.

NATHAN: It needs to heat up. The oil? It won't do anything until it's had time to get hot, to soften.

(*MARVIN nods. Returns to work. Dusting.*)

You okay?

MARVIN: Bin bags.

NATHAN: Top drawer.

(*MARVIN shakes out a bin bag.*)

You found them.

MARVIN: You need some more. I've put them on your list.

NATHAN: Thank you. You're finding everything okay?

MARVIN: I have a room at the hostel. Suits me fine. I can keep the same bed. If you pay in the morning you can keep the same bed.

NATHAN: And that's…

MARVIN: Suits me fine. I can keep the same bed. If you pay in the morning you keep the same bed.

NATHAN: That must be comforting.

MARVIN: That's all I need.

NATHAN: Yes.

MARVIN: You're not working…

NATHAN: Not today. (*Long beat.*) I won't get in your way.

MARVIN: That's fine. I was wondering about the ladies' things in the cupboard.

NATHAN: Yes –

MARVIN: It's just, they're taking up a lot of room, and I was wondering if you wanted me to move them down to the bigger one in the hall.

NATHAN: No.

MARVIN: (*Long beat.*) I won't bother hoovering today.

NATHAN: Thank you.

MARVIN: You need more polish as well.

NATHAN: You put it?

MARVIN: On the list.

NATHAN: Thank you.

> (*Silence.*)

> Marvin, you didn't always –

MARVIN: No… I've always been in cleaning of some kind but –

NATHAN: I thought not. I was thinking how's someone like him ended up –

MARVIN: I've been on a kind of holiday. Still on it really. This is my time out time. You should try it. Some time out time.

NATHAN: Yes.

MARVIN: Gives you a perspective.

NATHAN: (*Beat.*) Some things you can never get a perspective on.

MARVIN: Then you take time out until you do – (*Sniffing duster.*) Nice smell. There's nothing…there's nothing like a woman's perfume. I was just dusting some of those cupboards. It lingers.

NATHAN: There's a married man talking.

> (*Silence.*)

> My wife left – a while ago.

MARVIN: When you tell me that, I feel…

NATHAN: It's really very common.

MARVIN: That I understand you. That I understand what you must be going through. You didn't have…

NATHAN: Not having children makes it easier.

MARVIN: Not having children makes it possible. She wouldn't have left if you'd had children.

NATHAN: You think?

MARVIN: A child is innocent. A child is something small. Always, even when they are big, to you, a parent, they are always small. She wouldn't have left her child. That would be too much to ask you to bear.

NATHAN: Whatever.

MARVIN: It gets lonely.

(*Silence.*)

NATHAN: Opposite, you see there, the one with the blinds. There is a woman. I see her in the supermarket. She buys meals for two, enough for two people, but it's just her. I never see her with anyone. (*Looking out of window.*) Those windows out there become my friends. Those inroads into other people's lives. You must find that. As a cleaner. You are given a root in, to see the way other people live.

MARVIN: The lady who buys her meals for two buys so much because she has an elderly neighbour who can't get out herself. She divides everything she buys by two and shares it with her. I do the stairs outside her landing Tuesdays and Thursdays. The man, who you think is divorced, is not divorced. He is happily married but has chosen not to live with his wife, he spends every Sunday with her. I clean on Sundays when he is out. You see there are alternative ways of living, alternative families.

NATHAN: That's very reassuring.

MARVIN: Don't be cynical.

NATHAN: I'm not. I find that really very reassuring. People can be disappointing. Only the other week I was let down.

MARVIN: Right.

NATHAN: I had to cover for someone at work. (*Beat.*) Which was inconvenient.

MARVIN: (*Beat.*) Would you like me to do your bedroom now?

NATHAN: Yes. And in the afternoon…

MARVIN: In the afternoon?

NATHAN: I may go out.

MARVIN: And later?

NATHAN: I won't need you later.

MARVIN: I can go back to the hostel then. I don't like to be late. You can get tea between five to seven p.m.

NATHAN: That must be…

MARVIN: It's convenient. That's when I like to eat.

NATHAN: And what do you do in the evenings.

MARVIN: Sometimes I just lie on my bed and think. Or I sit at the window and listen to the different noises. Someone laughing or a shout down the corridor. And I try and work out what's happened. I set the scene in my head. The moment before, the minutes after. Or I just watch the flies zig zagging around the shade above. They move in a very definite way. Zig zag…zig zag… They leave an imaginary line, almost visible, they move so fast. Sometimes one of the other blokes, there are only men in our dormitory, sometimes one of them will go and cry out in the night and I'll go and sit at the end of whoever's bed, and share a fag, or talk, or just sometimes I just sit, even lie next to them, hold their hand, great big men holding hands, I never thought I'd see it, not like you think, just giving people company, being almost tender and I stay with them until the morning. They've normally pissed the bed or are shouting for a drink, whatever wakes me up first – The wet through the trousers or the great whisky breath on my neck.

NATHAN: (*Long beat.*) Are you happy?

MARVIN: …I don't think I've ever been happier in my life.

SCENE 14

Restaurant, London. SQUEAL, TASH, HEN and AL are midway through dinner. Chinese. Flock wallpaper. Shanghai Lil music.

AL: Amputation. That's hardcore.

SQUEAL: It's just one part of the surgery I do.

AL: Wow. What do people normally have –

SQUEAL: Mainly limbs.

TASH: Please.

HEN: Please.

SQUEAL: I'm mainly casualty. Dog biscuits up the nose, that kind of stuff –

AL: Hoovers stuck up people's arses.

HEN: Al. Stop talking like –

TASH: – a builder.

AL: (*To SQUEAL.*) She's a horror. You realise she's a horror. I have to work around her every day.

TASH: Not every day.

AL: She doesn't get out of bed.

TASH: This is not true. I get out of bed to make you tea and sandwiches?

HEN: You sound like an old married couple…

(*A ripple of laughter.*)

AL: You should get out more.

HEN: Why don't you go on holiday?

TASH: Maybe.

HEN: Kick start things a bit again for you.

TASH: I don't think we need to talk about this now. It's not your mission to get my life back on track.

SQUEAL: I don't mind.

HEN: Have you travelled?

SQUEAL: I did a year overseas as part of my medical training. Australia. Perth.

AL: I'd love to go to Australia. Did you know the indigenous Wallaby outnumbers the domestic dog by forty to one in the outback?

TASH: (*To SQUEAL.*) National Geographic. The Holy Grail.

HEN: I didn't know that. I didn't know you wanted to go to Australia.

AL: Yeah, you did. I'm always saying I'd love to travel.

HEN: I can't even get him to go out of London for a weekend and he's talking about Australia.

AL: That's proper travel. That's not like a weekend in Tenby. I'd like to do a lot of South East Asia as well. Malaysia, China… I've got a mate who's working on some apartments in Singapore.

SQUEAL: Singapore's fantastic. I spent a month there.

HEN: You never said this. You've never mentioned this before.

AL: I have. I've always said I'd like to travel. Maybe do India. I've always wanted to go to India.

SQUEAL: If you're doing India, you've got to head south. Sri Lanka.

AL: Yeah.

SQUEAL: It's an amazing country. I mean really amazing. I mean I'm not talking about all the tourism and the sleazy end of it but if you really spend some time there. It's Buddhist and yet there's a lot of Catholicism so you've got these two faiths side by side. You can be driving down the road and on one side you've got these fantastic Buddhist Temples, I mean really ornate and yet go in them and it's so humble, so peaceful. I mean I'm not religious, but there you start to believe in something beyond this, something linking us all then on the other side you've got all hell and damnation and then you start looking at the Buddhist temples again and you realise it's all just the same thing. They've got devils and demons and crocodiles eating elephants and its just everyone trying to believe in something beyond themselves. Know what I mean?

AL: Yeah. Yeah. And somewhere, I don't know where it is, there's this, there's this waterfall that falls down into this inland pool that's so deep that no one has ever actually got to the bottom and you can go there and stay days because all around the edges are these tiny caves and you build fires and sleep by the water at night and in the day you can do this trek to the top of the waterfall and people do these river jumps and they say if you do touch the bottom you've been touched by the hand of God and that if you survive it – you grow a third leg that turns into a fin over night.

(*AL starts laughing.*)

TASH: Funny. Very funny. Did anyone get that down?

AL: Sorry…mate… Sorry.

TASH: (*To AL.*) You're an arse.

SQUEAL: You're alright.

HEN: It sounds beautiful. It sounds amazing.

SQUEAL: It is.

HEN: (*Beat.*) We should go then.

SQUEAL: I've got some books on it if you want to have a look.

AL: It might be a bit hard with the baby.

TASH: You can do anything with a baby. I bet there were people out there with babies. Life goes on with a baby.

AL: It would with you, yeah. But then life goes on with whatever, doesn't it Tash? No job, you just get another, no bloke just pick up another fuck for the night.

HEN: Al –

AL: You do know she's incapable of sustaining anything she won't be able to rip down and replaster next week.

TASH: I'm not listening.

AL: When was the last time anyone said they'd loved you, Tash?

TASH: What's this turnaround?

AL: When?

TASH: You'll be the first to know.

AL: Not yet then. Point proven. Incapable.

TASH: That really is straight to the nuts even for you.

AL: It's what people say to each other.

HEN: Give it a rest, Al.

AL: It's what people feel for each other –

> (*Silence.*)

> When?

> (*Silence.*)

> When?

> (*Silence.*)

SQUEAL: I love her.

> (*Silence.*)

TASH: You hardly know me.

SQUEAL: I wasn't saying marrry me.

TASH: Don't give me the sympathy vote.

HEN: Tash –

TASH: You love me. Is that what you think I need? You think that does the trick? I'm not a charity.

SQUEAL: I didn't do that for a good cause.

TASH: Why did you then?

> (*Silence.*)

> I wasn't incarcerated and I wasn't abused. I have very nice parents and a brother with three kids. He's normal, too normal some might say. I have a healthy appetite, I don't get into abusive relationships, I don't get into relationships, I wasn't bullied and I had a fantastic time at college, career's a bit shaky but fuck it I've still got my own teeth, so the last thing I need –

SQUEAL: Forget it.

TASH: You're the one who's embarrassed yourself.

> (*Silence. TASH exits. SQUEAL, AL and HEN sit in silence.*)

HEN: (*Beat.*) You never said you wanted to travel.

AL: Someone was just talking about it at work.

HEN: Someone?

(*Silence. HEN scrapes her chair back and exits. AL and SQUEAL sit in silence until –*)

SQUEAL: Shall I get the bill?

SCENE 15

Flat, London. Morning. NATHAN is making breakfast. Coffee, bagels, cream cheese. Sound of a shower turning off. NATHAN waits until – TASH comes through in a towel.

NATHAN: You found –

TASH: Yeah.

(*NATHAN nods, pours TASH a cup of coffee. TASH picks up a shoe.*)

One more to go.

NATHAN: I've got bagels.

TASH: (*Beat.*) Great.

(*TASH exits. NATHAN starts to toast bagels, read the paper, flick around with the radio until – TASH comes back through, now half dressed, pulling on her shirt, the same clothes from the night before. NATHAN slides her over a cup of coffee.*)

Thanks. I'm sorry… I'm sorry I didn't show last week.

NATHAN: I had to cover –

TASH: Yeah.

NATHAN: I had to cover for you.

TASH: Yeah. I'm sorry.

NATHAN: It's probably, it's probably a sackable offence.

(*TASH laughs. NATHAN laughs. NATHAN goes to talk to her. TASH moves away.*)

TASH: Nice coffee.

NATHAN: Yeah.

TASH: Good.

NATHAN: Bagel.

TASH: Great.

(*TASH doesn't touch her breakfast.*)

I don't normally eat breakfast.

NATHAN: Right. Okay. Don't worry. Would you like cereal?

TASH: No, coffee's great.

(*Silence. TASH drinks, unsure what to do next.*)

I used some of your shampoo and a toothbrush as well.

NATHAN: Mia casa your casa.

(*Silence.*)

TASH: I might get a move on then.

NATHAN: Now.

TASH: Yeah.

NATHAN: I thought we could –

TASH: No. Sorry.

NATHAN: It's just last night –

TASH: I didn't want to go home.

NATHAN: I thought we could spend the day together.

TASH: Please. I know where this is going – I'm sorry but that's not the way it works. Why don't people get that? I don't know why you like me. Is it because I'm here? You seem like a very nice guy. A very nice lonely guy.

NATHAN: No.

TASH: Who thinks that I'm the answer. But I'm not…

(*Silence.*)

NATHAN: Right.

(*Silence.*)

TASH: I was lonely. I was lonely too last night.

(*Silence.*)

You live close.

NATHAN: Of course. Sure. Of course.

TASH: I feel a shit now.

NATHAN: Don't –

> (*Silence.*)

Why should you feel bad? We both got what we want.

TASH: Not exactly.

NATHAN: So shall we say Monday?

TASH: You serious?

NATHAN: You want a job don't you?

> (*Silence. TASH nods.*)

TASH: I used the hairbrush as well. There were a lot of blonde hairs and I'm dark so if she sees, whoever she is, can you apologise –

> (*Silence.*)

I wasn't really looking for anything more than –

NATHAN: Someone to lie with.

TASH: Yeah. (*Beat.*) So it didn't matter.

> (*Silence.*)

Everyone has that problem once in a while.

NATHAN: Not me. I bring girls back all the time.

TASH: Yeah.

NATHAN: Yeah. So really it made a change.

TASH: I should go.

NATHAN: Yeah.

> (*TASH wavers at the door. Silence.*)

TASH: I was out for supper last night. With a friend, my best friend and her boyfriend and we got into this sort of fight and I was with another friend and we were coming home and suddenly I just couldn't be on my own. I couldn't think where else to go.

NATHAN: (*Beat.*) Sure.

> (*TASH nods.*)

TASH: See you Monday.

(*TASH makes to go.*)

NATHAN: Looking forward to it. (*Beat.*) You know you really are quite a cunt.

(*TASH hesitates, exits. NATHAN sits on his own. He stares down at the second cup of coffee and bagel. He suddenly gets up, scoops up plates, bagel, cup in one move and shoves it in the sink.*)

SCENE 16

Bed and Breakfast, Scotland. GLORIA is standing brushing her teeth. She is talking to herself.

GLORIA: Not today. Please not today. Yesterday, when I needed you, where were you? Not today. I was walking and I was looking for you everywhere. Do you know how many pubs there are? Sitting on my own in a pub, hoping – Marvin? And I had this thought, it crossed my mind, it was more a feeling, a very strong sensation, that when you're in my mind, every moment that I'm thinking of you, every blinding, boring moment, that I'm carrying you close to me, talking to you, wanting you…you want no one. Not me. No one. You need no one. I feel sick. I want to vomit. I want to –

(*GLORIA looks at herself in the mirror, as she waits in expectation of some kind of response. She breathes heavy against the mirror.*)

Skye.

(*The squawk of gulls outside, making her turn and look out for a moment. She returns to cleaning her teeth, finishes, picks up a towel, her costume, contemplates with terror.*)

Come back. Come back. I don't know how much longer –

(*The lap of sea water.*)

SCENE 17

Bar, London. TASH and HEN sitting perched, drinking. Noise all around.

TASH: Forget it.

HEN: No, it was horrible of him.

TASH: I've know him too long. I've known you both too long. It was fine.

HEN: I felt terrible.

TASH: Friends, good friends have those kind of…scuffles.

HEN: He's cooking tonight.

TASH: He said. I saw the…

HEN: Curry. He always cooks curry.

TASH: And you always hate it. Why don't you say to him?

HEN: Too late. Should have done it years ago but now… I've been eating it and telling him I love it. We've bonded over that curry. We've made babies over that curry. (*Beat.*) You saw Al today –

TASH: (*Beat.*) He's almost finished the bathroom.

HEN: Well when he's finished with yours ask if he can knock ours on the head, eh? I don't know if we're ever going to get into that house.

TASH: You can have him back anytime you want.

HEN: Has it made it difficult?

TASH: It's fine. We both ignored it… It was ignored the next day. (*Beat.*) He had a point.

HEN: He cares about you. (*Beat.*) He cares about me, therefore he cares about you. (*Beat.*) He does.

TASH: Are you feeling – ?

HEN: Great… Fat… Fat and ugly…

TASH: No…

HEN: Yes.

TASH: This is when you say… 'He doesn't want to sleep with me anymore.'

HEN: (*Beat.*) He doesn't want to sleep with me anymore. (*Beat.*) Not.

(*A ripple of laughter.*)

Have you seen –

TASH: This bar is really noisy.

HEN: Deflection.

TASH: Overturned. I don't want to talk about –

HEN: I didn't say anything.

TASH: I don't want to talk about him. Do you need some kind of reassurance? Am I some kind of loose cannon like you want to partner me up?

HEN: It's okay… It's okay…

TASH: Why do you always say that? 'It's okay…it's okay…'

HEN: Sorry…

TASH: Stop it will you…

HEN: What?

TASH: Please, fight back a bit Hen –

HEN: This is not important enough. We've had a good evening. Why are you spoiling it now? You've had a bad day? I'm sorry if you've had a bad day.

TASH: I've not had a bad day… Stop accommodating me…

HEN: What have I done? I don't get it… This is what I do… I listen… You talk…

TASH: I know.

HEN: Is there something you're not telling me?

TASH: No…

HEN: Tash…

TASH: Just back off Hen. Your life's okay, alright?

HEN: I never said it wasn't. *I* never said it wasn't. Is Al sleeping with someone?

TASH: You're so fucking dramatic.

HEN: I'd rather know.

TASH: I was talking about me –

HEN: Is that why you brought me here?

TASH: No. Hen? (*Long beat.*) No… He loves you.

HEN: How do you know?

TASH: He does. Where's all this come from?

(*Silence.*)

He does.

(*Silence.*)

HEN: Liar.

(*HEN orders another drink.*)

SCENE 18

Flat, London. MARVIN entering the flat, pausing on seeing –

NATHAN: (*Calling out.*) Marvin –

(*A row of woman's clothes, dresses etc., hanging up, in bags as if ready to be thrown out as NATHAN comes through carrying more dresses on hangers.*)

If there's anything you would like take it.

(*NATHAN exits. MARVIN goes over and touches the dresses as NATHAN comes through carrying boxes of shoes.*)

Obviously that's not your colour but I thought maybe people at the hostel.

MARVIN: It's all men.

NATHAN: (*Beat.*) There's some good coats.

(*NATHAN exits. MARVIN opens one of the boxes, takes out a shoe as NATHAN comes back through, two big bin bags in hand.*)

I think it's a waste leaving them kicking around in the back of a cupboard when somebody could be getting pleasure out of them.

MARVIN: Right.

NATHAN: I could drive you to the charity shops if you don't want them.

MARVIN: That might be an idea.

NATHAN: We could pick up some supper after.

MARVIN: I have to be back at the hostel.

NATHAN: Let your hair down for a night, Marvin. When was the last time you went to a restaurant?

MARVIN: I go to Starbucks most days.

NATHAN: I want to take you out.

(*NATHAN exits.*)

MARVIN: (*Calling out.*) Oxfam is the nearest.

(*As NATHAN comes back through with the last bag.*)

NATHAN: Whatever.

(*Clocking MARVIN watching him.*)

You're always telling me to clear out that cupboard.

(*MARVIN nods, he looks at the shoe in his hand.*)

MARVIN: These are beautiful.

NATHAN: They've already dated. They're fashionable so I suppose they date quicker.

MARVIN: They're still beautiful.

(*MARVIN looks at the tiny straps of the shoe.*)

You forget how thin a woman's ankle is.

NATHAN: Yes.

(*MARVIN nods, carefully puts the shoe back.*)

MARVIN: My wife liked –

(*Silence.*)

I'll clean out that room then.

(*NATHAN nods. MARVIN makes to go, pulling off his coat.*)

NATHAN: And after we'll go out and eat.

MARVIN: I have to be back at the hostel before eight.

NATHAN: They don't lock you in. You can come and go, surely.

MARVIN: I like the routine.

NATHAN: For one night –

(*Silence.*)

MARVIN: I'll say no. But thank you.

(*Silence. MARVIN makes to go.*)

NATHAN: Marvin, I want you to come out to supper tonight. You've been a very good friend to me these last few weeks. Steak. You like steak I bet.

MARVIN: I don't eat meat much now.

NATHAN: Well tonight –

MARVIN: I don't really like going out. I've found a life that suits me. I don't mean to be rude, Nathan. You're a good boy but –

NATHAN: Say yes. Please say fucking yes Marvin. Say yes.

MARVIN: I'm your cleaner.

NATHAN: You're saying no.

MARVIN: I prefer to – I prefer just to work if you don't mind.

NATHAN: I'll pay you. How much do you cost for a night? Just for the company.

MARVIN: You must have friends. A man like you must have –

NATHAN: I want someone I don't know. I want a friend I don't know. Tell me about yourself Marvin. Your wife?

MARVIN: I'll clean the back room.

NATHAN: Twenty – twenty-five, I'll give you twenty-five quid. (*Beat.*) We could go to the cashpoint.

(*NATHAN starts trying to shove money into MARVIN's hand. MARVIN stands embarrassed.*)

MARVIN: Please –

NATHAN: I just want someone to have a fucking pizza with –

(*Silence.*)

It was just an idea.

MARVIN: A nice idea.

(*Silence.*)

Why don't you get one of your lady friends to take you out?

(*Silence.*)

I wouldn't be able to pay.

(*NATHAN shrugs.*)

Nathan, have you thought of going to talk to someone?

(*NATHAN half laughs to himself.*)

I'll clean the bathroom while I'm at it.

(*NATHAN nods.*)

NATHAN: I don't understand you. I don't understand people.

(*Silence.*)

I'll get changed then. I'm starving.

(*NATHAN exits. MARVIN is left standing looking at all the clothes. He goes to touch them and them stops himself.*)

SCENE 19

Bedroom, London. HEN and AL are lying in bed.

HEN: We don't do this –

AL: No.

HEN: We don't do this enough. Like being on holiday.

AL: A one hour holiday.

HEN: A lunch hour holiday. (*Sudden start.*) Did you feel it move?

AL: What?

HEN: It moved. More than a nudge, a real kick.

AL: I felt nothing.

HEN: Wait. (*Long wait.*) Feel?

AL: No, nothing.

HEN: Never mind.

AL: Footballer. It's definitely going to be a footballer.

HEN: Yes. (*Long beat.*) Have you talked to Tash yet?

AL: No.

HEN: You ought to say sorry.

AL: No.

HEN: It was cruel what you said.

AL: It was true.

HEN: She hasn't rung all week.

AL: Enjoy the peace.

HEN: Blokes never get, they never get girlfriends.

AL: I have mates.

HEN: Yeah but not like girlfriends. (*Beat.*) This is nice.

AL: Uh huh.

HEN: It's just…

AL: Something on your mind…

HEN: Someone finishing my sentences before I ever get to the end of them. Sorry. Sorry.

AL: (*Jumping up.*) Jesus… That was a Beckham punch. I felt it…

HEN: Did you?

AL: Right in the face. Really big boot right in the chops.

HEN: See. That's what I'm living with. That's what I'm waking up with.

AL: Uh huh…

HEN: To find you're not home… (*Long silence.*) Where were you Thursday night?

AL: Home.

HEN: No, you weren't. I woke up. I woke up at three and you weren't even back.

AL: It was eleven. You'd just gone to sleep. I promise you.

HEN: And I felt a kick in my stomach and I opened my eyes thinking it was you but you weren't home. So I waited up and when you did creep in at 4.30… I'd closed my eyes and pretended I was asleep, with it still kicking me, with me wanting to scream out and you just lay there with your eyes open, not moving…

AL: No…

HEN: And your face smelt. You hadn't even bothered to wash your face.

AL: Hen… This is mad…

HEN: Tell me then different. Tell me different…

AL: I don't know what you're talking about.

HEN: I do… I do…

SCENE 20

Office, London. GLORIA sits tapping details into a computer. NATHAN sits opposite. He shifts in his chair, as if short of time.

GLORIA: A natural blonde. That's very rare now.

NATHAN: I thought she was but after… When she'd gone, I discovered the hair bleach… She dyed it, and yet she'd always told me that it was her own natural colour.

GLORIA: A white lie. Husbands and wives need little white lies.

NATHAN: She was a very honest person. She was a very straight person.

GLORIA: It's a nice name.

NATHAN: It still has a kind of magic for me. I find it disturbing when I meet other people who have the same name. A lot of faces. (*Pointing.*) On the walls. A lot of people missing.

GLORIA: Yes. But they are found. Many of them, the majority of them are eventually traced. Do you have a job?

NATHAN: Yes… I'm freelance now… I work when I feel like it.

GLORIA: Who for?

NATHAN: Myself… People. I have been recording people. On film. Notating them down. Their habits.

GLORIA: For?

NATHAN: Clients.

GLORIA: You're an academic.

NATHAN: Yes... It's a kind of research...

GLORIA: Gloria.

NATHAN: Gloria. Do you get paid for this?

GLORIA: No... (*Beat.*) My husband has been gone now... 14 months and 12 days...

NATHAN: You count the days.

GLORIA: Without hesitation. It just happens.

NATHAN: It's the waiting...

GLORIA: We have to find a way of living in the waiting.

NATHAN: But if they don't come back.

GLORIA: Then your time hasn't been wasted. You should try a hobby.

NATHAN: I don't think so. I don't really have the time...

GLORIA: You have the whole of your life.

NATHAN: What if the person was your life? What if that one person was everything?

GLORIA: No one person is everything.

NATHAN: You were obviously married a long time. I don't mean to be rude. You have something to hold onto. We weren't married very long. I worry I'm forgetting her. I don't want to move on.

GLORIA: That's your choice.

NATHAN: You're very hard.

GLORIA: No.

NATHAN: Yes you are. You're hard.

GLORIA: I'm softer than I've ever been. I'm more open than I've ever been. I walk down the street and I notice people. Their pain. Their discomfort. Their happiness. I drink it in. I have my eyes open. I swim. Every day I swim. Back and forth. A routine. A boring routine that becomes so familiar I grow almost fond of it. I imagine myself swimming far out and not coming back. But how far away is forever?

How far away before that place becomes my life? So I stay. In my pain, in my vulnerability, in my isolation and in this nakedness I feel reborn. Like a baby. I am standing in the world like a dripping baby. More open than I have ever been. He has made me more open than I have ever been.

NATHAN: You're not grateful? You're grateful that he left you?

GLORIA: I live with a kind of understanding.

NATHAN: Until he comes back? (*Long beat.*) What if he never comes back?

GLORIA: I live with that.

NATHAN: I thought you were meant to give people hope. I thought you were meant to show me a way to find my wife.

GLORIA: How long has she been gone…

NATHAN: Nathan.

GLORIA: Nathan.

NATHAN: 2 years, 4 months. I don't do days.

GLORIA: That's a long time. Nathan…

NATHAN: (*Long beat.*) They found her with a belt around her neck. It always throws people. She's a banker. Was a… She fucks up on some shares. I tell her she won't lose her job. She does. I tell her I love her. I tell her… She mustn't have loved me. Professional suicide. I urinate on her boss's desk a week later. Piss all over the trading room floor. It seems a riot at the time. I lose my job. With sympathy and condolences. I come home and I sit down and I realise I don't like any of the furniture. I sleep around. It makes me feel liberated. I'm envied by all my mates. The best of both worlds. A taste of both sides of the coin. Married and single. 'You lucky cunt!' I miss my wife? 'No.' (*Long beat.*) I realise that I can't remember her face yet I find her features everywhere. Fixing her eyes with the lips of others. My cleaner tells me I am sick. I get her pissed and fuck her. She doesn't speak much English but I think we don't enjoy it. She leaves. I have a new one, a man working for me now. I get myself a new job. (*Beat.*) I try to work out my wife's thoughts. Retrace her steps. She comes home.

Has a sandwich. Doesn't even wash up after herself. She's lazy like that. Walks to the bathroom. Takes off her clothes, turns on the shower…

GLORIA: Your wife is dead?

NATHAN: She's missing, she's very much missing in my life.

GLORIA: (*Long beat.*) Is listening enough?

NATHAN: I don't know… I don't know if it helps at all.

(*GLORIA looks up from her work. NATHAN is staring out and beyond her. The lap of water building into a shower.*)

SCENE 21

Bar, London. TASH running in to meet HEN who sits at the bar, drinking a glass of red wine. It is raining outside. It's very quiet.

TASH: Did you not hear me? I was shouting at you half way down the street. You could have an accident driving like that. I was waving my knickers off. Did you not see me? Hen…

HEN: I saw.

TASH: I thought you worked late on Thursday. If you saw me you could have given me a lift. I'm wet now. I'm really wet.

HEN: I gave in my notice.

TASH: That thing's on the downward slope, I should hope so. (*Looking out for barman.*) Could I?

HEN: I had to wait…

TASH: Never mind…okay… So your time is now your own.

HEN: Yeah.

TASH: That's good. That's great. This is a treat.

HEN: You always…

TASH: Used to like this bar. Do not like this bar anymore. Do not like the lack of *service*.

HEN: Don't make a fuss.

TASH: I'm not making a fuss. At least it's quiet. I thought you'd like that.

HEN: Have you been drinking?

TASH: Celebrating. The flat. It's finished, I finished the back bedroom last night. Al was well miffed.

HEN: Uh huh?

TASH: He's an arse. He's charged me a fortune.

HEN: You love me.

TASH: I love you, therefore I negotiate around him but still…

HEN: I know.

TASH: I hope you do by now because I wouldn't last another week having him in my house. He better have done me a cheap deal.

HEN: I know about you and him.

TASH: Sorry?

HEN: I know where he is on Thursday night. I know what he gets up to. (*Beat.*) I know you're sleeping with him.

TASH: Right. (*Long beat.*) And you're going to leave him?

HEN: You weren't meant to take my husband.

TASH: Partner.

HEN: Did you do this on purpose? Did you want to hurt me? Are you very unhappy, Tash? Are you so unhappy that you couldn't…? Was it so awful to see me settled? What's in you that you have to destroy everything?

TASH: That's the way you see it.

HEN: Fact.

TASH: That's the way you see it.

HEN: I don't know what to do now. What am I meant to do now? Who am I meant to go to now?

TASH: You'll make yourself…

HEN: I have this thing to shit out. I have this thing to love and look after.

TASH: Why don't we go to mine?

HEN: And I try and understand that. I try and sympathise with you. Tash, I care if you're unhappy, but it is not my fault that you can't find a man of your own. Some people find love difficult. So I've tried to be there for you and you do something like this.

TASH: He told you?

HEN: I smelt you on him.

TASH: He told you?

HEN: He came home smelling of you.

TASH: Did he say?

HEN: He's being so sweet. So nice. So desperate. Last night he cried. He said *please don't leave me.* And I realise what you do. You go in and you scorch the surface of anyone else's relationship. I'm so angry with you. I don't know what to do. I want to love you, Tash. I want to love you, but you make it hard. Perhaps you should talk to someone. You should go and see someone and talk to them, because I can't love you anymore. This baby needs me now. Al needs me now. I've tried with you. (*Beat.*) I can't trust you anymore.

TASH: But you forgive him.

HEN: No, I don't forgive him. But this is longer than a friendship. We have to be bigger than this. If you'd just come and told me how you felt, Tash. I would have understood. If you just told me you were so jealous.

TASH: He told you?

HEN: I smelt you.

TASH: He told you.

HEN: *Please don't leave me.*

TASH: She's twenty-two. The foreman's daughter. I don't know her name.

HEN: I've loved you. I've cared about you. I've shared everything with you.

TASH: He fucks her over the photocopier. They're careless with the prints.

HEN: He said you'd say this.

TASH: The girl thinks she's in love with him. I found them in his bag.

HEN: Why are you doing this?

TASH: His foreman has warned Al he'll sack him if he finds him doing it again.

HEN: He said, you would…

TASH: Listen to me… I agreed he should work at mine to get him away from the site.

HEN: I promised him, I wouldn't leave him.

TASH: You can do it.

HEN: I promised him.

TASH: I didn't want to tell you.

HEN: He said…

TASH: I've never…

HEN: It's easier… (*Beat.*) Somehow it's easier if it is you…

TASH: No…

HEN: If it could have just been anybody…just anybody… then who's to say it's love with me? (*Beat.*) I smelt you on him.

TASH: No…

HEN: I smelt you on him.

TASH: Hen.

HEN: No.

TASH: My betrayal's easier than his? (*Long beat.*) There's nowhere to go then.

> (*HEN and TASH look at one another. HEN slides over her drink. TASH knocks it back.*)

SCENE 22

Loft, London. NATHAN is undressing as if getting ready for a shower. He drapes his shirt over the rail above. The sound of the shower throughout.

NATHAN: They fired her the day the market slumped. She never stood a chance. They're going bust. She calls me in high agitation. 'I've fucked them up the wall.' 'I'm busy, sweetheart. Can't we talk later?' (*Beat.*) Ask me how she looked that day and I struggle to remember her face. Doesn't that suck? Don't forget to look at your lover, don't forget to breathe her in, taste her, know her… She took a belt… Like this one… She hooked it over the shower head.

(*The sound of the hoover being turned off.*)

Why didn't the bastard break? She washed herself. Ready and then – (*Slipping the belt off around his waist.*) For a tiny moment I can feel her. Warm against my skin – (*Slipping the belt around his neck.*) I'm sorry. (*Beat.*) I get so lonely.

(*MARVIN enters as NATHAN swings from the rail above. MARVIN does not move for a moment until he struggles to get him down. He slips on the floor with him. He tries to revive him. He slowly realises that he is already dead.*

A build of a baby's wail.)

SCENE 23

Flat, London. HEN packing up a tea chest of china. AL enters. He's dressed down, shorts, trainers, a younger look.

AL: I didn't see your car…

HEN: Walked.

AL: I could help you with this.

HEN: No, I'm fine… (*Beat.*) You've let this place –

AL: I was going to tidy up.

HEN: Really get a mess.

(*HEN goes to pick up an empty tea chest.*)

AL: Let me.

HEN: No.

AL: (*Long beat.*) He's sleeping?

HEN: Right through. This easy I'll have another this time next year.

AL: Your mum?

HEN: Taking me in until –

AL: The house'll –

HEN: – never be finished.

AL: – not for a while yet. I never said –

HEN: – anything that wasn't true.

AL: – sorry.

HEN: No.

AL: Sorry.

HEN: (*Long beat.*) Not accepted…

AL: Hen…

HEN: There are random moments and moments of decision. You said that…

AL: I didn't mean…

HEN: Some of the biggest moments in my life have been founded on those two principles.

AL: Hen, if I could…

HEN: No… No… Yours was a moment of decision. (*Eyeing him.*) You going on –

AL: Holiday.

HEN: Yeah.

AL: Going to India.

HEN: Yeah. (*Beat.*) With? She's young enough to be your –

AL: It's only a –

(*AL starts to help HEN pack up. They work in silence.*)

What am I doing, Hen?

HEN: I don't know.

(*AL reaches out for* HEN'*s hand. She holds it.*)

AL: Please.

HEN: No. You can't come back. You can't.

SCENE 24

Flat, London. Late night. TASH *staggers in. She's pissed. She slams down keys and her bag and goes over to the fridge. She opens it. It casts its light, sending its hum around the room. She contemplates it.*

TASH: And then what?

(*SQUEAL sits in the half light.*)

SQUEAL: There are pockets of water, just spinning in space, small oceans of water which are lifeless, dead, or as we know it at the moment but which may well have the breadth and depth of some of our own larger seas.

TASH: But what glues them together? What holds them?

SQUEAL: Gravity.

TASH: Like a skin.

SQUEAL: A skin of gravity which envelopes them and changes form in motion.

TASH: Like amoeba.

SQUEAL: Like an amoeba.

TASH: Or a puddle.

SQUEAL: Not a puddle. But they can break up.

TASH: Like a worm.

SQUEAL: I'll go with a worm. (*Beat.*) You drink too much.

TASH: I don't drink enough.

SQUEAL: I'd like to see you. I'd like to talk to you. In the daytime. Not in the dark.

TASH: You wouldn't cope.

SQUEAL: You think?

(*TASH holds his stare, lets this moment hang between them.*)

TASH: Tell me the fighter pilot story.

SQUEAL: You've heard it.

TASH: Tell me it again.

SQUEAL: I'm useless at everything, except physics. I am the maestro of physics. I do all the tests. I'm top of it all. But I can't tell the difference between green and red. Stop or go. I fail.

(*TASH laughs to herself, finishing off her cornflakes, laughing to herself, letting it die between them.*)

It would be good to get further than this story you know. I'd like us to try and get beyond.

TASH: This is it.

SQUEAL: I don't believe that. I really truly don't believe that.

TASH: I wake up in the night and I'm almost breathless. Like I'm holding the exhale. Like to breathe out fully will kill me, shatter me, let me feel the full breadth of my empty bed. Just me and nothing. My thoughts. And sometimes the feeling is so desperate. And the only thing that gets me to sleep is to touch myself. Run my fingers over myself, bring myself to some kind of inner connection, do something that creates an involuntary sensation, shuddering through me, like the ghost of someone, the spirit of someone fucking me. It's not that I think that people always leave. I just don't contemplate they'll stay. (*Long beat.*) It's…painful.

(*SQUEAL leans forward in his chair, almost touching her. TASH sits motionless, suddenly frozen, trying to focus on his face.*)

TASH: (*Long beat.*) I've pissed myself.

SQUEAL: Lucky I'm here then.

SCENE 25

SQUEAL running, swimming towel in hand as if late for GLORIA.

SQUEAL: I'm sorry.

GLORIA: Keep your hair on. It's fine.

SQUEAL: I can't actually stay today.

GLORIA: Oh –

SQUEAL: It's just –

GLORIA: You're meeting someone? You're meeting someone.

SQUEAL: Yes.

GLORIA: Don't be miserable about it. It's good news isn't it?

(*Silence.*)

I might just do a few laps.

SQUEAL: This doesn't mean –

GLORIA: What? You're dumping me? Got you worried. It's a good thing.

SQUEAL: It might just be a meeting.

GLORIA: You might be –

SQUEAL: I'm not.

GLORIA: Yeah, I'm going to do a few laps today.

SQUEAL: Gloria –

GLORIA: Look at you. For a start, you better get your hair cut. I've been meaning to tell you for some time. Smarten up a bit for – Whoever.

(*SQUEAL shrugs, makes to go.*)

SQUEAL: From the back. The way your hair goes. The way the colour goes. First time I met you, you reminded me of my –

GLORIA: Cheeky bugger. (*Suddenly.*) I wish I had. Would have drowned you at birth. My luck.

SQUEAL: Yeah right.

GLORIA: Go on. She'll be waiting. I don't mean to be ungrateful.

(*SQUEAL looks away.*)

SQUEAL: Gloria, keep your thumbs with your fingers. It'll stop you splashing so much.

(*SQUEAL looks back. GLORIA has already gone, swimming away.*)

SCENE 26

Pool, London. TASH sitting reading her book, waiting for someone –
MARVIN dressed in black. He has clearly been at a funeral. He sits on
the bench next to TASH.

MARVIN: Good book?

> (*TASH nods. Continues reading.*)

> Long time since I read a good book.

> (*TASH nods. Shifts slightly in her seat. Ignores him.*)

> Talk to me. (*Beat.*) I've just watched them bury a man.
> (*Beat.*) Talk to me.

TASH: I'm sorry…

MARVIN: Say whatever you want. Say whatever comes into
your head. Just say something.

TASH: (*Long beat.*) Yes… It's a good book.

MARVIN: Adventure?

TASH: No… Sort of… A love story. Not a romantic love
story… It's a tragedy yet it also has hope. I haven't finished
it yet.

MARVIN: Of course.

TASH: Did you…

MARVIN: No. I hardly knew him.

TASH: Right. I hate funerals. It's alright if they have a lot to
drink. I've been to a wake before. You can't fail to have a
good time at a wake.

MARVIN: He was young. He was a young man.

TASH: That's awful.

MARVIN: Yes.

TASH: How did he…

MARVIN: He died because he wasn't loved, because he
thought he wasn't loved.

TASH: I see. I'm sorry…

MARVIN: I come here most days.

TASH: You must be very…

MARVIN: Yes… Shaken… Yes… I'm very shaken, but I understand it you see. You think you are not loved or maybe you have stopped being able to feel that you are so you withdraw. And the hardest place to be is with people but not with people. Alone in a crowded room. And sometimes it is your fault because you don't feel anything so you have to go away in order to decide if you want to come back. And when you don't. When what you have been looking for finds you, then you hope that they will forgive you. You hope they won't feel the pain that boy felt, you hope they'll understand that you do still think of them…

TASH: I'm sure they will.

MARVIN: Becaue you have to live with the not being sure. You have to…

TASH: I'm very sorry for your loss.

(*MARVIN nods. TASH gets up to go.*)

MARVIN: It's a nice park. It has a view of the pool.

TASH: Yes, I guess it does.

(*TASH gets up to go. She leaves her book. MARVIN picks it up and starts to read it. TASH comes back for it. He hands it to her.*)

MARVIN: I won't be staying long anyway.

(*TASH takes the book, smiles and exits. MARVIN stands up. His gaze follows someone very slowly in the distance. A gentle rhythm, barely visible back and forth.*)

(*Silent.*) Gloria –

(*He turns and exits. The lap of water.*)

SCENE 27

Pool, London. GLORIA is standing in her swimming costume and swimming cap, dripping wet.

GLORIA: And the sea is icy but I'm not scared. I wade in quickly. It is dark and I can see the shadows of clouds moving above. The water moves around me. It's cold and yet with every stroke I feel myself getting warmer. Like being held, suspended, above it all. And soon I can't see where I have come from or how far I have gone. Just me in the water in the middle of the sea, looking up at the dark sky above. And I think how easy it would be just to let go, just to keep swimming, until I am too exhausted and my legs and arms won't hold me. I could just let the sea take me, just wash me away, when I look up and there are a pair of eyes staring back at me. A seal, staring at me, circling me. And I feel no fear, no cold just utterly and absolutely not alone. Five minutes, ten minutes no more and it's gone. And without me even doing anything I'm suddenly turning and swimming back, not looking behind me, just swimming back to the bay, swimming back to land. Just a woman, too fat for her costume, dripping wet and cold, standing on a piece of Skye. Glad she didn't drown. Glad she didn't…

(*GLORIA turns slowly to look behind her, as if checking for someone for a moment. Nothing. She starts to dry herself, rubbing harder as the lights go down.*)

The End.

Note

In addition to the above play, short snapshot scenes were added during scene changes. These are an option and are to be placed at the discretion of the production.

INSERT 1

TASH runs back, hurrying after SQUEAL.

TASH: 8806 2424.

> (*SQUEAL stops, silently amazed.*)

> I changed my mind.

> (*TASH turns and runs off. SQUEAL stands, silently bemused in the rain, trying to remember a telephone number.*)

SQUEAL: Has anyone got a pen?

INSERT 2

NATHAN and MARVIN are bent peering over the fridge.

NATHAN: Fruit to the left. Dairy to the right. If you could clean it Monday, Wednesday and Friday, after you've done the surfaces and wiped through.

MARVIN: Right.

NATHAN: Hoovering thereafter.

MARVIN: Okay.

NATHAN: Good. Good.

> (*They sit.*)

MARVIN: Nice fridge.

NATHAN: Thank you. I don't like my dairy and fruit too close.

LOVESONG

For Dad.

Lovesong was first performed on 30 September 2011 at the Drum Theatre Plymouth produced Frantic Assembly and Drum Theatre Plymouth in association with Chichester Festival Theatre

WILLIAM	Edward Bennett
BILLY	Sam Cox
MAGGIE	Siân Phillips
MARGARET	Leanne Rowe

Creative Team

Writer	Abi Morgan
Direction & Choreography	Scott Graham
	& Steven Hoggett
Design	Merle Hensel
Lighting Design	Andy Purves
Sound Design	Carolyn Downing
Video Design	Ian William Galloway
Casting	Sarah Hughes
Singing & Voice	Helen Porter
Assistant Director	Geordie Brookman

Characters

BILLY
late 70s

MAGGIE
late 70s

WILLIAM
mid 20s-30s

MARGARET
mid 20s-30s

The play is set in a house and garden in a suburb of a city over several years.

A great love is perhaps incomplete without its decline, agony, without its conclusion.

Les Femmes et L'Amour, Sacha Guitry

SCENE ONE

Night.

A house, surrounded by an overgrown garden.

BILLY stands on a porch, smoking a cigarette.

BILLY: When I clean my teeth, I always clean them twice. This takes time. I use a little brush. I work between every molar, like a tiny chimney sweep. Because it is important. Because decalcification removes the enamel and yields decay. Because our teeth are our legacy, after bones and muscles have dissolved into dust and the earth, our teeth remain. Their value to archaeologist and paleontologist is infinite and undeniable. They reveal what we eat and how we live. I see it as my duty to preserve them.

A light goes off somewhere in the house.

Then I turn off the light and go to my bed.

I read. I wind my clock. I say no prayers.

A light goes on in a bedroom window.

I sleep.

And in my sleep…

BILLY flicks out his cigarette –

In my sleep…

A front door suddenly illuminated by WILLIAM holding a standard lamp.

I am young again.

MARGARET stands under a tree in the garden. She holds a kitchen chair and a tin bucket.

WILLIAM nods, heads inside. WILLIAM ascends the stairs, just visible through the hall window, holding the standard lamp. In the bedroom window, BILLY appears just turning on the same standard lamp. He readies himself for bed. He crosses to a bathroom window, turning on the light. He is visible brushing his teeth.

MARGARET: *(Calling out.)* Does the kitchen look smaller to you?

BILLY brushes his teeth. He spits out. Checks his teeth in the mirror. Turns off the light.

WILLIAM: No.

WILLIAM now stands in the bedroom window, by the now lit standard lamp.

MARGARET: Come down.

WILLIAM nods, exits downstairs. MARGARET stands in the kitchen below. She puts the chair down by a kitchen table, a bucket by the sink.

See. I counted twelve paces and now there are only ten.

WILLIAM: It's shrunk.

MARGARET: It's shrunk.

BILLY just visible in the bedroom window above. He stands winding up his clock. He turns off the light.

WILLIAM: Does that mean our repayments will be smaller?

MARGARET smiles, explores the sink. WILLIAM slips his arm around her waist; they peer out of the kitchen window.

The garden's still the same.

MARGARET: Yes.

WILLIAM: Want to pace it out?

MARGARET: It has a tree.

WILLIAM: It has a tree.

MARGARET: And grass.

WILLIAM: That is definitely grass.

MARGARET: Tall grass.

WILLIAM: I'll mow it tomorrow.

They look at one another, smile. They lean in to kiss –

WILLIAM: Is that a peach tree?

WILLIAM exits. MARGARET watches him.

(Calling out.) Come outside. They're ready.

MARGARET follows WILLIAM out. They stand picking peaches and laughing, putting them into a tin bucket in MARGARET's hand.

MARGARET: We have peaches.

She holds a peach up to him. He bites into its juicy flesh licking the juice as it drips down her wrist. They laugh, kissing one another, drawing one another into a laughing embrace until –

WILLIAM: What do you think they are?

Suddenly a sudden surge of birdsong, MARGARET and WILLIAM look up, eyes training across the sky.

MARGARET: Starlings.

Blackout.

SCENE TWO

Day.

BILLY stands in the kitchen doorway, holding a dead starling.

BILLY: The cat must have got it.

MAGGIE crosses the kitchen, pouring BILLY a cup of coffee. He goes to take the coffee. She tuts.

MAGGIE: Wash your hands.

BILLY nods, he carefully lays the starling on the table.

Don't leave it there.

BILLY washes his hands at the kitchen sink.

BILLY: I'll bin it.

MAGGIE: No. She'll get it again. You need to bury it.

BILLY hesitates, nods. MAGGIE picks up her coffee heading up.

BILLY: What time is your appointment today?

MAGGIE: It's fine. I can still drive myself.

BILLY: What time?

MAGGIE: Ten forty.

BILLY nods.

BILLY: I'll drive you.

MAGGIE: It's fine.

MAGGIE exits, heads upstairs. BILLY goes over to the table and pours himself a cup of coffee. He stands, drinks his coffee, staring out at the garden ahead.

BILLY: *(Calling out.)* We need to pick the peaches.

MAGGIE stops midway through creaming her face in the bathroom above.

They're going soft.

BILLY waits, the silence hanging until –

Wasps are getting them.

BILLY picks up the starling, heads out into the garden, picking up a trowel on his way out. MAGGIE looks out of the window, watching him. She finishes up in the bathroom, and crosses over into the bedroom. She opens a closet door, enters –

MARGARET: I have nothing to wear.

MARGARET comes out of the closet, holding two dresses on different hangers.

In this I look like my mother. And in this I look like a tramp.

WILLIAM lounges on the bed, reading a newspaper. She holds up the dresses to herself, considering.

Mother... Tramp... Mother... Tramp... Mother.

WILLIAM: Tramp... Tramp... Tramp.

MARGARET discards one dress, considering the other.

MARGARET: Mother.

MARGARET pulls on her dress, WILLIAM zips up the back of her dress. She sniffs.

WILLIAM: What?

MARGARET smiles, shakes her head –

MARGARET: How do I look?

WILLIAM: Beautiful. *(Beat.)* Your mother always looked like a tramp.

WILLIAM sinks back on the bed, resumes reading his book.

MARGARET: What are you reading?

WILLIAM holds it up for her to show her the cover, then he resumes reading. MARGARET watches him.

WILLIAM: What?

MARGARET smiles, exits into the closet. MAGGIE exits from the closet, now dressed.

BILLY: You ready?

MAGGIE looks at BILLY standing in the bedroom doorway.

MAGGIE: I said I could drive myself.

BILLY: What else have I got to do today?

MAGGIE nods, concedes, looks back at the bed, WILLIAM now gone.

Do you need to take anything with you?

MAGGIE: No. Not today.

BILLY nods.

I'm just picking up my prescription.

BILLY hesitates –

BILLY: I'll drop you and then wait outside the pharmacy.

MAGGIE nods, exits.

And after –

BILLY looks up, sees MARGARET smiling at him, coming out from the closet, fixing an earring.

MARGARET: What?

MAGGIE stands on the stairs.

MARGARET: Have you seen the blue heels?

BILLY shakes his head.

I can't find them anywhere.

MARGARET smiles, heading back into the closet.

MAGGIE: *(Calling up.)* Billy – ?

BILLY stands alone in the bedroom.

BILLY: I'm coming. I'm coming. I'm there.

Blackout.

SCENE THREE

Dusk.

The turn of the water sprinkler.

BILLY sits alone doing his crossword on the porch.

MAGGIE fixes a drink inside. The chink of ice, vodka poured in one glass, lemon and soda fizz poured in both. BILLY looks up, listens. BILLY resumes his crossword. MAGGIE exits out to the porch. She hands BILLY one of the drinks. They chink. She sinks down on a chair.

MAGGIE: Soda?

BILLY: Thanks.

MAGGIE stands looking beyond.

MAGGIE: Are you going to turn that sprinkler off or shall I?

BILLY does not answer, lost in his crossword. MAGGIE goes over to a tap on the side of the house. She turns it. The sprinkler goes quiet.

BILLY: You want a clue?

MAGGIE shrugs, sits on the front step.

Blue flower. Six letters. Something I –

MAGGIE: Violet.

BILLY shakes his head.

BILLY: Something I. Something N.

MAGGIE stands considering until –

MAGGIE: Zinnia.

BILLY looks up impressed. They chink.

BILLY: This soda's flat.

MAGGIE: There's another bottle back of the –

The swing of the door, BILLY gone.

…fridge.

BILLY enters the kitchen, goes over to the fridge, and opens it. He pulls out another bottle of soda, refills his glass, and adds ice. Drinks. He looks at the vodka bottle still resting on the table.

BILLY: I saw that boy today.

MAGGIE sits on the porch.

MAGGIE: Huh?

BILLY: While I was waiting for you to finish up at the doctors.

MAGGIE: *(Calling back.)* What boy?

BILLY: The kid who used to live next door.

MAGGIE: *(Beat.)* Adam?

BILLY: Adam

MAGGIE: Really?

MAGGIE: Wow.

Silence.

How old must he be now?

BILLY: He had his son with him and he looked... He must be forty at least now.

MAGGIE: *(Calling back.)* No he can't be that old.

BILLY: Yes... He must be forty-five, forty-six I swear.

He said I looked just the same.

BILLY closes the fridge door.

MAGGIE: He was lying. The young always say that to old people. I hope you told him –

MAGGIE enters the kitchen –

BILLY: Huh – ?

MAGGIE: ...you knew he was lying.

Silence.

MAGGIE: Adam.

BILLY: They're looking to rent. I don't think they've got a whole lot of money. His kid looked maybe nine.

MAGGIE: Wow.

BILLY: And two little girls.

MAGGIE: Girls.

BILLY: Yep.

Silence.

He remembered you.

MAGGIE: Really? That's nice...

BILLY: How did that happen? How did that happen that Josie's boy got so old?

Silence –

Huh?

Silence –

Looked like he was losing his hair.

MAGGIE: You hungry? What happened to the time?

BILLY shakes his head, eyes watching WILLIAM –

There's some cold meat in the fridge. I could make a sandwich. Do you want a sandwich?

MAGGIE disappears through a door into a larder.

BILLY: I might just go up.

MAGGIE coming out of the larder, carrying a plate of cold meat, and a loaf of bread.

MAGGIE: You always like a snack before you go up.

BILLY already gone, heading up the stairs.

BILLY: I'm fine. I'm good. I'm fine.

MAGGIE sinks a little.

MARGARET: *(Calling out.)* So are you going to say something?

MAGGIE spies the vodka bottle on the table. She picks it up, putting it back into the fridge. She reaches for butter and starts to make a sandwich, seemingly oblivious to –

(Entering.) Are you mad with me?

MARGARET enters but WILLIAM does not look up from his drink. She stands dressed up for the night, holding a clutch bag,

You've not spoke a word all the way home.

Silence –

OK, OK...

MARGARET sits down in the seat opposite WILLIAM.

You're mad.

WILLIAM does not speak. He eats the sandwich.

It was just a dance. I was being nice to him.

MAGGIE sits down, finishes her vodka, placing the glass on the table. She reads the paper, seemingly oblivious as she eats the other half of sandwich.

He's your boss for Christ sake.

MARGARET picks up the empty glass, goes over to the fridge, and refills the glass, drinks.

WILLIAM: You were all over him.

MARGARET: You're jealous.

WILLIAM: Please –

MARGARET: Yes, you are. You're jealous.

MARGARET smiles.

WILLIAM: He's ancient.

MARGARET: Forty-five... Forty-six.

WILLIAM: It was embarrassing.

MARGARET shrugs, playful.

MARGARET: I can't help it if he likes me.

WILLIAM: You never drink. Why tonight did you drink?

MARGARET: It was fun.

WILLIAM: It was work.

MARGARET: Some men would consider me an asset. I listened for a good hour and looked interested when he talked about advances in cavity maintenance.

WILLIAM: Thank you. No really of course thank you.

MARGARET: What does that mean?

MAGGIE stands, scoops up the plate, taking it over to the sink. She washes up.

WILLIAM: Had I known you were working for me I would have asked you to talk to his wife instead of leaving me stuck with her, scrabbling for conversation. It was awful.

WILLIAM gets up, goes to the fridge, and takes out the vodka bottle.

MARGARET: Go easy huh?

WILLIAM: Me go easy?

WILLIAM fills up his glass a little more. He drinks, looking at her.

MARGARET: Fine. It's your head in the morning.

MAGGIE exits, heading upstairs.

WILLIAM: Maybe I'm not getting up in the morning.

MARGARET stands, picks up the plate of cold meat, taking it back out to the larder.

MARGARET: Right.

WILLIAM: Maybe I have somewhere more important to be in the morning.

MARGARET comes through from the larder.

MARGARET: Like where?

Silence.

Like where?

WILLIAM: Like a meeting at the bank.

MARGARET hesitates –

MARGARET: For what?

WILLIAM: To discuss a loan.

MARGARET: Oh God.

WILLIAM: Don't do the face. Please not the face.

MARGARET: No –

WILLIAM: Listen

MARGARET: No –

WILLIAM: Listen to me.

MARGARET: We do not need a loan.

WILLIAM: Too bad. We got one.

MARGARET: Jesus... Please... Please –

WILLIAM: I've already seen the greatest place. It's down that back road. Past the café... Way past the café but –

MARGARET: Where the café used to be? Christ Billy. There's no footfall. No footfall, no people –

WILLIAM: People need dentists.

MARGARET: It's the worse place.

WILLIAM: You don't pass a dentist. You call a dentist.

MARGARET: There are millions –

WILLIAM: I like this place –

MARGARET: There are millions of better places than –

WILLIAM: We got this place.

MARGARET: Oh my God.

WILLIAM: Just say yes.

MARGARET: Billy?

Silence.

Were you even going to tell me?

WILLIAM: I'm telling you now.

MARGARET: We can't afford it.

WILLIAM: Not listening.

MARGARET: You're pushing us too far. I don't want us to be –

WILLIAM: It's not a stretch.

MARGARET: It's a stretch. We are stretched. Look at my lips. Hear what I am saying to you. Billy. We have been stretched ever since we arrived here.

WILLIAM scoops up MARGARET spinning her around.

No get off. Get off me.

WILLIAM: Come on… Come on.

MARGARET: Did you tell your boss?

WILLIAM: Yes, right after he'd finished groping my wife's ass.

MARGARET: You're pathetic.

WILLIAM: 'Screw you and your nasty practice. I will not be coming in any more. I will not be filling in your dull cavity extractions. I will not mop up your mess.' Did you see his face?

MARGARET: That's why we didn't stay for dessert.

WILLIAM: You know he's a fucking –

MARGARET: What are we doing?

WILLIAM: …asshole.

MARGARET: How much? How much did you borrow?

WILLIAM: Double this house.

MARGARET: Oh My God. No… No… N… NO…

WILLIAM: Breathe.

MARGARET: There are two of us –

WILLIAM: Yes.

MARGARET: In this. You and I. You promised –

WILLIAM: Yes but –

MARGARET: You promised. We have stretched ourselves too far. It was you. It was you who wanted to come to this country. Not me.

WILLIAM: And what did I say to you then. Maggie what did I say to you then?

WILLIAM stops her, gripping her wrists, looking her straight in the eye.

There are moments where you have to leap with me. There are going to be moments like this where I have to know you can jump when I ask you to jump. And you did.

MARGARET: Bill.

WILLIAM: I wouldn't do this if I didn't believe I could follow it through. I wouldn't do this if I didn't believe it was right –

A light flicks on in the bathroom overhead.

MARGARET: Asshole.

WILLIAM: Do you trust me?

MAGGIE stands for a moment, stuck, her hand still on the light chord.

Maggie.

MAGGIE hesitates –

MARGARET: I hate you.

MARGARET stands caught in his half embrace.

WILLIAM: I hate you too.

MAGGIE reaches for a pot of cream off a shelf, and opens it.

WILLIAM: So we're going to do this?

MAGGIE looks down at the pot in her hand.

MARGARET: Looks like it's already done.

WILLIAM spins her around, laughing and kissing MARGARET who slowly concedes, their whoops and shouts traveling through the house. Their laughter and embraces subduing into something more passionate as WILLIAM kisses MARGARET deeply, pushing her back against the wall. Her hand slipping upwards, reaching for the light switch. She flicks the light off as –

MAGGIE: Every night, I cream my face –

MAGGIE caught in the bathroom window, creaming her face.

As my mother did. And her mother did before that. Perhaps that's why I now see my mother staring back at me.

MAGGIE stares at her reflection.

I do this not just in an attempt to preserve my face. Though I like it when people say 'You're how old?' And then I tell them and they say 'No. No way.' And invariably they are lying. But I smile and look suitably flattered. They go away feeling good that they have bolstered the old girl and I go away knowing more than ever I look my age.

I do it because in doing it I am telling myself, 'your mother did the same.' She cooked. And she watched TV. And she raked leaves in her garden. And she creamed her face. And maybe just maybe if I do the same I will stave off the inevitable.

I can see it's a kind of madness now.

MAGGIE peers at herself more closely at the mirror.

…The world changes and you with it.

MAGGIE puts down her pot of cream.

It's inevitable.

WILLIAM and MARGARET running up the stairs, laughing, passing BILLY just coming out of the bedroom –

MAGGIE turns listening. Suddenly she reaches out a hand, gripping the shelf, knocking the pot of cream on to the floor.

BILLY: Maggie –

BILLY stands in the landing illuminated.

You OK?

BILLY taps on the door.

MAGGIE, her face contorted in pain, wincing.

Blackout.

SCENE FOUR

Day.

MAGGIE stands in the kitchen holding up a bright Chinese lantern. She blows on it. BILLY comes down the stairs carrying a box.

MAGGIE: Over there. Over there.

BILLY slides the box down on the floor.

BILLY: You want them all down?

MAGGIE is already rifling through the box.

MAGGIE: Yes…yes…

BILLY: You're not the one carrying them.

MAGGIE: What?

MAGGIE pulls out a pile of old records, peering at them.

BILLY: The boxes?

Silence –

Do you really want to do this now?

MAGGIE nods.

MAGGIE: I've been meaning to do it forever. We need to get rid of this stuff. I don't want it kicking around after –

Silence –

It makes it easier. For you.

BILLY sighs, heads back upwards.

BILLY: I'm bringing down moths and silver fish from that loft with every box that's all I'm saying.

MAGGIE does not look up from looking over the records. BILLY heads upstairs, leaving MAGGIE alone.

WILLIAM: You found them.

Suddenly WILLIAM appears, a portable record player under his arm.

WILLIAM: Will you bring the blanket?

He smiles with delight, scooping up the record in passing from MAGGIE –

(Calling back.) I'll wire it up from the back of the house.

The swing of the door, WILLIAM gone. MAGGIE looking on watching WILLIAM heading down to the end of the garden –

BILLY: Guess what else was lurking up there?

BILLY enters holding up an anatomical skull, with a smile.

The other woman in my life.

MAGGIE looks up.

MAGGIE: You're right. You're right. It's madness doing this today.

MAGGIE heads upstairs. She sits on the bed in the bedroom. BILLY looks back at the skull confused.

MARGARET: No... NO... NO... NO...

BILLY turns, MARGARET smiling at him.

You weren't meant to see it yet.

WILLIAM enters through the back door.

Do you like her?

WILLIAM smiles, peering closer at the skull.

WILLIAM: I love her. What's not to love?

MARGARET: Really?

BILLY looks on, MARGARET and WILLIAM oblivious.

Happy Birthday.

They kiss.

I thought you could put her in the reception.

WILLIAM: You don't think it will put patients off?

MARGARET: Really? No… She's got such a great smile.

BILLY smiles –

WILLIAM: Where did you find her?

MARGARET: I bribed someone who knew someone who met someone… Yard sale. *(Beat.)* I bumped into Josie.

WILLIAM: Josie. Just –

MARGARET: Moved in across the road.

WILLIAM: Married to that gas guy –

MARGARET: Oil broker.

WILLIAM grimaces.

We met them at that party across the street.

WILLIAM: Christ I remember him.

MARGARET: I think she's going to be my new friend.

WILLIAM: You've got friends.

MARGARET: Neighbour friends.

WILLIAM: What about Annie?

MARGARET: Married friends.

WILLIAM: Ah, married friends.

MARGARET: What does that mean?

WILLIAM: So many of your friends marry men I can't stand.

MARGARET: You like Don.

WILLIAM: Only because he's improved Kate.

WILLIAM hesitates, MARGARET smiles –

MARGARET: We went for coffee.

WILLIAM: Huh?

MARGARET: With Josie.

WILLIAM nods.

MARGARET: She's due a baby August.

WILLIAM hesitates, the silence hanging in the room.

Her second.

WILLIAM: That's nice.

MARGARET: That's what I thought.

WILLIAM nods. MARGARET smiles, looks away, spying the boxes.

Can you take these up to the loft?

WILLIAM: I'll do it later.

WILLIAM puts a hand on her shoulder. She stiffens then relaxes, leaning into him a little.

WILLIAM: It's only been eight months. It might just take us –

MARGARET nods –

MARGARET: Forever.

MARGARET laughs, smiles wiping away tears.

She looked exhausted.

WILLIAM: Exactly.

Silence –

They'll come. Children will come.

MARGARET: Names?

WILLIAM: Mustard and Teacup. Mustard older. Teacup younger, gap between her teeth.

MARGARET smiles. WILLIAM scoops up a picnic blanket from a nearby chair, ushering MARGARET holding the skull towards the garden.

Let's eat outside. *(Eyeing skull.)* Will your friend be joining us?

MARGARET laughs putting down the skull, following WILLIAM out, leaving BILLY on his own watching them through the window. He picks up the skull.

MARGARET: Be careful. She has a very jealous husband.

WILLIAM and MARGARET head to the end of the garden, BILLY looking on.

You find the hammock?

MAGGIE enters the kitchen –

MAGGIE: Huh?

BILLY looks up, sees MAGGIE standing in the doorway.

BILLY: The hammock? Where did the hammock go?

MAGGIE: Which one?

BILLY: The one we use to sling between those trees.

MAGGIE: It rotted a few years back.

BILLY: It never happened before.

MAGGIE: It happened every year, so I changed them every year. I just didn't bother telling you.

BILLY: Oh –

MAGGIE: Oh what –

BILLY: We should string it up. Have people over to dinner. Like we used to.

MAGGIE: Like who?

BILLY: Like Don and Kate.

MAGGIE: Don doesn't like to drive at night.

BILLY: What happened to everyone.

MAGGIE: They got old.

BILLY: Not listening.

MAGGIE: They're probably staying with Sally and the children. They always spend a month there –

This time of the year.

BILLY: Yeah.

Silence.

MAGGIE: Maybe another night.

BILLY: Sure.

> *BILLY looks away. MAGGIE spies the skull.*

MAGGIE: Where did you get that?

BILLY: You gave it to me on my 28th birthday.

MAGGIE: Did I?

BILLY: Yes. We ate in the garden.

> *MAGGIE looks at BILLY, smiles, shakes her head.*

MAGGIE: I have no recollection at all.

BILLY: And after we –

> *MAGGIE already lost in packing up the boxes. BILLY watches her.*

Perhaps we could eat outside tonight.

MAGGIE: Really.

BILLY: I'm going to find that hammock.

MAGGIE: No it's too cold.

> *BILLY hesitates, nods –*

The starlings are starting to scratch and gather.

> *MAGGIE resumes searching through the boxes.*

BILLY: Yes.

> *BILLY looks out the window.*

Cat's on the prowl.

Blackout.

SCENE FIVE

Night.

A beautiful Chinese lantern hanging from the tree in the garden.

WILLIAM lies in the long grass, MARGARET sits up next to him.

MARGARET: I want to be cremated.

WILLIAM: Now. Right.

MARGARET: It's cleaner.

WILLIAM: I don't think so.

MARGARET: It's quicker and easier. I think it's nicer.

WILLIAM: Cremation is nicer. Right. Than what?

MARGARET: Than being buried in the ground. I don't want to lie in a box and rot. I don't want anything left of me, after.

WILLIAM: You better write it down.

MARGARET: You'll remember.

WILLIAM: I might not be there.

MARGARET: Where will you be?

WILLIAM sits up smiles –

WILLIAM: Rotting in my box.

MARGARET swipes him away.

MARGARET: Then where will I go?

WILLIAM: They'll scatter you.

MARGARET: I don't want to be scattered just anywhere.

WILLIAM: Like I said, you better write it down.

MARGARET: I'm not planning on dying yet.

WILLIAM: That would make things a little easier.

MARGARET: You're so cold.

WILLIAM: No I'm not.

MARGARET: You're so clinical.

WILLIAM: What's more clinical than distilling an entire person into an urn, no, worse a cardboard box of ash.

MARGARET: Anything other is sentimental.

WILLIAM: And where do the children go? To grieve?

MARGARET: A beautiful mountain, a beach, this house, this garden, under this tree. I want to be scattered under this tree.

WILLIAM: Someone will cut down that tree one day.

MARGARET: No they won't. Mustard won't let them.

WILLIAM: What about Teacup?

MARGARET: She'll be into nature. She's very sensitive.

WILLIAM: Like her mother. Of course.

MARGARET: They will sit here with their children.

WILLIAM: We have grandchildren?

MARGARET: Several. All running around this house. Writing on the walls.

WILLIAM smiles. MARGARET smiles.

And they will never let anyone cut this tree down because you and I will be here –

WILLIAM: In my box.

MARGARET: Don't say that. Together. They'll scatter us together under this tree.

WILLIAM: What if we don't want to be? What if the years together have separated us? What if I can't stand you and you can't stand me?

MARGARET: Never. It won't happen.

WILLIAM: It might. One day we're laughing and the next I'm trying to work out how to poison your tea.

A light illuminates in a bedroom window. MAGGIE stands, a cup of tea in hand.

No worse, I smother you with a pillow in your sleep.

MARGARET: Is it a little cold?

WILLIAM: You're always a little cold. Or maybe I could strangle you. Creep up behind you when you're not looking –

BILLY suddenly visible in the bathroom cleaning his teeth.

MARGARET: Don't say it.

WILLIAM teases her, drawing her into laughing embrace, pulling her deep into the grass.

You're weird.

WILLIAM: You're weirder.

The light goes out in the bathroom window. BILLY enters the bedroom.

BILLY: Can't you sleep?

MAGGIE: I've just taken something. It will kick in in a minute.

BILLY nods, goes over to the bed. He winds up the clock, looks up, sees MAGGIE looking out of the window.

Silence –

BILLY: She'll come in when she's hungry.

He climbs into bed. Reaches for his book, reads until –

BILLY puts down his reading glasses.

MAGGIE stands by the window until –

MAGGIE: It's all right. Turn out the light.

BILLY hesitates, nods, and turns the light out.

I'll sleep soon.

Silence –

It's just so dark.

MAGGIE peers out of the window.

BILLY already drifting off to sleep.

MAGGIE: That fox was sitting on the wall again.

Silence –

MAGGIE peers out anxiously.

I'll just…

MAGGIE exits, heading downstairs, turning on the kitchen light. She comes out on to the porch, calling out –

Silence –

Puss puss… Biscuit…

MAGGIE walks across the long grass.

Where are you?

The drift of laughter, a record turning on a distant record player.

MARGARET: Don't ever let us become like them.

MARGARET sits up, WILLIAM lying next to her.

WILLIAM: Like whom?

MARGARET: Those couples you see facing one another over a cooling cup of coffee with nothing left to say.

WILLIAM: Maybe that's fine. Maybe they've said it all. Maybe they know one another so well that they're just happy in silence.

MARGARET: No one has ever said everything –

MAGGIE stands looking out until –

There's always more still to say.

The record catches on a fluff, stuck in an eternal groove.

MAGGIE: *(Calling out.)* Biscuit…

MARGARET sinks back into the grass. WILLIAM stands, goes over to the record player, to change it. He blows on the needle looking up at MAGGIE standing in the grass. He smiles at her.

WILLIAM: What shall I play next?

MAGGIE momentarily frozen until –

MAGGIE hurries back inside, the door swinging behind her.

She heads upstairs into the bedroom. She climbs into bed next to BILLY. She lies in silence.

Blackout.

SCENE 6

Day.

BILLY and MAGGIE sit opposite one another, eating breakfast.

MAGGIE: Did you sleep last night?

BILLY looks up from eating his breakfast.

BILLY: Huh?

MAGGIE: You were very restless.

BILLY: I slept fine.

MAGGIE: I woke at four and couldn't get back again.

BILLY: Did you take one of your pills?

MAGGIE: They don't help. Doctor Mace is giving me something stronger.

BILLY: I thought he did that last time.

MAGGIE: Yes.

BILLY: So he gave you something stronger then?

MAGGIE: Yes. But now he's giving me another one? Another prescription.

BILLY: When are you seeing him again?

MAGGIE: Tomorrow. I'll pick it up then.

BILLY hesitates, nods.

What?

BILLY: I can pick it up today if you like.

BILLY looks at MAGGIE, he resumes eating.

MAGGIE: Thank you. That would be great. If you could pick it up.

BILLY: OK.

A small package is resting on the table.

They eat in silence until –

BILLY: Aren't you going to open it?

MAGGIE: What is it?

BILLY: Open it and then you'll see.

MAGGIE: It's not my birthday.

BILLY slides the package closer to her. She smiles, hesitantly opens it.

You've stuck it too tightly. There's too much tape.

MAGGIE grapples with it at last tearing off the paper.

I'm all fingers and thumbs,

An iPod in a box. MAGGIE stares at it.

BILLY: It's an iPod.

MAGGIE: Thank you.

BILLY stands, going over to her, helping her by taking it out of the box.

BILLY: You can listen to music.

MAGGIE: Yes.

BILLY: Through these headphones.

MAGGIE: Thank you.

BILLY: See they go in here and then you put them in here and turn it on here. You turn this and...There's some music already stored.

MAGGIE: Stored?

BILLY: You can buy more songs. I'll show you how.

MAGGIE: Thank you.

BILLY: Yes you've said that. It's for when you can't read or if you're waiting at the doctors. You can just listen to music whenever you like.

MAGGIE: Yes.

BILLY: And you won't disturb me. If I'm reading, or sleeping, I won't hear a thing.

MAGGIE looks at BILLY.

MAGGIE: Thank you.

BILLY: Stop saying that.

MAGGIE: What do you want me to say?

BILLY: I want you to look happy, to be pleased.

BILLY hurls the box across the table. Suddenly WILLIAM enters, sinking down in the chair opposite.

I can take it back. It's fine.

WILLIAM slams down keys, in a fury.

MAGGIE: I'm sorry.

BILLY: Don't do that. Don't say sorry. I should have thought before I bought it. I should have realized –

MAGGIE silently scrolls down with the iPod. BILLY watches her.

I thought it would be useful.

MAGGIE: Useful, yes.

Silence.

It will be.

Silence.

Thank you.

MAGGIE puts down the iPod on the table.

BILLY: You will be all right while I'm out.

MAGGIE: Yes.

BILLY: Maggie.

MAGGIE stands, goes over to the stove, to pour herself coffee.

MAGGIE: Boring when you fuss.

BILLY nods, clears his plate, by the sink.

BILLY: Did you call Annie?

MAGGIE: I'll call her later.

BILLY: You said that yesterday. She keeps calling. She was checking if you needed anything.

The silence hangs –

MAGGIE: I'll call her later.

BILLY: She's a good friend to you.

MAGGIE: She's lonely.

BILLY: She should get a cat.

She can have Biscuit. Any time.

MAGGIE laughs –

(Calling after.) I'm serious.

MAGGIE exits. WILLIAM sits. BILLY stands. MARGARET enters –

MARGARET: Ssh. Did you have to bang the door like that?

In the bathroom, MAGGIE stands, creaming her face.

I'd just got him off.

MARGARET touches his hair in passing. He pulls away. MARGARET hesitates –

MARGARET: Bad day?

WILLIAM shrugs –

It will get better. People always need dentists.

WILLIAM: Not in this town. That's what happens when you come to the land of the *free*.

MARGARET: You need to advertise. Smile more. You've got good teeth.

WILLIAM: I don't think that will quite do it. There are four dentists in this town.

MARGARET: Three. Mr. Ashton retired.

WILLIAM: He did?

MARGARET: And that one by the library. He's nearly dead. So there are two. Nearly two.

WILLIAM catches MARGARET's hand in passing.

WILLIAM: I love you.

MARGARET: You hungry?

WILLIAM hesitates, goes over to the sink, and reaches for a glass in a cupboard above the shelf.

Do you have to?

WILLIAM: Yes.

WILLIAM goes to open the fridge door.

MARGARET: It's late. You should eat.

BILLY reaches a hand out, gently placing it across the fridge door. WILLIAM hesitates.

Billy.

WILLIAM hesitates, nods.

WILLIAM: What time did Josie say she'd pick him up?

MARGARET: She didn't. I told her to go out and enjoy herself.

WILLIAM: I hope she's paying you.

MARGARET smiles, folding a pile of baby clothes.

MARGARET: He's such a sweet boy. You should have seen him. I fed him and then I put him down and he looked at me and he held his arms up, honestly looking at me to pick him up. I sat with his little head on my chest, just sat with him until he fell asleep.

WILLIAM: You shouldn't have done that. He'll have a routine.

MARGARET: One night.

WILLIAM: You're not doing Josie any favours.

MARGARET: One night.

WILLIAM: She's his mother. He'll want that every night now. And it's not just one night.

MARGARET: She never gets any time to enjoy herself. He's always away working and…I like to give her a break.

WILLIAM drinks. She watches him.

I'll make you something to eat.

WILLIAM: I'm not hungry.

MARGARET: Have you stopped once today?

WILLIAM: Ten cavities. Four extractions. I enjoyed ringing up that till.

WILLIAM tops his glass up.

MARGARET: I could work.

Silence –

There's a job at the library. It's two days a week.

Silence –

I dropped down yesterday. They don't need qualifications. I mean they're saying they don't.

WILLIAM: A librarian. You need a degree for that.

MARGARET: No... No... How difficult can it be to check a book in and out.

WILLIAM: You're not qualified.

MAGGIE enters, passing WILLIAM exiting upstairs.

MAGGIE: Haven't you gone yet?

BILLY nods –

BILLY: Going.

BILLY exits.

Gone.

MAGGIE and MARGARET stand alone in the kitchen, oblivious to one another. MARGARET stands, finishing folding up the baby clothes until –

She slams the last piece of clothing into the basket.

MARGARET: *(Shouting up.)* Funny. Because they asked to interview Friday.

Silence –

WILLIAM sinks down on the bed.

You can't stop me. *(Shouting up.)* We need the money.

WILLIAM stands, comes downstairs, enters.

I'm not stupid. I've looked at the accounts.

WILLIAM goes over to the fridge; MARGARET tries to stop him. WILLIAM takes out a bottle of vodka.

Don't.

WILLIAM ignores her pouring himself a glass.

I'm doing nothing here. Nothing. I'm waiting for nothing.

WILLIAM: What do you mean?

MARGARET: Three years Billy. Three years since we arrived here. And it's still not happened.

WILLIAM: It's not long.

MARGARET: It's three years. I'm the only one –

WILLIAM: Annie –

MARGARET: Annie doesn't want children. I do.

Silence.

You should have seen him. Holding up his arms, just looking at me... *Hey Adam...*

Silence.

WILLIAM: It will happen.

MARGARET: Will it?

Silence –

WILLIAM tops up his glass.

We need the money.

WILLIAM: But a few more patients and –

MARGARET: Two days a week. That's all I'm asking for.

WILLIAM: No.

MARGARET: You can't tell me what to do. It's the 20th century.

WILLIAM drinks –

WILLIAM: Stamp a book? You don't read a book.

MARGARET: Is that the best you can do?

WILLIAM: Hemmingway. Let's start with Hemmingway.

MARGARET: I'm not talking to you.

MARGARET scoops up the washing, makes to go. WILLIAM bars her way.

WILLIAM: OK, let's go back to basics. Carver, Fleming, Graham Greene. Do you even know who Graham Greene is?

MARGARET: I'm not listening.

WILLIAM: Updike? Orwell?

MARGARET: There's no money in the account, Billy – ?

WILLIAM slams his glass against the wall.

WILLIAM: If you get a job then you'll only have to leave again to take maternity leave...

It will happen.

MARGARET makes to go. WILLIAM grips her arms, stopping her.

MARGARET: When?

Silence.

Do you even want them?

Silence.

MARGARET exits upstairs carrying the basket of clothes.

WILLIAM exits out of the house.

MAGGIE stands, clearing up the last of the things off the table.

She stops, picking up a small child's dusty sock.

Blackout.

SCENE 7

MAGGIE on the telephone –

MAGGIE: …Annie… Are you there?… No you're not… Billy said you called… I'm fine… Not great but… We've been clearing out the loft… The things we have kept… It's shaming…really shaming… Remember that skull Bill had in his office…we've still got it… I found a load of Chinese lanterns… What do I want Chinese lanterns for… Anyway…I was wondering… Remember we talked about Biscuit… If the time came you'd take her…Well I think… Yes…I was thinking… It's time… It's nearly time… So would you… I can't think of anyone better I'd want to have her and…I'd leave her with Bill…but you know what he's like…I'm hoping…I want him to feel free after… He really should travel again… So I was thinking Sweetheart… Could we drop her over before Sunday? I have her basket and her bowl and her blanket… So you won't need to get her anything…She's had her jabs of course… She's really very easy… And you're the only one I know will love her as much as we have… Billy always says he'll be happy to see the back of her but… He gives her prime salmon when he thinks I'm not looking… They share a tin. *(Silence.)* Funny huh… Is that alright? Annie dear… OK… There's the beep…I've been rambling and –

The line goes dead. MAGGIE puts down the phone.

Lights up –

BILLY stands holding a prescription bag.

MAGGIE sits in the chair looking on.

BILLY puts down his prescription bag.

BILLY: You didn't get dressed?

MAGGIE looks down at her silk dressing gown.

MAGGIE: What time is it?

BILLY: Ten after noon.

MAGGIE nods –

MAGGIE: Still early. I called Annie.

BILLY: Thank you.

MAGGIE: She's going to take Biscuit.

BILLY hesitates, sweeping up –

I want to cook something special on Sunday.
Something you'd really like.

BILLY: Maggie.

MAGGIE: It's this house I worry about. I walked around the other day and I counted twenty-eight windows. They all need sanding. You used to sand every other year but we've just left it and left it and –

BILLY: I'll call Robert.

MAGGIE: Robert's fine for plumbing but –

BILLY: Robert'll sand it again.

MAGGIE: Twenty-eight. We've cleaned twenty windows for over forty years.

It's this house I worry about.

BILLY: Don't.

Silence –

MAGGIE: Lamb or beef?

BILLY: I don't mind.

MAGGIE: Just say.

BILLY: Really I'm easy.

MAGGIE: I told her it was time.

They stand in silence –

So – ?

Silence –

BILLY: Lamb.

Silence –

MAGGIE: Lamb it is. And after –

BILLY looks up –

BILLY: Yes –

MAGGIE nods, exits to get dressed.

MAGGIE: I'll make ice cream.

BILLY: Great.

BILLY smiles, waits until she has exited then sinks down on the chair.

MARGARET enters from outside, holding a pile of books and a pen.

She is wearing a summer dress.

She paces, then sinks down at the table opposite BILLY, resumes working, clearly distracted by noise from outside.

WILLIAM enters going over to the fridge, filling up his glass with ice.

MARGARET: They've filled that paddling pool too deep.

WILLIAM scoops up a book.

WILLIAM: It's ninety degrees out there. Let them have the cool.

Distant laughter, the sounds of a party far off at the end of the garden.

Josie's stripped off.

MARGARET: Yeah, I saw you looking.

WILLIAM: Me? Not me –

WILLIAM slips his hands around MARGARET's waist.

They offered me a beer. It was neighbourly.

MARGARET pulls away.

MARGARET: Liar.

WILLIAM: What does that mean?

MARGARET: You spent the last half hour talking to that poor young thing who lives with Sandy Nichols.

WILLIAM: Who?

MARGARET: The blonde girl? Looks after Sandy's kid when she's not home. Apparently she is an au pair.

WILLIAM: Oh her...

MARGARET: Yeah her you were *just* talking to while ten six-year-olds nearly drowned. Some au pair.

WILLIAM: There are fourteen adults out there and it's less than a couple of inches of water. It's not our party. Why do you care?

MARGARET: You're drunk.

WILLIAM: I'm not drunk.

MARGARET leans in close to him, sniffs.

WILLIAM: I had a beer. I've moved on to lemonade.

MARGARET: Liar.

MARGARET pours herself a glass from the jug in his hand. Drinks.

Liar. Liar. Liar. You have stood out there for the last hour, giggling like a teenager. You got her number.

WILLIAM: No.

MARGARET: Yes.

WILLIAM: I didn't.

MARGARET: Liar.

WILLIAM: When did you get so old?

MARGARET: When I married you. I got old when I married you. You make me old Billy.

WILLIAM: Please –

MARGARET: I never know when you're coming home. I never know where you've been. I call the office and they tell me you left an hour ago, and then you don't get home until three hours after that. It's Adam's birthday. It's our neighbour's six-year-old's birthday and you are working that poor delusional twenty nothing girl into believing you can offer her a good time. Well you can't Billy I should pack my bags tonight, and just leave, get away from this fucking country, really I should. Sell the house and –

WILLIAM: It's in my name too. This house is in my name too.

MARGARET: Great. We'll split it. Your half will pay back the money you owe my dad.

WILLIAM: And I'll enjoy paying it.

Silence –

Distant sound of voices singing Happy Birthday.

Did he like the bat? Adam? Did Adam like the bat.

WILLIAM: He did. We had a knock about.

MARGARET: That's good.

Silence.

They're moving.

WILLIAM: Yeah.

MARGARET: Josie... And the family.

WILLIAM: Yeah. They just said.

MARGARET: Right.

Silence.

Apparently it's a big promotion. She's very excited. They didn't think he'd get it. But he did. They've been looking at schools.

WILLIAM: Yeah.

MARGARET: Five, six hours away.

Silence.

WILLIAM: Good for them.

MARGARET: Yes. That's what I said.

Silence.

WILLIAM: You know we should go on a trip.

MARGARET: Where?

WILLIAM: Asia. I've always wanted to see Asia.

MARGARET: I've got an exam.

WILLIAM: After.

MARGARET: I'm not so –

WILLIAM: We should do it.

Silence.

Life is for living.

Silence.

MARGARET: Asia.

WILLIAM: Asia.

The distant noise of kids' laughter –

MARGARET: You should go out. Get some cake.

WILLIAM: You come too. It's chocolate.

MARGARET: In a minute. I just want to finish up...

WILLIAM nods. MARGARET resumes working.

Anyway your au pair is waiting.

WILLIAM hesitates by the door.

WILLIAM: I want you. You are still the only woman in the room for me.

MARGARET buckles a little.

You are always, you will always be the only woman in the room for me.

MARGARET turns to look at him.

MARGARET: Chocolate?

WILLIAM nods, MARGARET smiles, puts down her pen, stands, a hand brushing his as she exits.

WILLIAM reaches in his pocket, searching for matches, finding instead a folded piece of paper, a telephone number. He looks at it –

(Calling back.) Billy –

WILLIAM bins the piece of paper, scooping up the matches in passing held up by BILLY.

MAGGIE: *(Calling out.)* Did you pick up my prescription?

BILLY hesitates, opens a cupboard, adding it to a half-filled shelf of white prescription bags, quietly stockpiled. BILLY slides the bag inside the cupboard, closing the door.

BILLY: Yes.

MAGGIE enters now dressed in a beautiful summer dress, like MARGARET earlier was wearing.

BILLY just looks at her. She is beautiful.

MAGGIE: *(Seeing his look.)* What?

BILLY shakes his head, nothing.

BILLY: You look beautiful.

MAGGIE smiles –

MAGGIE: Liar.

Blackout.

SCENE EIGHT

MARGARET stands brushing her hair in the bedroom.

MARGARET: There are these paintings in a cave in France. I read about it in National Geographic.

They were found by an old schoolmaster in 1901. They're somewhere in the Dordogne Valley.

WILLIAM: South West France.

Margaret: ...Yeah that was it.

MAGGIE stares back at her from the other side of the mirror.

Prehistoric people first settled there around 25,000 BC. 25,000 BC. Amazing huh?

Lights up to reveal WILLIAM getting changed for bed.

There are bison and wooly mammoths and horses just etched into the stone...with I don't know what...Charcoal... flint... Whatever. But it was the way the journalist described them... Like a child again, running his fingers over the rocks, squinting up in the half light, fascinated by these tiny markers of a former life. I read it and suddenly I was crying... Isn't that crazy?

WILLIAM: Really?

MARGARET: I want to go there. I want to go there one day.

WILLIAM: France?

MAGGIE: Yeah.

WILLIAM smiles, resumes getting changed for bed.

There's all these theories why man did this. Why he drew like this? To notate nature. For pleasure. For storytelling. Because they could. But there's this one idea that they drew them out of sensory deprivation. That in this lightless place they drew almost in a trance. Perhaps to remind themselves of a world beyond, a world they've left behind, they can no longer see. Perhaps they knew, perhaps they knew in that moment that if this is all there is, they must leave something behind. Some guide. Some marker of their existence. Some legacy.

Silence.

WILLIAM: National Geographic?

MARGARET: Yeah.

WILLIAM: I didn't know you looked at National Geographic.

MARGARET: It's always out on display. Just when I'm tidying around. Helping the new guy.

WILLIAM: New guy?

MARGARET: He's cute, works on non-fiction.

WILLIAM: Oh non-fiction. Now if you'd said fiction I would have been standing at his desk, pistol drawn.

MARGARET: Thank you for tonight. It was fun.

WILLIAM: Don shouldn't sing.

MARGARET: Kate shouldn't provoke him.

WILLIAM: Annie was quiet.

MARGARET: She was fine.

WILLIAM: I thought she would hook up with Robert.

MARGARET: Robert? The gardener?

WILLIAM: He tiles and plasters as well.

MARGARET: Not her type.

Silence.

She's happy.

WILLIAM: It was a good night.

Silence.

WILLIAM lies in bed and reads.

MARGARET: I called by today. You weren't there.

WILLIAM: No.

MARGARET: Susan said you were very busy.

WILLIAM: Yeah... Yeah... Busy week.

MARGARET: But that you keep going AWOL.

Silence.

Where do you go?

WILLIAM: I –

MARGARET: She says some days you're gone all day.

WILLIAM: I –

MARGARET: ...presumed the worse and then I realized where you might go. You come back here. To the house. So I drove home and I saw you. You were just sitting in the garden.

Silence.

Billy.

Why? What do you do here all day?

WILLIAM: I read.

MARGARET: You read.

WILLIAM: Yes.

MARGARET: You've got a waiting room of patients and you come back and read.

WILLIAM: Yes.

MARGARET laughs –

Sometimes I take a shower. A really long cool shower.

MARGARET: Great.

Silence.

You can do that anytime.

WILLIAM: No. I can't. I can't because you're here.

MARGARET: What do you mean?

WILLIAM: Because you're here and you need me. To fix a bulb or to look at something in some stupid magazine you've found. And sometimes... Sometimes I just want to be alone... It's like at work, all the drills... Suddenly they are too loud… People's conversation it's just all too loud. Don tonight.

MARGARET: He was fine.

WILLIAM: Talking...talking and I just want to say will you please shut up... Will you please stop talking about your holiday? 'Yes we've done Asia, and Africa... Yes we travel a lot too... Car? I don't know... I was thinking about the Chrysler?... What do you think? You going for 3.5 or 4…I don't know... Did you hear Tom's got Cancer? Such a great guy... His poor family... The kids... Yeah, they're doing great… Really great… Oh he's going to college... We're very excited…Yes she's a sweetheart… You know what she did for me on our birthday… Daddy...I love you… embroidered on a cushion… Isn't that great? Isn't that great?' And all we can talk about is our garden, and our trips to Sardinia and where we are going next year… 'You want a cat! What you guys need is a cat!… That would be nice for you... Something to look after…'

Silence.

'Something to look after… You guys need something to look after.'

WILLIAM goes into the bathroom.

MARGARET: We have each other.

MARGARET exits to follow him.

Billy?

WILLIAM looks at MAGGIE.

WILLIAM: I'll go to work tomorrow.

MAGGIE finishes creaming her face, WILLIAM enters the bedroom, stands by his bed, winding up his clock.

MARGARET: We have each other.

WILLIAM climbs into bed, reaching for his book. MARGARET enters the closet, picking up WILLIAM's shirt en route.

Isn't that enough?

MAGGIE exits out of the closet as MARGARET enters. MAGGIE stands at the end of the bed. She climbs into bed.

MAGGIE: Are you going to read?

Silence –

Billy –

BILLY sits up in the bed, WILLIAM now gone.

BILLY: Yes –

MAGGIE: Oh OK.

MAGGIE nods –

BILLY: Did you want to turn off the light?

MAGGIE sinks back into bed.

MAGGIE: It's fine.

BILLY reaches for his book. Reads.

BILLY: Maggie need to –

MAGGIE: Not tonight.

MAGGIE winces, clearly in pain.

MAGGIE: Not tonight.

BILLY nods, resumes reading.

Tomorrow.

Silence –

BILLY: I found the hammock.

MAGGIE: You did?

BILLY: I'll string it up in the morning.

MAGGIE: That will be nice.

BILLY: For Sunday.

Silence.

MAGGIE: I invited someone.

BILLY turns and looks at MAGGIE already settling down to sleep.

The scratch of starlings overhead, moving around in the loft. BILLY looks up. BILLY looks back, MARGARET has gone.

BILLY: Maggie –

BILLY looks back, MAGGIE stirs a little –

MAGGIE: Huh?

BILLY turns off the light, sinks back into bed.

BILLY: It's OK. Go to sleep.

The scratch of starlings louder overhead.

It's just the starlings.

MAGGIE stirs, restless.

It's OK Maggie, go back to sleep.

Blackout.

SCENE NINE

Day.

The garden. MAGGIE stands watching BILLY string up the hammock in the garden.

MAGGIE: See. It's nearly rotted through.

BILLY ignores her, MAGGIE turns to head back in.

BILLY: You were up again last night?

MAGGIE nods –

MAGGIE: It's always if I mix the blue with the yellow and black. If I take blue on their own, I'm fine but with the yellow and black then that's it...I'm up til five.

BILLY: Then don't mix them. Take more blue.

MAGGIE: Take more blue and I never wake up.

Silence –

BILLY nods, resumes stringing up the hammock.

MAGGIE: You want some help?

BILLY shakes his head.

BILLY: I dreamt last night I was talking to you and you looked –

MAGGIE hesitates, smiles, in expectation –

MAGGIE: I looked – ?

BILLY shakes his head, dismissive.

BILLY: Rope's gone on this. I might go into town and get some more.

MAGGIE nods.

MAGGIE: Can you pick up the meat?

BILLY: Sure.

Silence –

I'll get some wine.

MAGGIE smiles, nods.

MAGGIE: Do you think they'd prefer red or white?

BILLY: Red maybe.

MAGGIE: You think red.

BILLY: Red? White? How would I know, Maggie? I haven't seen the kid in –

Silence.

BILLY: Was he surprised? When you called?

MAGGIE: No… Perhaps a little. I said 'Adam, do you remember me. Bill said he bumped into you?' He said 'Of course Mrs Alton. I remember the house and the tree. And the paddling pool.' And I said 'No we never had a paddling pool. Your mother had one. You were in it all the time.' Then I said 'How's your mother?' 'Josie died six months ago.'

Silence.

Then I said 'So Bill says you're back in town and you're looking for a house to live in… And so we thought…we thought…'

Silence.

And this house… This house has got too big for us… And we're hoping to travel again.'

Silence.

BILLY and MAGGIE look at one another.

BILLY resumes unwinding the rope from the tree –

MAGGIE holds out a peach picked up from the ground to him.

BILLY shakes his head.

BILLY: I'll get all sticky.

MAGGIE shrugs, scoops up a second and a third.

MAGGIE: I'll make pie. The rest I'll put in the freezer.

BILLY: I know.

BILLY winds up a reel of old rope, unwinding it from the tree.

MAGGIE: I'm just reminding you. So you'll know they're there.

BILLY: You don't have to keep telling me this.

MAGGIE: OK, but I've left a list in the kitchen drawer and another in the –

BILLY: Study. I know…I know.

MAGGIE: It's important, Bill, it's important that you know where everything is,

BILLY: I'm not a fucking baby.

Silence –

MAGGIE: Well they're there if you need them. Or we could always give them to Annie when we drop Biscuit off.

BILLY: I can look after the fucking cat.

MAGGIE: Do you have to – ?

BILLY: This is not a fucking holiday.

MAGGIE: Do you have to fucking swear?

BILLY: This is not some fucking...fucking...fucking...fucking –

BILLY slams down the rope.

...holiday where you come back.

Silence –

MAGGIE: I just worry. How you'll look after yourself?

BILLY: I won't –

MAGGIE: Bill.

BILLY: I won't. I'll grow my hair long and never get it trimmed the third Saturday of every other month as you've booked it all my life. I'll leave out the milk, let it go warm on the front step, let it pile up with the newspapers. I'll let the grass grow. I'll never pull hair out of the plughole when it clogs up. I won't wipe up after I've washed the dishes. I won't wash up dishes. I won't eat. I won't. If I do I'll eat straight from the freezer, with a spoon, fingers if I feel like it. Frozen pie mush. And the endless cans of salmon. For the fucking vanished cat. Which I'll open with a penknife. Why not? I'll stop opening mail. I'll stop opening anything. I won't answer the phone. If people ring I won't pick up. I won't open the front door much at all. I won't shovel snow like a good neighbour should do. I won't pick up my clothes. I won't wash my underwear. I'll wear the same socks. I'll stay in the house and if I do venture out I won't say hello to that kid with his fucking skateboard banging back and forth up and down the fucking kerb like a fucking moron. I will live as someone who used to have a life, who used to have a life with someone but that someone isn't here anymore. I will live my life as I fucking want. Without you.

Silence.

Without you.

Silence.

MAGGIE: Might you brush your teeth?

Silence.

You'll brush your teeth.

Silence –

BILLY: Always.

Silence.

MAGGIE: Thank you.

Silence.

MAGGIE turns, heads in.

BILLY: Maggie?

Silence.

Wasps are biting, put some shoes on. Maggie, how many times do I tell you. Can you never ever just put some –

BILLY stops –

MAGGIE heads into the kitchen. BILLY resumes winding the rope around the tree.

MARGARET: I like the feel of the grass.

MARGARET stands in a suit, her shoes kicked off. WILLIAM appears from the other side of the tree, rope in hand.

WILLIAM: What time did you get in?

MARGARET: Seven.

WILLIAM: Why didn't you call me?

MARGARET: I got a taxi.

WILLIAM nods, finishing stringing the hammock up. MARGARET lies on it.

WILLIAM: How was it?

MARGARET: It was OK. There were a couple of decent seminars.

WILLIAM: I called your room, but you never picked up.

MARGARET: Did you? They never said. Reception never said.

MARGARET smiles, sits up. WILLIAM kisses her. MARGARET smiles, pulls away.

You should have left a message with reception.

MARGARET heads into the house, heading upstairs.

Something smells good.

MARGARET enters into the kitchen, lifting a lid on a pot. WILLIAM watches her in the garden.

You cooked.

WILLIAM finishes stringing up the hammock, he heads into the kitchen.

You never cook.

WILLIAM: I did today.

Silence –

MARGARET: How was your week?

WILLIAM: Good. Fine. The usual.

MARGARET heads upstairs.

Let me change and I'll

WILLIAM follows her upstairs.

WILLIAM: I did call.

MARGARET enters the bathroom, closes the door, runs a bath.

I did call reception.

WILLIAM stands outside the bathroom door.

At your hotel.

MARGARET hesitates, sinks on to the side of the bath.

They said they'd not seen you all week.

MARGARET: Weird.

The silence hangs –

Bill.

MARGARET opens the door. WILLIAM stands, waiting.

Silence.

WILLIAM: I don't want to know his name.

Silence –

MARGARET: It's not –

WILLIAM: Do you love him?

Silence –

MARGARET: Billy –

WILLIAM: Do you love him?

Silence –

MARGARET: I love you more.

WILLIAM exits, into the kitchen. MARGARET goes to follow, stopping on hearing –

Don't drink.

The slam of the fridge door open, the chink of ice, the glug of a vodka bottle as WILLIAM pours himself a drink in the kitchen. MARGARET enters the kitchen.

Please don't drink.

BILLY exits, passing MARGARET.

Billy –

WILLIAM: I read an amazing article today. About time… Our notion of time. For most of us it is linear, based on the bible, beginning with the act of creation but as we know there is no God… Then that notion of time is redundant… Anyway… It got me thinking, you know how I hate all those bumper stickers saying *One Life Live It* and *Don't Die Tomorrow and Not Live for Today*… You know how much I hate those…

MARGARET: Bill –

WILLIAM: What if time is part of a fundamental structure of the universe. What if there's a dimension where events occur in sequence. Newtonian time they call it. It would make time travel a possibility. If your life was wired like a filmstrip. Spread out across the timeline. Or what if our notion of time is all wrong. We've seen it as this kind of container where events and life is something we 'move through' but what if it doesn't flow. What if instead we are part of a fundamental intellectual structure within which humans sequence and compare events. What if time is not an event, nor a thing? What if it can't be measured? Or travelled?

MARGARET: God you've been drinking all night.

WILLIAM: Don't you think that's interesting?

MARGARET: What?

WILLIAM: About time?

MARGARET: I don't know what you're talking about.

WILLIAM: I thought it was fascinating.

MARGARET: Yes.

WILLIAM: Because I was thinking perhaps I've got boring to you.

MARGARET sits at the table, head in her hands. WILLIAM enters from the larder, with a knife and a bag of carrots. He starts chopping.

Is it someone you work with? Is it that nerdy guy on non-fiction – ?

MARGARET: No –

Silence –

I met him last year. He was at the literature conference I went to in August. We kept in touch.

WILLIAM: How? How did you keep in touch?

MARGARET: The odd call.

Silence.

WILLIAM: What was it like?

MARGARET: It was –

WILLIAM: What was it like?

MARGARET: It was nice to be wanted.

WILLIAM laughs –

...to be wanted by someone else.

WILLIAM: Did you – ?

MARGARET: And when he asked me up to his room... Finally...I was excited. Nervous but –

WILLIAM: I don't want to –

MARGARET: So I went upstairs with him. There was a mini bar.

WILLIAM: What?

MARGARET: We drank. And when he tried to take my clothes off –

Silence.

I declined.

Silence.

Time is linear. When we die. I think we die. But until we do...I want that time to be with you.

Silence.

Billy –

Silence.

I declined.

WILLIAM: Right –

Silence –

Is it going to happen again?

Silence.

Is it?

MARGARET: No. I said I loved my husband.

MARGARET slips her hand around his hand. BILLY's hand stills.

That I wanted to grow old with my husband. That it was with him I would be with until I died.

Silence –

WILLIAM: Dinner will be ready in half an hour.

It's only soda.

MARGARET nods, exits.

Blackout.

SCENE TEN

BILLY lies in bed, next to MAGGIE.

BILLY: Starlings are mimics. Car alarm, water sprinkler, the high, screeching pierce of a fox howl in the dark. They are ventriloquists, effortless in their counterfeit. The human voice can try but next to the starling, it is an amateur. Sometimes when I am lying awake, unable to sleep, I listen, searching amongst their scratchings, listening to these interlopers to see what messages, what voices they have brought from their travels to far off places, what places they will take the inconsequential moments, the endless random snatches of conversation from this house. It comforts me. That somewhere my snoring is being carefully considered, examined by these dark little birds, sitting deep in my loft or the woods that surround this house. Somewhere there is an oral document of our voices. It's the voice that one struggles to hold on to after, the memory of it. It is the voice that is the first to decay.

WILLIAM suddenly appears, peering upwards as if at a cave.

WILLIAM: *(Calling out.)* Maggie –

BILLY: A lifetime held in the song of a bird, a lifetime embedded in that loft. A lifetime carried in a voice, carried in a silence.

WILLIAM: *(Calling out.)* Maggie.

MARGARET approaches WILLIAM smiling, peering up, the wall covered in cave drawings.

MAGGIE: Bill, are you awake?

BILLY: Yes.

MAGGIE: Do you remember that cave we visited in France?

BILLY: Yeah.

MAGGIE: It was so hot outside but as we climbed down it got colder and colder and yet it still felt so alive. And we ran our fingers over the walls. Marvelling at those pictures of –

MARGARET turns smiling at WILLIAM peering up at the cave.

BILLY: ...bison...

MAGGIE: Put our palms against the cold stone. Do you remember?

BILLY: Yes.

MAGGIE: And after we went to that weird place... And we drank too much and –

BILLY: You sang...

MAGGIE: Yes...

BILLY: And it was beautiful.

MAGGIE: Yes. Go back there run your hands over those walls again... Remind yourself... Remind yourself what you are part of...

MAGGIE's hand reaches up, catching BILLY's hand, lying restless in bed. BILLY turns as MAGGIE sinks back into the bed, to be replaced by MARGARET now sitting up.

MARGARET: Sleep…sleep.

MARGARET and BILLY caught in an embrace in the bed, the twist and turn of sheets, until at once, BILLY is now WILLIAM, lost in lovemaking with MARGARET and then with another twist MARGARET is now MAGGIE and then WILLIAM and then BILLY until –

BILLY: *(Calling out.)* Maggie –

And at once, MAGGIE is sitting up in bed, wracked in pain, screaming out.

Blackout.

SCENE ELEVEN

Day.

MAGGIE sits opposite BILLY at the kitchen. There are several bottles of pills laid out on the table.

MARGARET: Are they here yet?

MARGARET enters the kitchen carrying a pie, from the pantry.

WILLIAM: Not yet.

WILLIAM stands on the porch.

MAGGIE does not look up. BILLY resumes counting the pills.

MAGGIE looks at him, nods.

MARGARET comes through on to the porch.

MARGARET: Bill, you haven't even got the table up.

WILLIAM: Doing it… Doing it…

WILLIAM exits.

MAGGIE: Go get changed. It's nearly noon. They'll be here by one.

MARGARET re-enters the kitchen, sliding the pie down on the side.

BILLY looks up from counting the pills.

BILLY: Huh?

MAGGIE: Don't be scared.

When I jump I have to know you're with me Bill.

BILLY nods, stands.

BILLY: Yes…yes.

BILLY passes MARGARET. She puts a hand on his arm. He stops and looks up at MAGGIE.

MAGGIE: Wear the blue shirt I bought you.

BILLY smiles, nods –

It's in the closet, I ironed it yesterday.

BILLY: Thank you.

BILLY exits upstairs, to the bedroom.

MARGARET: *(Calling out.)* Can you carry out some chairs?

WILLIAM just visible in the garden setting up a wooden table under the tree. He looks up, not hearing her.

(Laughing.) Chairs.

WILLIAM nods, enters the kitchen –

WILLIAM: People won't be sitting, they'll be dancing. It's your birthday.

WILLIAM picks up two kitchen chairs.

MARGARET: Don will sit.

WILLIAM: Then he'll sing.

MARGARET: Then he'll sit and drink and Kate will get ratty. And Annie will watch and not say much –

WILLIAM makes to go.

They're good friends. We've got good friends, haven't we Bill.

WILLIAM: Yes.

From upstairs –

BILLY: *(Calling out.)* Maggie – ?

MAGGIE picks up the pie, heading outside.

MAGGIE: *(Calling back.)* What?

BILLY: *(Calling out.)* Blue shirt?

MAGGIE: *(Calling back.)* Closet.

BILLY enters the closet. MAGGIE stands in the garden putting down the chairs.

WILLIAM smiles, her hand brushing his arm in passing.

WILLIAM: Beautiful day.

MAGGIE looks up –

MARGARET: Yep. It's going to rain.

MARGARET now standing on the porch.

WILLIAM: Maggie –

WILLIAM shakes his head wearily –

Can you not worry for just one day?

MARGARET picks up a peach, offers it to him.

WILLIAM: No, I don't want to get all sticky.

MARGARET: You're about to take a shower.

MARGARET holds it out to WILLIAM. WILLIAM refuses. BILLY bites the peach. He exits upstairs towards the bedroom.

MARGARET: *(Calling out.)* One day we'll sell this house –

WILLIAM stops on the stairs –

Silence –

WILLIAM enters the bathroom, it is now BILLY brushing his teeth. He is alone.

MAGGIE: *(Calling out.)* You hung the lanterns.

MAGGIE reaches up, touching a Chinese paper lantern from the tree.

MARGARET: And then where will we go.

BILLY turns off the bathroom light. WILLIAM enters the bedroom now wearing the blue shirt.

After.

WILLIAM hesitates, resumes dressing.

Where will we go after?

WILLIAM hesitates, steps out on to the landing –

(Calling out.) Bill?

WILLIAM comes down the stairs.

BILLY enters the kitchen, doing up the last button on his shirt.

BILLY: I lost a button.

MARGARET looks up, BILLY looks at her, seemingly missed it all.

MAGGIE: Give it here.

MAGGIE moves past MARGARET –

MAGGIE: I'll sew it.

MAGGIE hesitates, laughs, reaching for his shirt. MARGARET now gone.

Give it here.

BILLY takes off his shirt. MAGGIE takes the shirt, heads upstairs passing WILLIAM on the stairs. WILLIAM looks at her as she passes –

Blackout.

SCENE TWELVE

Dusk.

The aftermath of dinner.

BILLY and MAGGIE sit at the table in the garden. BILLY wears the blue shirt.

The hammock now strung up.

Overhead starlings circle, casting their shadows.

BILLY: When people ask us –

MAGGIE: When people ask us –

BILLY: How did you two –

MAGGIE: …meet?

BILLY: They want a story, a good story.

MAGGIE: So together, over the years, we have built ours.

BILLY: A quiet shared mythology.

MAGGIE: It was raining.

BILLY: I was reading a book.

MAGGIE: He looked intellectual. He was reading a book. I thought –

BILLY: Good teeth. I like a woman with –

MAGGIE: Good teeth.

A light goes on in the kitchen. MARGARET stands washing up.

Was it love at first –

BILLY: Sight...

MAGGIE: No... No...

BILLY: She wasn't –

MAGGIE: Educated.

BILLY: ...interested in a –

MAGGIE: A dentist. I was impressed. He was very –

BILLY: Shy –

MAGGIE: Inconsequential. But there was obviously –

BILLY: Something.

MAGGIE: There was definitely something.

BILLY: She said –

MAGGIE: *What are you reading?*

BILLY: I could have so easily caught an earlier train.

MAGGIE: *Hemmingway.*

BILLY: I knew she'd never read him.

MAGGIE: He was very very –

BILLY: Romantic. I had a romantic idea that women like men who read.

MAGGIE: They do. They did. I did.

BILLY: And that is the story of –

BILLY and MAGGIE look at one another, smile.

BILLY: ...our beginning.

MAGGIE: And this is the story of –

BILLY: ...the end.

MAGGIE and BILLY look at one another.

MAGGIE: And on this day –

BILLY: On this last day, we invited a boy –

MAGGIE: Now a man. For lunch. Who we once knew.

BILLY: With his wife –

MAGGIE: Martha who we liked –

BILLY: Who we liked very much.

MAGGIE: With their children.

BILLY: Their children –

MAGGIE: Josh and –

BILLY: Josh and Ava and Ruby.

MAGGIE and BILLY look at one another.

MAGGIE: And they stayed.

BILLY: They stayed all day until the sun –

MAGGIE: …until the sun was just skimming –

BILLY: And the starlings were –

MAGGIE: …circling overhead. And that's when we told them.

BILLY and MAGGIE look up.

'We'd like you to have this house now.'

BILLY: At first they didn't believe us.

MAGGIE: Because it's not what you do.

BILLY: But who else –

MAGGIE: …who else is going to live here but –

Adam.

BILLY: The boy we once knew.

MAGGIE: And they thanked us, unsure at first, smiling. But in the end –

BILLY: They said yes.

MAGGIE: And why?

BILLY: And we said –

BILLY and MAGGIE look at one another. MAGGIE smiles.

MAGGIE: 'Why not?'

Suddenly the sound of starlings. BILLY and MAGGIE look up.

WILLIAM crosses the grass, stands looking up at the starlings.

WILLIAM: Come out here.

MARGARET finishes up, coming out on to the porch.

MARGARET: What? It's got cold.

MARGARET crosses over, placing a glass of water on the table.

WILLIAM: Just... Look.

MARGARET looks up, watching the starlings circling overhead. They stand in silence.

MAGGIE: You will travel.

BILLY: There's still so much I have to say.

Silence.

Maggie –

MAGGIE: Ssh… It's all been said my –

BILLY grips MAGGIE's hand.

BILLY: Darling.

MAGGIE: My boy.

BILLY: My girl.

MAGGIE: My love.

BILLY nods, slides across a plate of pills.

BILLY: Yellow black –

MAGGIE takes a handful of pills from the plate, puts them in her mouth, drinks from the glass, swallows.

Yellow black.

MAGGIE takes another pill from the plate, puts it in her mouth, drinks from the glass, swallows.

Blue.

MAGGIE takes another pill from the plate, puts it in her mouth, drinks from the glass, swallows.

BILLY: Blue.

MAGGIE takes another pill from the plate, puts it in her mouth, drinks from the glass, hesitates –

Blue.

BILLY grips her hand, smiles, she looks at him suddenly uncertain. Then smiles, reassured.

MAGGIE: Blue.

MAGGIE takes a fourth handful of pills from the plate, puts them in her mouth, drinks from the glass, swallows.

And on that night –

MAGGIE: Shall we – ?

BILLY nods, MAGGIE stands, BILLY takes her arm, leads her, and then at once it is WILLIAM leading MAGGIE, and then MAGGIE leading MARGARET and then MARGARET leading BILLY and then BILLY once more leading MAGGIE, gently easing her on to the hammock.

The swing of the door, MARGARET already gone.

BILLY: And on that night –

MAGGIE takes out her iPod. She fiddles with it. BILLY takes it off her, turns it on, gently placing one earpiece in her ear and the second in his own.

BILLY and MAGGIE look at one another as they lie together on the hammock.

They were playing our song.

WILLIAM flicks out his cigarette, heading back into the house. The bedroom light goes on, MARGARET just visible undressing for bed. The light goes on in the bathroom, WILLIAM stands brushing his teeth.

Blackout.

The End.

27 was first performed on Tuesday 25 October 2011 at the Royal Lyceum Theatre, Edinburgh in a co-production with the National Theatre of Scotland.

Cast

Maureen Beattie	SISTER URSULA MARY
Emma Hartley-Miller	AUDREY MARIE
Finn den Hertog	DR SAM PARKER
Molly Innes	SISTER RUTH AUGUSTINE
Libby King	DR HELEN JARVIS
Colette O'Neil	SISTER MIRIAM THOMASINA
Nicholas Le Prevost	DR RICHARD GARFIELD
Benny Young	DR JONATHAN LEES

Creative Team

Abi Morgan	*Writer*
Vicky Featherstone	*Director*
Merle Hensel	*Set Designer*
Nick Powell	*Composer & Sound Designer*
Natasha Chivers	*Lighting Designer*
Nick Sagar	*Sound Associate*
Jenna Watt	*Assistant Director*
Anne Henderson	*Casting Director*

Characters

DR RICHARD GARFIELD *(60s)*
American, Epidemiologist, University of Alabama

DR SAM PARKER *(early/mid 30s)*
British, Epidemiologist, University of Edinburgh

DR HELEN JARVIS *(late 30s/early 40s)*
American, Neurophysiologist. University of Alabama

DR JONATHAN LEES *(early 50s)*
British, Neurologist. National Institute of Ageing

SISTER MIRIAM THOMASINA *(late 90s)*
Mother Superior

SISTER URSULA MARY *(late 40s/early 50s)*
Sister Procurator / Mother Superior

SISTER RUTH AUGUSTINE *(late 40s)*
Sister Portress

AUDREY MARIE *(early/mid 20s)*
Aspirant.

SETTING

The play is set in a modern Catholic Convent somewhere in West Scotland over five years.

/ Denotes when lines intercut

Act One

An office.

A desk. A filing cabinet. Three chairs. There is a vase of roses in full bloom on the desk.

RICHARD stands, a cup of tea in his hand.

HELEN stands looking out of a distant window, distracted.

It is summer.

HELEN: Is that someone swimming?

> *RICHARD follows HELEN's gaze out of the window. HELEN takes in the room, leaning forward to look at a painting on the wall.*

MIRIAM: *'Joshua Roll'.* The original's preserved in the Vatican.

> *MIRIAM enters, ready to greet them.*

HELEN: It's beautiful.

MIRIAM: A picture is to the illiterate what the religious word is to the educated. *(Beat.)* I don't remember who it was who said that.

> *The action freezes –*

RICHARD: *(To audience.)* So this is how it started –

> *The action springs back into life –*

MIRIAM: I'm so/

RICHARD: No/

MIRIAM: …sorry. Ruth should have/

RICHARD: It's not a problem. /

MIRIAM: …told me you were here. Normally word gets around. /

RICHARD: Really… We only just arrived/

MIRIAM: Dr Garfield.

RICHARD: Please, Richard *(Introducing HELEN.)* And this is Dr Jarvis.

> *HELEN smiles in greeting to MIRIAM.*

HELEN: Helen's just fine.

MIRIAM: …There are always whispers. How long have you been – ?

RICHARD: …five, ten minutes that's all.

MIRIAM: Really someone should have at least got you/

RICHARD: They have. They did.

RICHARD holds up a teacup.

MIRIAM: …tea. *(Beat.)* Good. *(Calling out.)* You sure you wouldn't prefer coffee? *(Beat.)*

RICHARD: Well…/

MIRIAM: I knew it. I knew it.

MIRIAM reaches for her phone, tapping buttons –

… *(As phone answers.)* Charlotte, I just called Ruth… Is she…? …Never mind. Could we have coffee please? I know but…tea is a poor cousin, Charlotte, that you should know. Thank you. Can someone please tell Ursula to come and find us seeing as she invited these guests here? And root out a digestive if we have one. You're a dear. *(As puts down the phone.)* Don't let us get away with that again. If we can't give you something decent to drink… Or would you prefer a cold drink?

RICHARD: There was talk of –

MIRIAM: It's Friday. On Friday, there's always lemonade.

A distant ripple of laughter.

(Beat.) You came –

RICHARD: Plane, then train.

MIRIAM: From Euston?

RICHARD: I think…

HELEN: Heathrow to Paddington, Paddington to Euston, Euston to –/

MIRIAM: The train must have been a nightmare/

RICHARD: …No.

MIRIAM: …for an American.

RICHARD pauses, mid sip. MIRIAM smiles, a certain mischief to her –

JONATHAN: Miriam –

Lights up on JONATHAN greeting MIRIAM enthusiastically as if he has just entered –

MIRIAM: Where have you been skulking?

JONATHAN: I was just saying to Ursula… The roses smell, wonderful… Ursula's just coming.

URSULA enters, her hair dripping wet, drying with a towel.

URSULA: I'm sorry…I'm sorry…I couldn't understand why Ruth was waving and by the time I had swum back/

MIRIAM: You're dripping.

URSULA: …I found Jonathan wandering in the garden, stealing strawberries.

JONATHAN: That river…

URSULA laughs.

URSULA: It's very low at this time of year.

URSULA holds out a handful of strawberries to JONATHAN, who takes one and eats.

URSULA: The ducks don't even try. I beat them at breaststroke.

JONATHAN: Still. You get caught in those reeds and –

URSULA: There's hardly a tug until you're down to the weir.

HELEN: I'd love a swim.

URSULA: Have one? Really it's the only thing that saves me whatever time of the day.

JONATHAN: Now have you all met?

URSULA looks to RICHARD and HELEN shaking hands in greeting.

RICHARD: We saw you from the window.

MIRIAM: She's in a world of her own. Head down, arms going, fixed on a point straight ahead.

RICHARD: I've heard so much about you.

URSULA: Jonathan? It's all flannel. He knows how to butter us up.

JONATHAN: That's not true. Ursula is Jackie to Miriam's JFK.

MIRIAM: She's my right hand. You are. She takes over at the end of the year.

URSULA: Though I'm not letting her go far.

MIRIAM: We're easing her into the job gently.

URSULA: It's a fairly new suit so I apologise before we even begin. Jonathan believes I affect this air of chaos but really –

MIRIAM: Nonsense, you'll be running this place long after I'm in the ground. Ursula's been with us since she was –

URSULA: 1970…something too long ago for me to repeat in public.

MIRIAM: She was fifteen and shaking all the way on the drive here. In artistic circles I think one would call her a protégé.

URSULA: Thank the Lord we're not in artistic circles then.

RICHARD: Fifteen. So young.

URSULA: My aunt brought me. I was practically an orphan. Thankfully, Miriam took me in.

MIRIAM: The roses are beautiful, Ursula.

URSULA: Ruth/

RUTH enters with a jug of lemonade. URSULA throws her hands up, gesturing to RUTH –

MIRIAM: At last…

URSULA: …is to be congratulated for all flower arranging.

RUTH: *(To URSULA.)* There you are. We almost sent out a search party.

MIRIAM: I asked Charlotte/

RUTH: Coffee. On its way.

MIRIAM: See, word travels.

MIRIAM takes the jug of lemonade from RUTH –

Lemonade is our consolation.

…and starts to pour.

Drink –

MIRIAM hands a glass to JONATHAN.

You're quite purple with the heat.

RUTH: There's a young man downstairs. He says his name is Dr Parker –

JONATHAN: Damn –

JONATHAN looks to RUTH, senses her quiet disapproval.

He's early. *(To RICHARD.)* Edinburgh were keen to provide one of their own. *(Beat.)* Don't give me that look, Richard. Just don't. They're funding a large slice of the study. Diplomacy is the key.

RUTH: Shall I bring him up?

MIRIAM: If you would.

MIRIAM nods, RUTH makes to go.

MIRIAM: Ruth is Sister Portress. She knows everything that comes in and goes out.

RUTH exits passing AUDREY as she enters with a pot of coffee and a tray of biscuits. URSULA swipes a biscuit in passing.

URSULA: Audrey, you're a good girl.

AUDREY: Bourbons. I couldn't find digestives.

URSULA: Remind me to write a memo to the board.

URSULA grins, sinking down into a chair, taking a cup of coffee and swiping a biscuit.

Audrey's been with us six weeks. We're trying to convince her of the virtues of a contemplative life.

AUDREY goes to put down the pot of coffee, scalding herself.

AUDREY: Ah shit!

URSULA: She's a great mind.

MIRIAM: *(To AUDREY.)* Have you seen Aileen about?

AUDREY: Downstairs, wrestling with some chickens in the kitchen. They got stuck together in the freezer. Bernice is trying to gouge them apart.

MIRIAM: Audrey, would you?

URSULA: I'll go. I'll go.

MIRIAM: Ursula –

URSULA makes to go.

URSULA: She wanted to do crab but Ruth and I convinced her that it doesn't smell like that if it's fresh. She bought them off that friend of Robert's. I've already told him not again. It's fish that's not seen sea in six months.

MIRIAM: No really. Let Audrey do it.

URSULA finishing up her tea, and exits.

(To AUDREY.) Tell her to lay for four more while you're at it.

AUDREY exits.

She's going to kill us with a chorus line of poultry…

MIRIAM shrugs, smiles.

We've had three sisters down with the runs only last week because someone didn't defrost the meat through. There was a time when we had our own livestock but – It was that or a new TV room. TV was the victor. Now it's a monthly trip to Iceland. I love it but some of the others get upset. They like meat that's had a pulse. We tell them it's organic. They're all God's creatures. That's what I console them with.

SAM enters.

JONATHAN: Here he is. Sam.

JONATHAN goes over to greet SAM.

SAM: Sorry…sorry… Sorry… –

JONATHAN shakes hands with SAM as he takes off his jacket and puts down his briefcase.

…I've been standing since Edinburgh… The heating stuck on full blast.

SAM goes to greet HELEN. HELEN smiles, wiping her hands on a tissue.

HELEN: Don't come too close. Some guy in the next seat, sat with his dog, its butt in my face.

SAM: You got an earlier train.

HELEN: I got an earlier train.

JONATHAN: You've met?

HELEN: We have.

SAM: Strasburg. Last autumn.

MIRIAM: Just fish out the lemon.

MIRIAM hands a glass of lemonade to SAM.

SAM: …Thank you… I can't quite believe I am here. *(Drinks.)* This is good.

JONATHAN: Miriam, Dr Sam Parker, a rising star in our field.

MIRIAM: We're honoured.

SAM: That's just Jonathan. He exaggerates. Thank you for having us here.

JONATHAN: And of course Dr Garfield.

JONATHAN introduces RICHARD. SAM shakes RICHARD's hand enthusiastically.

SAM: *(To RICHARD.)* We met in Berlin. I came to hear your paper/

RICHARD: I remember…

SAM: 'The Legacy of the Depressive Mind.' Your argument for pre-condition screening was very –

RICHARD: You challenged me on my figures.

SAM: …convincing.

RICHARD: *(Beat.)* I'm not a natural speaker.

JONATHAN: He lies.

RICHARD: No, really I hate those things.

JONATHAN: Your speech at/

RICHARD: That was my wedding.

JONATHAN: …was rather funny, really rather funny.

RICHARD: No one laughed.

JONATHAN: I laughed. /

RICHARD: Exactly.

JONATHAN: Beautiful wedding. We made a holiday of it. It was only –

RICHARD: Six… Seven…Yes nearly seven weeks ago now.

MIRIAM: Congratulations.

JONATHAN: It's ridiculous. Can you believe he's never been married before? Laura's – ?

RICHARD: Fine. Laura's great. We're settling into married life. She doesn't like my taste in shoes. Or cutlery. Out with the old in with the new.

JONATHAN: That woman is a saint.

RICHARD: It has been duly noted.

JONATHAN: Richard is the only man I know who takes his new bride to Leeds for her honeymoon.

RICHARD: The neurology unit had asked me to speak. *(Beat.)* We saw a castle…

JONATHAN: A castle. *(Beat.)* How terrifically romantic. *(To MIRIAM.)* Sam will be overseeing the study and assisting the UK arm of the project, shadowing Richard.

URSULA enters, with a smile.

URSULA: The poultry are parted. Dinner might be a little late. So if anyone needs a snack. Aileen's up for making sandwiches.

SAM: The view is/

RICHARD: …stunning.

URSULA: Yes.

JONATHAN smiles, gesturing to SAM.

JONATHAN: Ursula? Sam?

URSULA: Yes, we crossed on the stairs.

URSULA follows RICHARD's gaze, looking out.

Do you have a view, Dr Garfield?

RICHARD: No. I have a wall.

URSULA: That can also be…

MIRIAM: We should get started. Only time is…

URSULA: Sorry. Sorry. *(Beat.)* You just have to tell me to shut up.

URSULA closes the door, goes to sit but instead pours herself another cup of coffee. She holds up the pot to RICHARD.

URSULA: More coffee?

RICHARD shakes his head.

It'll be my fifth of the day, although apparently, there is just as much, if not more caffeine, in your average cup of Earl Grey.

MIRIAM looks at URSULA.

…Silence.

JONATHAN: *(To RICHARD.)* Will you?

RICHARD: If you prefer.

JONATHAN: I would.

RICHARD: Ok… *(Beat.)* Sister –

MIRIAM: Miriam.

RICHARD: Miriam, you'll have already heard of our work in the States, I think Jonathan sent you some papers –/

MIRIAM: Yes.

RICHARD: My apologies, if you found them a little dry.

MIRIAM: I confess they defeated me somewhat.

JONATHAN: I'm pushing for them to publish but Richard believes –

RICHARD: Despite Jonathan's best efforts, we've managed to keep it pretty quiet so far.

Beat.

The study's in its ninth year, working across seven of the mid-Western states. Your sisters in the US have been very generous with their time.

URSULA: We're in contact with our sisters in Missouri. Only last August. Sister Loretta/

RICHARD: …Sister Loretta Hope is a particular favourite.

URSULA: …She's a marvel. Her letters are a hoot. The last one detailed how she built a BBQ. She did all the brickwork herself. And she's 89 –

RICHARD: 89.

URSULA: Did you know she's doing a masters in Islam?

RICHARD: I didn't.

URSULA: We'd be hard pushed to match them though Sister Mary Jane Brody hits her 103rd birthday this September and she can do every word on *Countdown*.

MIRIAM: Ursula.

URSULA: Am I doing it again? Sorry. Words just spill with me.

URSULA takes a seat, determinedly silent. RICHARD smiles.

RICHARD: I'm not exactly sure what Jonathan has told you./

JONATHAN: I thought it would be better if the sisters hear the core of the proposal from you.

RICHARD: As head of the Institute of Ageing, I know that Jonathan has been visiting you. The institute's US arm has provided a large proportion of our funding. *(Beat.)* We're already talking to your sister convent in – .

URSULA: …Aberdeen. We had a call last week.

RICHARD: Jonathan may have mentioned we've met a little resistance so far.

JONATHAN: The key is someone leading, someone seen to be leading the way –

MIRIAM: Jonathan, you're jumping around like a grasshopper.

JONATHAN: Sorry. Sorry…I just thought… Sorry –

JONATHAN sits, drinks his coffee.

…It drives my wife mad.

RICHARD: We're keen to establish a second study in the UK. To build upon what we've already learnt in the US. *(Beat.)* We need to find at least 200 willing candidates. You currently have 16 –

MIRIAM: 17. If you consider Audrey.

RICHARD: 13 of those sisters are in the relevant age bracket.

MIRIAM: Age bracket?

RICHARD: *(Beat.)* He hasn't told you a thing.

JONATHAN: Not exactly. Not entirely. I wanted the whole team to be here today to answer any questions you may have.

RICHARD: *(Beat.)* Our study sisters range from 75 to 106. Thirteen of your sisters are in the relevant age bracket to participate in our study. With the fourteen at your sister convent, we would have 27 potential candidates in total in the UK so far. In particular we're interested in the effect of ageing on the human mind and developing our understanding of what constitutes a healthy life.

JONATHAN: You're getting all of this, OK, Miriam?

MIRIAM: Yes, Jonathan, thank you, Dr Garfield's English is surprisingly good.

JONATHAN: I'm just ensuring everyone is up to speed…

URSULA: Absolutely.

JONATHAN: It's just –

URSULA: We're fine.

RICHARD: For an epidemiologist like myself, your religious order provides the ideal study group. Your lives have been carefully regulated. Copious records have been maintained. …To be frank as a community you're easy to track. The noviciate autobiographies alone –

MIRIAM: Yes?

RICHARD: …are very exciting to us. A detailed insight to a sister's early life, a biography written in as an aspirant about to take her vows which we can use to compare language skills, idea density with that of the same sister today. *(Beat.)* In particular we're trying to further our understanding of Alzheimer's in the ageing mind.

JONATHAN: It's a very attractive proposition, Miriam. The Institute would of course make some kind of covenant, a bi-yearly donation of some kind.

MIRIAM: You want to work here?

URSULA: Now wait and hear what they have to say.

JONATHAN: Richard's team would monitor the physical and mental effects of ageing through a series of simple well-established tests.

URSULA pours herself another cup of coffee, watching MIRIAM. JONATHAN holds out his cup.

MIRIAM: Tests?

JONATHAN: Sam?

SAM: These are called MMSE or mini-mental state exams.

JONATHAN: They're approved by the National Institute of Ageing in both America and over here.

HELEN: They're designed to assess verbal fluency, word recognition etc.

RICHARD: This is Helen's particular area of expertise. They offer some kind of prognosis. It's not a definitive analysis of Alzheimer's per se but –

JONATHAN: All findings remain confidential, known only to the sister if she wishes.

Silence. URSULA looks to MIRIAM, sees she is clearly struggling.

We appreciate this might be a lot to take in in one go.

MIRIAM: 'Exam'. The word 'exam' is –

SAM: …misleading.

MIRIAM: Most of our sisters haven't taken any kind of qualification since their masters or teaching diplomas. Many of them have found vocation in say the garden or the kitchen. Any kind of exam –

RICHARD: …certainly don't compare. The last thing I want to inflict are exams on anyone. I was the worst student in my class.

MIRIAM: Still. Then what are they?

HELEN: They're small exercises, almost like games to stimulate and assess processing, language or let's say memory skills, designed to create some kind of criteria to examine levels of physical and mental coherence.

SAM: They last no more than an hour over two days, and are carried out on a yearly basis. This is then compared with the pathology of a sister after –

JONATHAN: Sam –

MIRIAM: After? *(Beat.)* Ursula?

RICHARD: This is a very sensitive request…

URUSLA: They want our brains.

JONATHAN: Tissue.

RICHARD: One can't deny this is a highly provocative – /

URSULA: Our sister convent will agree if we do as well.

MIRIAM: Right.

URSULA takes another biscuit, eats.

RICHARD: The co-operation of the sisters in America has been dependent on their benevolence and genuine belief in our work. The donation is essential for those agreeing to participate in the study.

URSULA: *(Eats.)* I'm eating all these bourbons.

URSULA puts down the biscuit. JONATHAN shifts in his chair as RUTH enters with more coffee.

RUTH: Aileen was asking if anyone's vegetarian.

JONATHAN: We're weren't expecting supper.

MIRIAM: We can't not feed you, now you're here.

RICHARD goes to speak but hesitates on seeing RUTH still loitering.

Everything alright Ruth?

RUTH: Yes… Sorry.

MIRIAM: No vegetarians I think.

Silence. MIRIAM looks to RUTH waiting for her to go until –

URSULA: Ruth is a trained nurse.

RICHARD: Really?

RUTH nods, letting the silence hang.

URSULA: She's read a lot about your work in America.

MIRIAM: *(To RUTH.)* You have?

RUTH: Ursula and I talked a little.

URSULA: She's a demon with her articles. Let her loose amongst the broadsheets with a pair of scissors...

RUTH: It seems very interesting... Your study I mean?

RICHARD: We're hoping so.

URSULA: She worked in Africa.

RUTH: It was years ago. *(Beat.)* I aided some of the smallpox vaccination programmes for a little while in Eastern Africa and the Niger through most of the late 80s.

RICHARD: Then you must understand more than most –

RUTH: ...the benefits of such work. Yes.

RUTH starts to pile cups on a tray, MIRIAM waits. RUTH nods, making to go.

MIRIAM: So you'll let Aileen know?

RUTH nods then exits.

How many have you so far? *(Beat.)* Donations?

RICHARD: There are 700 sisters participating in the programme in the US. 128 have passed away since we started in '97. Of which actual tissue donations are 49. We allow for a certain number of sisters to drop out nearer the time due to family wishes or through a change of heart of some kind. We would need tissue... Plus unlimited access to all noviciate autobiographies, medical records and relevant documentation held on each sister participating. *(Beat.)* As Jonathan mentioned, your sister convents in the UK, have certain reservations but –

JONATHAN: If you were seen to be leading the way/

MIRIAM: We've had a recent rise in the popularity of the open casket –

JONATHAN: It's a very simple procedure.

RICHARD: The sisters would still be able to be viewed even after –

MIRIAM: That sorts that one then.

MIRIAM absently follows the sound of footsteps, of someone passing.

URSULA: Miriam?

MIRIAM: *(Beat.)* The brain is not just –

RICHARD: …an organ of the body, no.

MIRIAM: The brain –

RICHARD: Yes.

MIRIAM: …it's the very essence of being, of who we are.

RICHARD: Yes I can see that.

SAM: *(Beat.)* Richard, do you mind if I?

RICHARD hesitates, nods. SAM takes a seat opposite MIRIAM.

No one underestimates what we're asking you to consider. But does it help if I tell you that in the last nine years, it's widely believed Dr Garfield's work has come closer to answering some of the fundamental questions on brain degeneration than any other study currently being undertaken…

RICHARD: You're being a little too kind.

JONATHAN: Ssh.

SAM: Why is it that one sister ages gracefully, all faculties in tact through into late life often passing her centenary and yet another, who has lived a comparable in many cases almost identical life in terms of education, socialisation, medical care, nutrition, lifestyle, seem to lose herself with a steady degeneration of her mental faculties? A sister who can't recognise her own family or even what time of day it is and yet whose life has been identical to that of the other?

JONATHAN: Sam's unit of memory and ageing at Edinburgh are doing some very interesting research on folic acid, its beneficial effect on the brain in early life.

SAM: We're hanging on the US' coat tails. But in Richard's work…I genuinely believe he will find a cure.

RICHARD: That's not strictly –

JONATHAN: Do you think Louis Pasteur could afford to be this modest?

RICHARD: Understanding, understanding will suit me fine.

MIRIAM: What do you think, Ursula?

URSULA: I told you we should eat more liver. That's packed with folic acid. We eat the odd takeaway burger, but don't go spreading that around. It breaks up the nun run from town and back.

JONATHAN: You're not taking this seriously.

URSULA tidies the last of the things on the tray, going to take JONATHAN's cup.

I know how important your opinion is to Miriam.

URSULA: *(Beat.)* I am just heir in waiting.

JONATHAN: Nonsense you are the rock star of the ecclesiastical world.

MIRIAM laughs.

URSULA: And now you're encouraging him.

JONATHAN: It's true.

URSULA looks to MIRIAM, sensing her waiting.

URSULA: Most of them will take their lead from you. You've run this place since God began…

MIRIAM: You invited them here.

URSULA: They made their vow of obedience to you.

MIRIAM: And soon to you.

URSULA hesitates, pouring herself more coffee.

JONATHAN: Now take your time – Really don't be rushed on this.

URSULA: No. You don't want to catch us on a different day.

MIRIAM: How many of us would it affect?

RICHARD: Thirteen here. 27 in total.

URSULA: But with time –

RICHARD: You're a long way off being old enough for our study.

URSULA: I'll hold on to mine a little longer then.

HELEN: In some of the convents we've visited, the sisters have put it to a ballot. We've found it can be very helpful in uniting these communities.

MIRIAM: These communities?

Distant sound of bells.

I presume you'd want to start quite soon.

RICHARD: We'd monitor the sisters on a yearly basis. The time varies, it could be summer it could be the fall. Dr Jarvis and I would conduct the assessment here over say a two week period.

HELEN: We would clinically examine the sisters as well as conducting the tests with our team. This data along with all other documentation kept through their lives is collated and stored on our computers. Following death the data would then be definitively compared to assess where there is a correlation with MMSEs scoring, the other forms of testing and changes in the brain tissue.

RICHARD: The American Psychiatric association have laid out detailed guidelines to distinguish non-Alzheimer's dementia from possible or probable Alzheimer's but there is no definitive test, no scan, no blood test that can provide absolute certainty until after death.

MIRIAM: Whatever the sisters may be to you, to us they are still very much in the living.

RICHARD: No one doubts that.

URSULA: We were born to serve our fellow man, I can't think of a better way of helping him, Miriam.

MIRIAM: You decide.

URSULA looks to MIRIAM.

You invited them here, Ursula.

A beat.

URSULA: A ballot it is. Though it would be best to address the sisters straight after supper. They have an hour's recreation at 7.30 and you would be advised to get in before their soaps start. For some the order of *Eastenders* carries greater comfort than a whole evening of prayer. If we over run, I'll hide the remote, that normally foxes them.

The bell passes as if moving just past MIRIAM's office.

You can amuse yourself for the next hour? Audrey will show you around if you like. We still have the gardens in full working order. August is the best time, there's plums if you can find them and of course if you fancy a dip in the weir.

MIRIAM goes to exit.

MIRIAM: The necessary arrangements would be put in place by you in the event of a death of a consenting sister?

RICHARD: Yes.

SAM: The brain would be removed, boxed and posted and be on a lab slide within six weeks.

JONATHAN and RICHARD both turn to look at SAM.

JONATHAN: Christ, Sam.

SAM: Sorry…sorry.

URSULA: You might want to phrase it a different way once you get in there. One or two of them are a bit queasy and they would've been even more so if Aileen hadn't got those chickens apart.

RICHARD: Four million people in America currently suffer from Alzheimer's disease. There will be 7.7 million by the year 2030. There will be 115 million by 2050, worldwide.

MIRIAM: That's a lot of lost people.

MIRIAM goes to exit. SAM, HELEN and JONATHAN follow. URSULA goes to tidy the last of the tea things, following RICHARD's gaze, looking outside.

URSULA: Go to the weir if you can make it. This time of day, it's the quietest place you'll find around here. Everyone's always surprised how noisy it is when they visit. You're never really ever alone, even if you wanted to be.

URSULA exits. RICHARD stands, the cup still in his hand.

RICHARD: *(To audience.)* A healthy adult female brain usually weighs between 1,100 and 1,400 grams. That's about 2-3lbs in old money. Hold it in your hand and you soon appreciate the weight of this gift, feel it. The brain of most Alzheimer's patients is noticeably smaller. They often shrink below 1,000 grams, as the disease destroys the brain tissue. You become adept at knowing this just by looking. As you lift it out of the box, already telling you something. The surface already confirming or destroying what you thought you'd already had pinned down. Like a beautiful landscape that you've painted in your mind though you've never actually been to. Now you get to visit, to see all its ruts and curves and valleys, the odd rogue crevasse that you hadn't expected to find. You get to photograph it and slice it and hold it up to the light and look at it under a microscope. You know the person it belonged to. You probably laughed with them over a game of scrabble, or been surprised when after weeks of blind staring in the corner of some convent hallway, they wink at you. Like the first smile of a baby, delightful. As if they're saying 'Hey there is someone in here, everything is still firing, just maybe in a slower gear.' You've got all of it, right there. I think of it as my friend. I think of it as someone I once knew. I think of it as the key to the most secret part of someone's life, and that someone has left that key with me. And I'm grateful. I'm always grateful. But it's still a weight, an ever present weight, just there, a constant in my hand.

RICHARD puts down the coffee cup, sliding it onto the tray.

Act Two

A library.

A long table. Chairs. A low wide bowl of pomegranates on the table.

HELEN sits working, talking into a Dictaphone, reading from a pile of documents in front of her –

It is winter, three years on. 2009.

HELEN: *(Reading/into Dictaphone.)* I was born in Greenock. Though my da was a Corkman. Eleven words. Punctuated on the fifth and the eleventh word – End. Note to self predominately monosyllabic bar the colloquial noun 'da'. I was one of six. Two boys and four girls, a seventh, Michael died in childbirth. Five. Five. Two. Punctuation – Comma. Two. Punctuation – Comma. Five. Punctuation – Full stop.

HELEN takes notes throughout, talking into a Dictaphone –

MIRIAM: Am I in the way?

HELEN smiles, flicks off her Dictaphone.

HELEN: No.

MIRIAM: Don't be shy to say.

HELEN: Really Miriam. It's fine.

MIRIAM nods. HELEN resumes working, turning the Dictaphone back on.

(Reading/into Dictaphone.) I was one of six. Two boys and four girls, a seventh, Michael died in childbirth.

SAM enters, sinking on seeing MIRIAM.

MIRIAM: Sam, now you promised me…

HELEN smiles, amused –

SAM: Rats! Found.

MIRIAM holds up the lamp.

SAM: I swear you save these jobs up for me.

SAM goes in search of a socket, plugging them in. Nothing.

MIRIAM: Yes I do. I think it's the plug.

MIRIAM hands him a screwdriver.

And can you try and mend my desk lamp after, please. It's on then it's off, as if one is under visitation from a poltergeist.

HELEN smiles, resumes working.

HELEN: *(Reading/into Dictaphone.)* Five. Five. Two. Punctuation – Comma. Two. Punctuation – Comma. Five. Punctuation – Full stop.

HELEN hesitates, aware of MIRIAM hovering close by. She flicks off the Dictaphone, works on.

MIRIAM: It's a foreign language.

HELEN: It's pretty impenetrable.

MIRIAM: Though linguistics has always been a passion.

MIRIAM peers over HELEN's shoulder, reading.

HELEN: Please. I give a scoring every ten or so words based on grammatical complexity –

MIRIAM: I see, yes.

HELEN: Richness of vocabulary,

MIRIAM: Fascinating.

HELEN: Density of ideas and positive or negative emotion –

MIRIAM: Searching for the embedded clauses.

HELEN watching MIRIAM, absorbed in reading.

HELEN: Exactly. The verb phrase infinitive complexes, incidents of repetition and anaphora…

MIRIAM: Anaphora.

HELEN: Reading them is like striking gold. Whole lives, so perfectly notated, really. It never fails to humble me.

MIRIAM: Yes, words do last, yet what they say is not always the same. For example Anaphora, a rhetorical device, rhetoric. A referential pattern in linguistics… Yes… Then there is Anaphora…part of the divine liturgy in Eastern Christianity.

MIRIAM watches HELEN working. MIRIAM looks over her shoulder again reading.

And what one writes as a young woman one perceives as something so entirely different I find…with time…with age.

MIRIAM moves across the room.

HELEN: It's quite a library you have down there.

MIRIAM: We're very lucky. We've built it up over the years.

HELEN: A real legacy.

MIRIAM: *(Beat.)* That's something then.

HELEN: I've been trying to teach Audrey. It's laborious I know but if she knows the phrases when she types them up then it will make life a lot easier, for her. It's all useful experience for her resume.

MIRIAM looks at her bemused.

For when she works outside?

MIRIAM: Is Audrey leaving?

HELEN: I don't…know…I just meant.

MIRIAM: She arrived here in quite a state. She'd not had a bath in two months. A bed maybe longer. She'll leave when she wants to.

HELEN: And if she stays?

MIRIAM peers at a book on the shelf.

MIRIAM: *Playboy of the Western World.* What a play!

MIRIAM takes it out of the shelf, considers, smiling to herself.

JM Synge. Have you ever seen it?

HELEN: No.

MIRIAM: Neither have I. But we've read it. Time and time again. Before we had a television.

HELEN clocks MIRIAM's cardigan, the label visible at the base of her neck as she walks away.

Ursula and I.

MIRIAM smiles, looks over HELEN's shoulder.

Such dedication.

MIRIAM smiles, makes to go –

HELEN: You have your cardigan on inside out?

MIRIAM: Hmm.

MIRIAM feels for a label, laughs –

Oh yes, so I do –

MIRIAM points a finger at SAM before she exits.

MIRIAM: I will be back.

MIRIAM exits. SAM looks to HELEN.

SAM: A catalogue of little jobs every time I sit down to start work.

HELEN: I'm not saying anything.

SAM: I mean why do they even employ Robert?

HELEN: He lives with his mother and it gives him a chance to get out.

SAM: You speak to him?

HELEN: I'm very fond of Robert.

SAM: Fond is not a word I'd associate with you.

AUDREY enters carrying a pile of files, heading towards HELEN.

AUDREY: Biscuit, table, airplane, handbag, dog, envelope, policeman, lake, pencil… I know it…I know it…

SAM reaches one hand across a desk and holds up a card with the word 'tambourine' on it.

AUDREY: Tambourine. …I would have got that.

AUDREY laughs, snatching the card off SAM. HELEN looks up, clearly irritated to be disturbed.

Sorry… Sorry. Those ready to go up.

HELEN nods.

HELEN: I was just telling Miriam how hard you've been working learning all the terms. To help you later.

AUDREY starts sorting through the files, putting them into different piles.

Don't you want to be able to work outside?

AUDREY: I have work.

HELEN: I thought it was a 'vocation'.

AUDREY: Aspirant. I'm an aspirant.

HELEN: Still –

AUDREY: You make it sound like a prison. Inside, outside, I can still go out. I drive the van sometimes.

HELEN: Audrey, I'm sorry I –

AUDREY: I'd rather be here than slaving in some office, trying to get a bigger house, a bigger car, ending up divorced and lonely and –

HELEN stops her note taking. AUDREY hesitates.

HELEN: *(Beat.)* I just think you're too young –

AUDREY: I'm 24 next March. *(Beat.)* Ursula thinks I could… I'm going to take a Higher next month. *(Beat.)* It's better than being smacked out nicking scratch cards all your life.

AUDREY scoops up another pile of files.

That to go up?

HELEN nods.

Is this Aileen's?

HELEN nods, catching on AUDREY looking at the file.

You know I found her. She was blue. Must have been dead ages. It's shaken them all up a bit. 78's not a bad age but she's one of the youngest. They were all checking their pulses that day.

HELEN: A stroke's a stroke.

AUDREY: She used to eat double cream frozen, straight out of the bag. Heart must have been like a sponge of fat. But God I miss her pies. Sister Maria Angelica is a f'ecking awful cook. I mean Aileen was bad but Maria…

SAM and HELEN look to one another, smile. HELEN slides a pile of files towards AUDREY.

AUDREY nods, scooping them up, making to go.

AUDREY: I didn't mean you. Divorced and lonely.

HELEN hesitates, smiles.

Sam, would you talk to Ursula because we're still using that crap PC. It took me months to type the biographies last time.

SAM: I think Jonathan might have sorted that.

AUDREY: He hasn't.

SAM: Looks like an Apple Mac to me. Of course I can't be sure because it's still inside the box, waiting in the hall for someone with a modicum of computer literacy to open it but… Think of it as an early Christmas present.

AUDREY: Hallelujah!

AUDREY is gone.

HELEN: You're flirting.

SAM: I'm not flirting…much.

SAM peers over HELEN's shoulder, close, teasing her.

So it came through at last.

HELEN: Signed the paper's August.

SAM: How is George?

HELEN: He took the cat. *(Beat.)* It's fine. I hate the cat. So does he. So he either took it as an act of selfless love, or an act of mean-minded revenge, thinking I cared… This and other irritations dog my day. How's Elizabeth?

SAM smiles, HELEN smiles, both dangerously close.

URSULA: Samuel.

URSULA enters. She is carrying a mug of coffee, and a pile of books. A plate of cake rests on top.

There you are. Ruth said you were helping out with the decorations and I find you hiding up here. Where were you this morning? You promised me. I was up early and –

SAM: I nearly drowned last Christmas –

URSULA: And the year before that.

SAM: I swam. It was August. November, you need a ice pick. There are icebergs.

URSULA: The Norwegians –

SAM: See you said that last year and I figured the Norwegians have saunas.

URSULA: …find it very good for the circulation. You're a big disappointment.

SAM: You build a sauna…?

URSULA: Now that would get them talking. When are you going to get a new suit?

SAM: As soon as someone starts paying me more.

URSULA: I will talk to Richard. Who is normally here. It's a waste of good coffee.

URSULA slides a cup of coffee down.

HELEN: I'll have it.

URSULA: Don't.

HELEN drinks winces.

HELEN: Wow. He likes his sugar.

URSULA: I've tried cutting it down, but he sniffs it out if you put in less than four spoons. Was Miriam just here?

HELEN: Yes.

HELEN barely looks up from her work. SAM tinkers with the plug on the lamp.

URSULA: I don't know why you changed it all around. August was always great, it was the best time for you to come but November. It's cold and damp and…a nothing month –

HELEN: Orders from above. They want us to work faster.

URSULA: They'll have you clocking in and out next.

HELEN: Richard's trying to keep them at bay but Jonathan is hovering eager. He's excited by the results we're getting. We all are.

SAM tinkers some more with the lamp, then plugs it in. It turns on.

URSULA: And that is why we look forward to you coming every year.

SAM: A loose bulb fitting. I'd like to take the credit for more.

SAM unplugs the lamp, making to go.

URSULA: Rumour has it you've been published.

SAM: Someone has to get us out there... It was nothing...

HELEN: That's not what Richard says.

SAM: He's read it?

URSULA: It was four columns more than Dr Kaufmann and cirrhosis of the liver. Ruth pinned it up on the notice board.

SAM makes to go, hesitating as he passes HELEN.

SAM: Can I borrow these? I want to compare the Braak scores.

HELEN scours through her pile of documents.

SAM takes them.

HELEN: If Richard finds you doing that –

SAM: Richard doesn't need to know.

URSULA: Are you going downstairs?

SAM stops mid step, cornered.

The radiator? It's that beast of a thing in the hallway.

SAM: Next time I am charging.

URSULA busies herself, tidying books back into the shelves.

URSULA: Don't mind me.

HELEN resumes talking into her Dictaphone.

HELEN: *(Reading/into Dictaphone.)* 'The sisters of Poor Clare were running the church school. Come fourteen, my Aunt, Tattie Pol as we were calling her, got us a place.'

URSULA hovers, searching for a book.

Sixteen. Punctuation – Comma. Eleven. Punctuation – Full stop. Note to self, simplistic idea density, left-sided branching, 2-3 g.c. score –

HELEN resumes reading.

(Reading/into Dictaphone.) Tattie Pol said I must. My ma's mind was gone and my da's was close behind.

HELEN hesitates.

A terrible sickness, that left them both lost for reason or words. Ma was gone 19th May 1964.

HELEN hesitates, the Dictaphone still running. HELEN suddenly flicks the Dictaphone off.

URSULA: Raphael.

URSULA holds up the book she is reading, deflects.

It's an ongoing love affair. I don't know what it is about his frescoes but I just…

HELEN nods, lost in reading, flicking the Dictaphone back on.

HELEN: *(Reading/into Dictaphone.)* I made a visit to Da a week after for he was housed now at the Landsdowne Infirmary. He howls when he sees us, and would not stop that I was a wicked girl and no good would come of me and that he was wanting his own little daughter back though I says it was me, Geraldine to him twice.

HELEN slides the Dictaphone down on the desk, still running, searching through the files, looking for something.

URSULA: Have you lost something?

HELEN: I asked Audrey for all the sisters pre 1945 so I don't know quite why this one –

HELEN holds up the document in her hand.

(Reading.) Geraldine. February 9th 1971. Way out.

URSULA: Audrey must have –

HELEN: Yes.

URSULA: Mixed up the batch or –

URSULA reaches across for the file, HELEN is working on.

I'll put it back.

HELEN snaps the document shut in her hand, resisting.

HELEN: No…you're fine. I'll do it later.

URSULA: Post 1945, we've moved to the basement, you shouldn't have that. I can take it down.

HELEN gently places a hand over the file, stopping URSULA from taking it.

HELEN: Really. It's fine.

URSULA shrugs, conceding defeat, resuming her search.

URSULA: A picture is to the illiterate what the religious word is to the educated. Pope St Gregory.

HELEN: Miriam?

URSULA: She had a terrible cold, last month. She took to her bed for four weeks. She still thinks she runs the place, and now with the wheeze on her chest.

HELEN: I was looking at her file only yesterday. Her writings are quite brilliant.

HELEN goes through the files, pulling out a particular document.

Every time we visit, I find myself pulling out her noviciate biography again, just to have a look. There's a level of vocabulary, grammatical complexity and density of ideas that is quite extraordinary –

URSULA: The 'contemplative' life certainly ekes out time and space, to educate the mind.

HELEN: I don't doubt that but… Where is it?

HELEN rewinds the Dictaphone.

Miriam's the morning after she's taken her vows –

the sun rose through my window, casting its glorious light across my bedspread, my wall was patterned with a heavenly glow that the less rigorous minded might have taken as a sign. My preference is that I need no divine intervention for this is the start of the rest of my life.

HELEN stops the tape.

HELEN: It's pure poetry. We're discovering, the early notes are a good marker, the reserves of the brain have perhaps been built in very early life. Miriam has clearly had an expansive vocabulary from early age.

URSULA: Her mother was very educated, she read a lot. I think there was a lot of healthy debate.

Beat.

URSULA: Her cold. It's left her a little scattered.

HELEN: Even so. Her tests were fine last year, though slightly less good than the year before. I will be curious how she is this time.

URSULA stands awkward, the last of her pile of books in her hand.

URSULA: T.S. Eliot.

URSULA goes to return the small poetry book.

It's signed…

HELEN takes the book.

People leave bequests.

HELEN flicks through –

We didn't have a single book in our house except the bible, though half of it was missing, and the odd sports journal my father would bring home. He was brought up by my aunt, she was the religious one, she didn't approve of 'literature'. If it wasn't in the name of our Lord then it was ungodly to her. That was twaddle Miriam said, and I was to banish that thought if I was ever to open my mind to anything. There is nothing more godly than 'literature' … *'If ever you want him, just look, you'll find him on every page.'* Though to be frank, there's a couple of Henry James down there in the library where he's a bit sparse. Sister Bernice has a sweet tooth, she slips them in when she thinks we're not looking mixing up the Barbara Taylor Bradfords. I don't think it does much harm but –

RICHARD enters, RUTH close behind.

RICHARD: We're on a mass exodus from Siberia. Even the tea in our mugs is freezing over.

URSULA: Ruth has the right idea.

RUTH close behind in gloves and scarf, clutching a pile of papers, pen in hand.

You should at least wear a scarf. Promise me you got your flu jab this year.

RICHARD: I did.

URSULA: Flu jab in August and –

RICHARD: Not even a cough.

HELEN: You'll be making him soup next.

URSULA: That was Aileen's domain.

RICHARD: Are we good to stay?

RICHARD looks to HELEN, hovering.

I can't ask the sisters to sit down there much longer.

HELEN: Oh…yeah, that's fine…I want to finish up the last of the reading in my room anyway.

HELEN clears her things, scooping up her documents.

Though can I catch you later – ? Say five?

RICHARD: Five should be –

HELEN slides the file across to RICHARD in passing.

HELEN: I found you something. Try and take a look at it. Geraldine. 1971.

HELEN exits.

RICHARD takes it and starts to read until –

URSULA: Cake.

RICHARD looks up from reading, as if realising something to see –

URSULA holds out the plate of cake to RICHARD.

RICHARD: Cake is good. We don't get cake…

URSULA: Laura told me –

RICHARD: You've been talking –

URSULA: …that you cut out carbohydrates.

RICHARD: *(To RUTH.)* This woman, this woman talks to my wife more than I do.

URSULA: She also said –

RICHARD: I stop at dairy. I cannot not eat dairy.

URSULA: …That you are sneaking cheeseburgers at the weekends and that she hasn't seen you since –

RICHARD: I've been working late.

URSULA: You must be nice to her. Otherwise she'll leave you Richard, then where will you be? *(Beat.)* She called on the main phone. I told her you'd call her back. Why don't you ever pick up your phone? *(Beat.)* There is only so often that you are taking a walk outside.

URSULA holds out a plate of cake out to RICHARD.

And then we had the American –

RICHARD: American?

URSULA: I think they make aspirin or something. I do not remember. I told him he had the wrong extension –

RICHARD: You're remarkable, Ursula do you know that?

RUTH: Shall I bring Miriam up now? She's wandering around a bit lost. Sister Anna Maria was going to go first, but it might be better if we see Miriam. I know that there was some work she wanted to do in the garden later.

URSULA: I would skip Miriam this year.

RICHARD: Really?

URSULA: She's not been herself this last month.

RUTH: It was just a cold.

URSULA: I know but I really don't think she is at her best. I don't think it would be fair. In fact I think she would be relieved if you did not test her this time.

RUTH: That's not what she says.

URSULA: You talked to her?

RUTH: Dr Garfield. I think Dr Garfield had a word.

URSULA: You did?

RICHARD: She seemed fine.

URSULA: It might have just been a cold but it was evil.

RUTH: That was six weeks ago.

URSULA: It's exhausted her. And it was four weeks.

RUTH: Six. It was six weeks ago.

URSULA hesitates, looking to RUTH, quietly challenged. URSULA shrugs, smiles.

URSULA: Still. She's not been right.

RUTH: I was saying to Dr Garfield about our concerns.

URSULA: She's just tired, Ruth.

RUTH: No Ursula.

URSULA: Ruth and I will now disagree.

RUTH: I am simply saying that we need to acknowledge –

URSULA: There is nothing wrong with Miriam.

Silence.

I hope she's been behaving herself.

RICHARD: Exemplary.

URSULA: No religious literature or tracts from our favourite saints left lying around?

RICHARD: I don't think you can count the odd copy of *Private Eye.*

RUTH: Why must you two tease me so?

URSULA: Because it's so much fun.

RUTH: Have you ever had to question my work, Dr Garfield?

URSULA: For the love of God, Ruth, it's Richard's third year here. Robert is Robert. Sam is Sam. Even Mr Hadlow the butcher is Mick. You can call him Richard.

RICHARD: I could not manage without you Ruth.

RUTH: Thank you…Richard.

URSULA: You know your visits save her don't you? *(Seeing RUTH's look.)* What? The other 351 days of the year you are polishing the knocker on that front door so many times, it's ready to march itself off to a more upmarket location.

RUTH: I keep myself busy.

URSULA: Oh yes, we're all so busy doing nothing.

RUTH: It's not nothing, Ursula.

Silence.

Every day is our prayer to Christ.

URSULA: Did you read Sam's article? Eight columns. Not bad. Though it's yours I'm waiting for.

RICHARD: I promise when I think there is something worth saying, you will be first person who will read it.

URSULA: Thank you, Dr Garfield. Even so you should read Sam's.

RICHARD: I'll look it up.

RUTH suddenly pulls an article out of her pocket, handing it to RICHARD.

RUTH: It displays some of the study's best work.

RICHARD flicks a hand into his top pocket, pulling out his glasses ready to read.

The metaphor of the brain as the placemat at life's table, I thought that was quite brilliant.

RICHARD: *(As reads.)* Yes… Yes I can see that.

RUTH: It's the discovery of miracle that I was just sorry he didn't flag up.

RICHARD looks up from the article, taking in RUTH's obvious delight.

RUTH: I mean as the article says. May I?

RUTH holds out her hands, RICHARD returning the article.

RUTH: Sister Philomena… Last time you were in Missouri… I remember you all talking of this that she was translating… the letters of…here it is.

RICHARD: Poor Clare into English from the French.

RUTH: According to this she scored near perfect on both her physical and mental MMSEs. I mean Sam says here that some of the assistant sisters used to try and shuffle the cards up a little just to try and catch her out but –

RICHARD: Yes, her mind was one of the smartest and most alert we'd come across until the day she died.

RUTH: And yet, in autopsy the pathology of her brain revealed a surprising fact. *(Reading.)* Sister Philomena was marked as a Braak stage VI an absolute confirmation of severe Alzheimer's pathology based on your methods of diagnosis. Death revealed that her brain was severely damaged and yet in life…

RUTH smiles, almost elated.

She was still teaching elementary class well into her 80s.

RICHARD: She also had an abundance of grey matter, formed by the cell bodies of neurons in the neocortex. 90 per cent more than we had seen in any other sister.

RUTH: Her brain was damaged, severely damaged and yet she passed all your tests with flying colours?

RICHARD: Yes.

RUTH: It's a miracle.

RICHARD hesitates, smiles.

RICHARD: I like to think it's a miracle that we haven't found the answer to yet.

RUTH: I understand you believe that your work may one day find a cure for Alzheimer's. That's commendable. But this need for science to colonise this miracle for itself… Don't you ever think that just maybe there is no scientific answer, that the answer is God's work?

RUTH looks back over the article.

These *'escapees'* that you refer to –

URSULA: Ruth.

RUTH: Ursula does not agree with me that's why she's interrupting.

URSULA: I'm not. I am. *(Beat.)* I'm sorry. *(To RICHARD.)* Ruth is about to highlight a difference of opinion.

RUTH: I mean three years here and in America, you've been working for how long –

RICHARD: Twelve years…

RUTH: Twelve years over in America and you still don't have a scientific answer for these phenomena?

RICHARD: *(Beat.)* Nothing concrete –

RUTH: So you have no answer?

URSULA: Ruth, the Catholic Church has had centuries of miraculous occasion that we've laid claim to. We can afford to have one or two challenged.

RUTH: I'm asking Richard.

The action freezes –

RICHARD: *(To audience.)* I say –

… I cannot deny the presence of miracle. The very essence of all life is formed from a miraculous multiplication of a single cell. The work of the scientist works several steps behind this obvious sign of something beyond science and yet –

(To audience.) I say –

…The answer may lie in brain reserve. There's a couple of scientists in Minneapolis who've been monitoring it over the past few years.

(To audience.) I say –

The action springs back into life.

It's to do with the way the brain develops in the womb and during adolescence which may lead to a stronger or weaker structure. A stronger brain may have more reserve, more grey matter. This may combat the effects of structural damage to the brain tissue, so that though the brain may have all the pathology of Alzheimers the symptoms are not displayed. These 'stronger' brains find new ways to establish connections between the nerve cells, like re-patching the wiring of a cowboy electrician, Sister Philomena displayed a high level of this grey matter. If I'm right it could be argued that she had a 'fighting' brain, may have more ammunition in 'reserve'.

RUTH: And if you are wrong? I know you're not Catholic. I mean I've never discussed it with you but I know you're not religious.

RICHARD: My mother was a Methodist.

URSULA: And your father?

RICHARD: Jewish.

URSULA: That will not be good enough for Ruth.

RUTH: *(Seeing URSULA's look.)* I don't understand why you don't support me in this.

URSULA: I support you in your belief of miracle, Ruth. I struggle but I support you in *your* belief of miracle.

RUTH: It's the basis of our faith, Ursula.

URSULA: Yes, and I struggle with that.

Silence.

RICHARD: Our study is exactly what it says it is, Ruth. It's a study. If we don't see it, then we don't say it's there. If it is a miracle, then no man can own it.

Distant ring of bells.

RICHARD: *'The study of mankind is man.'* That's all we're doing Ruth.

RUTH: And the study of a sister is her God.

RICHARD smiles, handing the article back to RUTH.

So we agree the jury's still out?

RICHARD: I'll do you one better. Find me a sister with a genetic link on both sides of her family to early onset Alzheimer's, who may be carrying one of the three defective genes that cause this kind of dementia and yet who's displaying no signs of cognitive failure and you might have that miracle. Now that's a pathology I'd be interested in looking at. A sister with a genetic link both sides showing no cognitive failure –

The bell passes as if moving just past URSULA's office.

RUTH: *(Beat.)* What do I get if I win?

RICHARD: You show a surprisingly mercenary edge, Ruth.

URSULA: We could do with a new television. I swear Sister Rachel has been sucking on the wires again. *(To RICHARD.)* You are so easy to wind up.

RUTH: I'll get Miriam.

RUTH exits. RICHARD lays out his things preparing to work.

URSULA: Your coffee's gone cold. Even Helen couldn't drink it.

RICHARD: You look after us so well.

URSULA: It's the highlight of our year.

RICHARD reaches for the coffee cup.

Let me get you a fresh cup.

RICHARD: Really.

URSULA: Please.

RICHARD holds out the cup. URSULA takes it.

RICHARD: I won't test Miriam if you don't want me to.

URSULA: No, Ruth is right. I'm being silly.

RICHARD: She was a little…pale.

URSULA: Ruth was saying… I know you're not meant to talk about these things but Aileen… I was wondering –

RICHARD: She was fine. The stroke had clearly been damaging but her Braak scores were fine. Everything correlated before and after –

URSULA: That's good then. That's… Only what I already thought. I mean 78. She was practically a teenager. I mean she's our first.

RICHARD: Yes.

URSULA: I can't imagine what it's like. I mean you can travel, see the world but to travel that deep into someone's mind. That's…

RICHARD: It is.

URSULA nods, returning to putting books back on the shelf. RICHARD watches her.

RICHARD: Ursula –

Distant voices.

URSULA: That'll be Miriam. Go gentle with her, OK?

RICHARD: Yes.

URSULA: I don't know what it is but… You'll see… Something's not… Something's just not –

RICHARD: It's the highlight of my year, too. Coming here? It's the highlight of my –

MIRIAM enters, carrying a radiator.

MIRIAM: You've to thank me –

URSULA: I asked Sam.

MIRIAM: It was headed downstairs but I said you need…we need it far more up here.

SAM enters.

SAM: She's like a whippet.

SAM takes it off her, moving over to plug it in.

I had my back turned for one minute and she was off.

URSULA goes to take the radiator off her, hesitating, seeing MIRIAM's nails encrusted with earth, mud on her shoes.

URSULA: What have you been doing? You've half the garden under your fingernails.

MIRIAM: I was just pulling up the bulbs. Robert leaves them to rot in the ground.

URSULA: Because they come back, Miriam if you take them out of the earth they won't come back in the spring.

MIRIAM: Now you say that but the squirrels are little monsters. It's delicious Christmas booty. I told him lay them down on newspaper in the shed and he didn't and the front bed was nearly bare this time round. I rescued them.

URSULA concedes, smiles –

URSULA: Then we are to be grateful.

MIRIAM smiles. URSULA smiles.

We were just looking over your noviciate biography, Miriam.

MIRIAM: Hmm.

URSULA: *…the sun rose through my window, casting its glorious light across my bedspread, my wall was patterned with a heavenly glow that the less rigorous minded might have taken as a sign.*

MIRIAM: Did I write that?

URSULA: Yes…

RICHARD looks up from his notes, with quiet surprise.

…My preference is that I need no divine intervention for this is the start of the rest of my life.

MIRIAM: Trust in the Lord with all your heart and lean not on your own understanding; In all your ways acknowledge Him, and He will make your paths straight.

URSULA nods.

URSULA: *(Beat.)* I was just saying you haven't been well.

MIRIAM: What?

URSULA: I was just saying you haven't been well.

MIRIAM: Just a cold –

URSULA: But –

MIRIAM: I'm much better now.

URSULA: But if you don't want to Miriam, if you don't feel like being tested this morning.

MIRIAM: It's never been more important that I am tested, we both know that.

Silence.

Now where shall I sit – ?

RICHARD: Perhaps over here.

MIRIAM nods. URSULA crosses the room, pulling out a chair for MIRIAM.

Just give me a minute and we'll be ready for you Miriam.

RICHARD slides the flash cards SAM has been using earlier off the desk offering them to SAM.

A word of advice. The card tricks? *(Beat.)* Don't do them outside of the study. I've mentioned this before. It reduces what we do to a side stall show.

SAM: If I've offended –

RICHARD: You haven't. But you might.

SAM looks at the article resting on the side.

SAM: You read it.

RICHARD: Yes.

SAM: Was it?

RICHARD: It's fine.

SAM hesitates, nods preparing to set up, RUTH enters.

RUTH: There you are.

RUTH comes over to MIRIAM, starts to lay out cards in front of her, clearly preparing to begin.

URSULA: She's been outside.

URSULA squeezes MIRIAM's hands, concerned as she sits in silence.

Feel her…I'm making more tea.

URSULA makes to go.

Now is there anything else you need, Miriam –

MIRIAM: Don't fuss. There's nothing to be frightened of, Ursula.

URSULA: I'm not.

MIRIAM: Good.

URSULA nods. RUTH and SAM sit with URSULA starting work.

RUTH: Shall we begin Miriam?

MIRIAM: Yes. Begin… Yes…begin.

RUTH and SAM lay out cards in front of MIRIAM, taking notes on a clipboard as she observes –

Silence until –

Biscuit, table, airplane, handbag, dog, envelope, policeman, lake, pencil…

URSULA looking on waiting –

…and… Tambourine.

URSULA moving on.

Act Three

The library.

Later.

Distant sound of television, Newsnight or the like from a distant room.

URSULA enters, crossing the room in the half light, searching amongst the pile of documents resting on the table. URSULA hesitates, leans forward reaching for the Dictaphone. She presses play.

From the Dictaphone, HELEN'*s voice.*

> (On the Dictaphone.) *I was born in Greenock. Though my da was a Corkman. Fifteen words. Punctuated on the sixth and the fifteenth word – End. Predominately monosyllabic bar colloquial pronoun 'da'. I was one of six. Two boys and four girls, a seventh, Michael died in childbirth. The sisters of Poor Clare were running the church school. Come fourteen, my Aunt, Tattie Pol as we were calling her, got us a place.*

> *RUTH enters, not seeing URSULA in the darkness. She scoops up a coffee mug, placing it on her tray.*

URSULA: How's the new arrival?

RUTH turns surprised by URSULA.

RUTH: Richard's tinkering as Audrey shouts instructions from the manual. It's as thick as a brick.

URSULA: One day Audrey will be running this place.

RUTH: One day this place will be a Pizza Express and Audrey will be waitressing.

URSULA: That's not true. The World needs people like you, Ruth.

RUTH: No. The World needs fast food. And now Jonathan thinks he can butter us up, with the latest Apple whatsit.

URSULA: It's just a Christmas present, Ruth. A very generous Christmas present How long are you going to keep this up?

RUTH: What?

URSULA: This disapproval.

RUTH: Why didn't you say us? Why didn't you say 'the world needs people like us'?

URSULA: *(Beat.)* That's what I meant. Did someone drop by to check on Miriam and –

RUTH: Yes, Charlotte's reading to her now.

URSULA: I was just on my way there.

RUTH: She called me Ruthie today. She's not called me that in years.

URSULA: I am going to insist she stays in bed tomorrow. She's not thinking straight.

RUTH: Sam thinks there's a problem.

URSULA: You've talked to him.

RUTH: Yes. He's good to talk to.

URSULA looks at RUTH with a smile.

URSULA: I've seen you chatting with him.

RUTH: What do you want from me, Ursula? Some mornings I look at this place and I wonder what are we doing? For what purpose? A scrubby garden, a few classes a week, this study. I look at them sitting, growing fat, staring at the TV and I want to scream, but… I'm not tempted. I see miracle everywhere. I do, tiny miracle everywhere. *(Beat.)* It's not *me* that's lost my way.

URSULA: What does that mean? What are you trying to say? *(Beat.)* Ruth?

RUTH: Don't flutter around Richard so.

URSULA: Flutter?

RUTH: One day they'll be gone, Ursula.

URSULA: I don't know what you're talking about.

URSULA looks up; AUDREY is standing in the doorway, a computer print out in her hand.

AUDREY: We are officially online. You have a user name.

URSULA: I do.

RUTH: Everyone needs a user name to log in.

AUDREY: Aphrodite. That's your name.

URSULA: You're kidding me?

AUDREY: It was Richard's idea.

URSULA: The old fool.

RUTH exits. URSULA suddenly scoops up a book resting on the table.

Have I ever shown you…?

URSULA flicks through the pages –

Where is it? There…

URSULA pauses on a painting of the Virgin Mary.

I could look at this again and again… I love the way her face… It's luminous. Do you see?

AUDREY: Yes.

URSULA: First painting Miriam ever introduced me to. I used to sit up late and –

AUDREY: It's beautiful.

URSULA: Didn't I tell you, you had an eye?

URSULA and AUDREY silently flick through the art book.

To paint something so – All those brush strokes, it must have taken such sacrifice. It must have been so hard, when there's so much to distract –

Silence. They continue to look at the book.

Sister Aileen used to be a demon for the horses. That's what used to spirit her away. That's why we moved her to the kitchens, we couldn't trust her with the van. Right up until the end, Bernice used to count the change when it was Grand National day. 2.30 at Newmarket, that's what always spirited Aileen away. The trick is getting back. That's what we all battle with sometimes. *(Beat.)* It's a fight. I don't believe it's for you, Audrey.

URSULA closes the book, putting it back.

There are arrangements that can be made.

AUDREY: No.

URSULA: There's a small allowance that we can sub you. Just until you're up and on your way… St Margaret's still runs its hostel, and has rooms.

AUDREY: Ursula –

URSULA: No one is judging you if you don't stay.

AUDREY: Where else would I go?

URSULA: We can get you a place.

AUDREY: I won't last. I never last. Not until here. Please –

I have no one, Ursula. I'm changing. Really I am.

URSULA: Audrey.

AUDREY: I feel for the first time… Not since I was small… have I felt this…but I feel as if my blood is…I'm alive again.

Silence.

I can't leave. I can't.

URSULA hesitates, nods.

URSULA: Then the drinking has to stop.

URSULA gently holds out a hand.

We can't take you any other way.

AUDREY: I'm sorry.

URSULA: It's not a pastime. Not some well-meaning retreat. You will scream inside until your teeth ache with gritting them tight trying to hold it in some days, Audrey.

AUDREY: I want to stay.

URSULA: It's hard –

AUDREY: I'm ready.

URSULA: Sleep on it.

AUDREY: No, I –

URSULA: It's a long life, Audrey.

AUDREY hesitates, nods, makes to exit.

AUDREY: I can only try to be as good as you, Ursula.

URSULA: Goodness has nothing to do with it.

AUDREY exits.

(Beat.) God Bless.

URSULA pulls the Dictaphone out of her pocket, flicking it on once more. She listens.

(On the Dictaphone.) Predominately monosyllabic bar the colloquial noun 'da'. I was one of six. Two boys and four girls, a seventh, Michael died in childbirth. The sisters of Poor Clare were running the church school. Come fourteen, my Aunt, Tattie Pol as we were calling her, got us a place.

URSULA looks up, RICHARD stands in the doorway.

URSULA flicks the Dictaphone off.

RICHARD: It's official, I am a computer loser.

RICHARD stands, pulling his reading glasses off, a computer manual in hand.

Satan's tract. Shall I burn it now or later – ? Jonathan is definitely trying to earn his place up there.

URSULA: Sam says the sisters in Aberdeen were given a minibus.

RICHARD: Sam doesn't know what he's talking about.

URSULA: He promised me he'd swim.

RICHARD: It's freezing. *(Beat.)* You swim too far.

URSULA: You watch me?

RICHARD: You should swim closer to the bank.

URSULA: That's for pussycats.

RICHARD smiles. URSULA smiles.

Will you thank Jonathan. It's very kind, but we don't need gifts.

RICHARD: It's Christmas, Ursula.

URSULA: Still.

RICHARD: You give us so much of your time.

URSULA: Our charity knows no bounds as long as it's after *Midsomer Murders* and before *Newsnight*.

Distant murmur of a television.

Sometimes I think if it was a toss up between watching telly and… Put it this way it would be quite a squabble. My greatest fear in this world is to be left, the last nun standing, remote in hand, shouting quiz answers at the TV screen.

RICHARD laughs, clocking the Dictaphone in her hand.

RICHARD: Helen shouldn't have left that out. *(Beat.)* She's worried you don't like her.

URSULA: Helen? I like her well enough.

RICHARD: I see she's right.

URSULA: It's not that I don't like her it's just… Her analysis is very harsh. She talks about brain reserves… I mean I'm no scientist but to insinuate that the brain has a better chance of survival depending on our education, on the quality of our early lives – Some of these biographies, were written… were written…by sisters who could barely read, let alone write when they first arrived.

RICHARD: It's not definitive.

URSULA: But a sharp brain is a healthy brain?

RICHARD: It's like any muscle. A little exercise can't do any harm.

URSULA: So what do you say to a sister like Charlotte? She can make pastry as light as a feather but ask her about the state of the current economic climate… It could be hurtful to those sisters, to those sisters who haven't worked their minds in the same way.

RICHARD: Do you have fillings?

URSULA: You know I do. I smile, and a ring of steel. We can't all have braces when we're young.

RICHARD laughs. They look at one another, enjoying the moment.

RICHARD: There are a couple of scientists in Michigan who are convinced that the mercury in your average filling can seep into the brain and may be a trigger for Dementia. Then there's aluminium in coke cans. A predilection to cannabis? That won't have helped those cells much. All theories. No positive confirmation yet. A hundred and one different theories, nothing proven yet. *(Beat.)* That's why I don't answer the phone.

URSULA: Now cannabis I've never tried.

RICHARD: You really should.

URSULA hesitates. RICHARD smiles wickedly.

I'll sneak some in next time.

URSULA: How were Miriam's scores?

RICHARD: I can't discuss –

URSULA: Richard.

RICHARD: There is some decline.

URSULA looks at RICHARD.

….Some significant decline.

URSULA: Right… Right…

RICHARD: Ursula –

URSULA: If Miriam's mind is going there is no hope for any of us.

RICHARD: You have nothing to worry about.

URSULA: I'm Geraldine? 1971? You read it. You know I'm...

Silence.

…Geraldine…Geraldine Mary Louise Thomas Grey Hague if one is to be absolutely correct. Though don't ask me why. My mother had a couple of sisters who died young so I know that's why I ended up with a couple of them but… Miriam gave me the name Ursula but Geraldine is my Christian name.

URSULA flicks on the Dictaphone in her hand.

(On Dictaphone.) Tattie Pol said I must. My ma's mind was gone and my da's was close behind.

URSULA flicks off the Dictaphone.

URSULA: You've found your perfect case.

Silence –

Why else do you think I was curious about your work?
I put my file out for you to see.

RICHARD takes the Dictaphone from her.

RICHARD: You're not dead yet.

URSULA: Both parents.

RICHARD: I could take a swab.

URSULA shakes her head.

It doesn't mean you'll carry the gene.

OK so maybe the odds are stacked a little higher. It might
mean –

URSULA: Your study is more important to me than you think.
(Beat.) If Miriam… Miriam had the best 'fighting' brain I
know. Miriam, if Miriam can't survive this then… There is
no one with a brighter mind.

She had a cold in September, it moved onto her chest. She
stayed in bed for weeks. She stopped reading. I noticed a
change when she didn't want to read anymore. And the
laughter… There was always laughter here. She always led
the laughter.

RICHARD: She could be depressed. That can cause some
distraction.

URSULA: The black dog gets us all, but that's not Miriam. You
and I both know that. It's like slowly being evicted from
your own life.

RICHARD: It's a pretty Godless place.

URSULA: If it's Godless, we might as well all renege on the
lease. If Miriam can't survive it –

RICHARD looks at URSULA waiting. She stops herself.

RICHARD: Your life here. This place –

URSULA: Could do with a lick of paint.

RICHARD: Your love and dedication to this place shines
brighter than anyone could ever ask for.

URSULA: Audrey is the first intake we've had in fourteen
years.

RICHARD: That's very difficult.

URSULA: Ah well. She's surprisingly committed to building a life with us.

RICHARD: Is that fair?

URSULA: What do you mean?

URSULA looks at him a sudden tension hanging –

RICHARD: I'm sorry –

URSULA: It must be very surprising to you that a young woman would want this life –

RICHARD: I'm sorry. I stepped out of line.

URSULA: You're Jewish. To you Jesus was just the son of a carpenter with big ideas.

Silence.

Now I've stepped out of line.

RICHARD: *(Beat.)* It comes through the mother's line.

URSULA and RICHARD look at one another. They laugh.

URSULA: There is no justice if Miriam –

RICHARD: It's nothing to do with justice –

URSULA: *Her* faith shone –

The distant ring of a bell, passing just outside of the office.

…shines.

HELEN enters. RICHARD and URSULA pull apart.

HELEN: Sorry, Laura was on the phone. I said I'd get you but –

RICHARD: I'm coming –

HELEN: She hung up.

RICHARD: Right.

URSULA: You should – Tonight, it's very cold…I'll…You should all, you should all have –

URSULA makes to go –

…hot milk.

URSULA exits. Silence.

HELEN: Did you talk to her?

Silence.

Richard?

Silence.

Ursula's file?

Silence.

For God sake. Can we use it?

Silence.

RICHARD: She's not in our age bracket.

HELEN: Both parents, Richard. She shows no cognitive decline. Yet. Admit it you. You are excited.

RICHARD doesn't move.

RICHARD: No.

Silence.

HELEN: Jonathan called. Edinburgh have been onto him again. You need to copy in Sam, Jonathan's already told you.

RICHARD: He's been bleating again.

HELEN: Sam's just ambitious.

RICHARD: And too young for you.

HELEN: *(Beat.)* This from the man whose wife was at high school with my cousin –

RICHARD: I know what I'm talking about.

HELEN: He's brilliant. *(Beat.)* He's got a brilliant mind.

RICHARD: Yeah, and a job waiting for him. I read his article.

HELEN: This is our fourth year, here Richard. Jonathan wants answers. None of us are getting any younger. Sam's just getting a feel for what's out there.

RICHARD: Like endorsing the next magic pill? *(Beat.)* It's corrupting and gives false hope.

HELEN: But blind faith is OK? *(Beat.)* Four years here and nine years before that in the US? That's thirteen years. We could be publishing our findings.

RICHARD: We have nothing conclusive.

HELEN: Even though there is something in what we're finding Richard.

RICHARD: We don't need that kind of press yet.

HELEN: *(Beat.)* Jonathan wants you to go to the Zurich conference at the end of the month. Go Richard.

RICHARD: And say what? That there are things we still don't understand? There are mysteries of humankind that I have no answers for at this current time.

HELEN: We understand some stuff. You could say we understand some stuff – A little flashy piece in the Sunday broadsheet would do us no harm.

RICHARD: About how some dopey Beagle has barked at a picture of a bone that he couldn't recognise last week until that shot of God knows what in his butt got him thinking for a five second dog minute?…Yeah, you're right, that wouldn't be too hard, maybe slip the sisters a quick shot of something. *Dr Richard Garfield recommends* – 'After one spoon of '*I can't believe you've got your brain back*', Gloria can now name eleven types of vegetable a minute instead of ten.

HELEN: Sam didn't write that –

RICHARD: No? But I bet you some schmuck will read it, that's $500 dollars in medication for a month that some poor desperate fuck has to shell out.

HELEN scoops up the last of the papers.

HELEN: I thought it was a fine piece.

RICHARD: Well you're fucking the guy. You would say that.

HELEN: Where did that come from?

Silence.

RICHARD: I'm sorry. That was. I'm sorry… *(Beat.)* If you're happy, then I'm happy.

Silence.

HELEN: *(Exits.)* You should talk to Laura.

SAM: Hey Richard.

SAM enters, looking over some paperwork, smiling on seeing him.

Those pathology reports.

RICHARD: I'm still going over it.

SAM: Only I really would like to compare those Braak scores, so –

RICHARD: Yeah, I'll go over with you later.

SAM: Thank you.

RICHARD makes to exit. He suddenly stops.

RICHARD: Sam, are you leaking our results to Tycon?

SAM: Sorry?

RICHARD: They make aspirin, the contraceptive pill, some of the AZT stuff, the CX516 compound you like to push so much?

SAM: I don't like what you're inferring.

RICHARD: They call. I don't pick up.

SAM: Whatever desire I may have –

RICHARD: Are you?

SAM: *(Beat.)* No.

RICHARD makes to go.

Is it so wrong to want a little more, Richard? To want to share what we're finding here. I wrote an article, no shit and you can be as angry as you want Richard, but I think what pisses you off the most is that you didn't get there first.

RICHARD: I'm a scientist not a journalist, Dr Parker. Unlike you, I'm in it for the long ride. I don't presume I'm going to find answers. It's the act of asking the questions that I believe in.

SAM: Is that why you've agreed to write a book? Good on you Richard. Get a book out before they cut your funding because they will. If we don't start to translate what we are finding here they will move on to some other research programme, to someone who's got the balls to convert their findings into some kind of conclusion, Richard.

RICHARD: So they can use it to licence the next miracle cure?

SAM: Maybe.

RICHARD: Bad luck. We're not there yet.

HELEN comes back in, clearly something forgotten.

RICHARD: You shouldn't leave all this stuff out –

RICHARD hands the Dictaphone to HELEN.

HELEN: I'm sorry, I just –

HELEN hesitates, hands the file to him.

At least think about it Richard.

RICHARD hesitates, exits.

SAM: So it went well then? He won't use her.

HELEN: He won't even ask her.

SAM: So it's true then.

HELEN: What?

SAM: Haven't you noticed the two of them?

HELEN: She's a nun for Christ's sake Sam.

SAM: So was Maria… Have you never seen the movie?

HELEN: Ursula? No.

The distant sound of a bell passing as lights go out –

SAM: I wouldn't be so sure.

SAM sidles up behind HELEN as she tidies away her things. She slaps him away but he pulls HELEN closer, and starts to kiss her, pushing her up against the wall, her resistance slowly turning to laughter. The giggling subsides, as they fall into a passionate embrace.

HELEN: Have you no shame.

Through the half light of the corridor, URSULA stands, a cup of hot milk in her hands. She stops, hesitating for a moment before stepping back into the shadows, watching –

SAM: I leave that to the sisters.

The slam of a book as it falls to the floor from one of the shelves. HELEN looks up. URSULA has gone. A cup of warm milk, resting on the table, HELEN looks to SAM. SAM hesitates, picks it up and drinks. They exit. URSULA steps out of the shadows.

URSULA: *(To audience.)* If you go to the Sint-Jan hospital in Bruges, and visit the old hospital infirmary, it's not in use anymore, but… You will come to the shrine of St Ursula. It's a gilded wooden reliquary in the shape of a small chapel with a saddle roof. Pinacles, gilt goblets, croquets, tralery and tromp l'oeil. But what catches your eye are the six panels painted by the Flemish Master Hans Memling denoting the journey of the young Ursula. From Breton Princess to religious martyr –

I am not a lover of Flemish art.

The first panel shows Ursula, arriving in Cologne, the second in Basel, the third in Rome. The fourth denotes her…I can't remember but the fifth and sixth are the most memorable. In the fifth you have Ursula refusing to denounce her Christian faith to Julius leader of the Huns. Around her stand the ten virgins who have accompanied her on her pilgrimage to Rome, each one representing one thousand other virgins that have also journeyed, a constant at her side for an audience with the Pope.

10,000 virgins, that's some boat.

In the sixth Ursula dies. A thin white whippet sits at her feet. It represents fidelity. Dogs always represent something. The King of the Huns, rebuffed by Ursula and angered that she has given herself to God, shoots her straight through the heart. She's got the most beautiful golden hair, twisted in braids, facing her fate, the last of her virgins still around her, hands splayed. Yes…

URSULA absently flexes her fingers.

…accepting her death. *(Beat.)* If I'd been her I'd have taken the train.

It sticks with you. There's a sister in Cardiff who sent me it on a Christmas Card. I dislike it with a vengeance. It's very …cold…Flemish art. But still. There are 759 schools and churches with the name Ursula worldwide. …My favourite are the Poor Virgins of St Ursula, a sorry group of ladies somewhere in Bangkok who do little conversion but a lot of dancing on tabletops. They were on television. Some of the sisters talk about it still.

Ursula. It's not a perfect fit.

Mary, you're safe with Mary. Angela or Bernadette? I like both of those. But 'Ursula'? Why give me a name like Ursula?

'Because she did not step down.'

There are life's natural heroes and then there are those who prefer to run, when challenged, when truly challenged. I tell myself that faith is all we have if we are to be truly strong. *(Beat.)* I stand before my fourteen now and I think of her. Her hands splayed accepting…

I want to run. I want to –

The distant ring of a bell. URSULA exits.

Interval.

Act Four

The Refectory.

JONATHAN stands lent up against a table, a plastic cup of champagne in hand.

A wide window, the late afternoon sun, shuttered out behind blinds.

An old television on a stand to the left.

A vase of snowdrops, in a jam jar on the table.

It is early spring, two years on.

JONATHAN: Sister Hilary was amazing.

URSULA: She wiped the floor with them, she really did. Didn't she?

URSULA, RICHARD and JONATHAN stand drinking champagne in plastic cups.

RICHARD: Undoubtedly.

RUTH enters.

URSULA: Ruth you had to see Hilary. I said 'you're not nervous.' 'Nervous, I'll have him for breakfast.' Have you taken her some tea?

RUTH: *(Nods.)* She's lying down. *(Eyeing URSULA.)* Are you wearing make-up?

URSULA: You have to wear make-up. On the camera, make-up is obligatory. Even Richard –

RICHARD: *(Beat.)* Just to take the shine away.

URSULA: It was fun, Ruth. Really good fun. Doesn't Jonathan look smart in his new suit?

JONATHAN: My wife warned me you put 10 lbs on on the TV screen. I thought dark might be better. As a scientist one is not prepared for public outings in front of the media. But we are modest people, Ursula we really are. Albert Einstein was well versed in his achievements. When people would ask what he did he would answer 'I changed your life.'

RICHARD and URSULA smile.

Quite brilliant. She was... Really...Hilary. Really Ruth, she is wasted on crochet.

URSULA: Don't bother. Ruth disapproves.

RUTH: Ursula.

URSULA: She fails to see that we are reaching out to a whole world of different people, a wide audience that...we never meet.

RUTH: No. Exactly. We don't meet. But we pray for and we think of and we live our lives for. We don't need to go out and court the world, to tell them what we're doing. They'll find us soon enough.

URSULA: Is everyone sitting down?

RUTH: Well... One or two haven't quite grasped the concept that you can have been interviewed this morning and already be on television by late afternoon. The sisters were worried you wouldn't be back in time.

URSULA gives up on her search, returning to pouring more champagne.

URSULA: Have they all got a glass at the ready?

RUTH nods.

RUTH: Helen's agreed to sit with those in the nursing wing.

URSULA: That's very good of her.

JONATHAN: What has this place done to that woman? There was a time she wouldn't babysit a cat, now she's reading bedtime stories.

URSULA goes to pour some more champagne in RICHARD's cup. He waves it away.

URSULA: Richard was fantastic. Wasn't he Jonathan?

JONATHAN: Made for the camera.

RICHARD: They ask such dumb questions.

JONATHAN: 'So you're actually telling our viewers that those sisters who have done something with their lives, who haven't sat around all day praying, who've stayed active and on the go, they may hold the answer to preventing this debilitating disease?'

I was floundering. Quite frankly floundering but you… Marvellous… The Erroll Flynn of the scientific world… 'I'd rather talk about the study in process. Our data is throwing up certain trends, similarities and correlations with our work in the US but I don't feel that we can positively confirm anything yet.'

We had an eight minute slot, that's longer than most of them.

URSULA: Tell Ruth how many viewers.

JONATHAN: 4.1. /

URSULA: 4.1 million viewers. Could we ever get better publicity? *(To RUTH.)* One young woman watching that – It's life changing.

RUTH: Yesterday they had a woman on discussing training dogs for police dramas and a lady who had just won some prize for… I don't know for quite what. The point is what?

AUDREY enters. She is wearing plainer clothes, a cross around her neck.

JONATHAN: Audrey –

AUDREY: Dr Lees –

JONATHAN goes to greet AUDREY.

JONATHAN: I've not seen you since –

JONATHAN goes to pour AUDREY a cup of champagne, she declines.

AUDREY: October last…I've been away on teaching leave.

RUTH: We have a mission in Ghana.

JONATHAN: That's wonderful. Wonderful.

AUDREY: It's all on our website, you should look it up. *(To URSULA.)* Miriam's gone off again.

URSULA: She'll turn up. *(Beat.)* She always does.

AUDREY: Sister Charlotte is very disapproving of the alcohol. She's taken to her room and refusing to do the Angelus at supper.

URSULA: Charlotte is disapproving of Easter eggs and Maria's Don McLean CD. It's barely a thimble in each cup.

RUTH: I'll talk to her.

AUDREY: It's not just that.

RUTH: One or two of the sisters are worried that your interview might reflect badly on them. Those like Charlotte and Margaret in the garden. The study's findings do point to the fact that those sisters who have not led perhaps such academic or intellectually rich lives –

AUDREY: That's not what's bothering Charlotte.

RUTH: I spoke to her, to insinuate that they have less of a chance of escaping this disease. For many of these sisters, the implication that –

AUDREY: Charlotte's not upset about that. She's read that... she's concerned, she has a brother in Toronto. Since her diagnosis she's afraid that he might worry that he has inherited the same gene.

JONATHAN: There was that question…

RICHARD: APOE gene has three variants. Sister Charlotte's DNA has shown no sign of any such gene. Her Alzheimer's is not inherited. Her brother's fine. *(Beat.)* I'll talk to her.

AUDREY: That's not the only question they have –

RICHARD: I'll talk to all of them.

JONATHAN: Let's hope they cut that bit.

RICHARD: *(To JONATHAN.)* This is why we don't go on TV.

JONATHAN: Don't be ridiculous, Richard. Really it is false modesty. You write a book, you have to promote that book. You have to go on TV.

URSULA: Lets not get dramatic. Audrey, you lead the Angelus tonight. We'll let Richard talk to Charlotte and after supper, we will talk to the rest.

JONATHAN: You do newspaper articles.

RICHARD: I don't like doing those either.

JONATHAN: Well if it bothers you, Richard, you better brace yourself, this is only the beginning.

AUDREY: That's what Sam said.

RICHARD: Sam's here?

AUDREY: He's down with the sisters, now.

RICHARD: How long has he been?

AUDREY: He arrived after lunch.

RUTH: You should see the car.

URSULA: Tell them we'll be down in *(Checking watch.)* ...a minute.

AUDREY and RUTH exit.

JONATHAN: *(To RICHARD.)* He was giving a paper in St Andrews I mentioned if he was passing by... Richard, it's time to let this one lie.
Tycon wanted to see the book, I take it as a good sign if they sent Sam. I've asked the publishers to send over a box of the first print run. They should be here, by, certainly by the end of the day. Your funding cannot last forever, Richard. We have to explore other avenues. And even if it just reminds those who have been giving us money then it does no harm.

RICHARD: No. No. I don't agree. With any of it. Today, yesterday, you invited someone from Tycon here?

JONATHAN: Not just anyone. Sam has been a loyal member of our team.

AUDREY: Ursula –

AUDREY enters, carrying a prayer book.

I was thinking I might read one of the Acts with the Angelus...The Act of Self-Dedication.

URSULA: Nice choice.

AUDREY searches through her book as URSULA recites.

Take O Lord and receive my entire liberty, my memory, my understanding and my whole will. All that I am and all that I possess you have given me.

RICHARD listens, pausing as he does battle with the DVD player.

I surrender it all to you and to be disposed of according to your will. Give me only your love and your grace, with these I will be rich enough and will desire nothing more. Amen.

URSULA catches RICHARD watching her.

JONATHAN: That was beautiful.

URSULA: Yes.

JONATHAN: Would it surprise you to know that I was once an altar boy?

URSULA: It would surprise me.

JONATHAN: My mother had great plans for me. Science was always second best.

URSULA: I never knew that.

JONATHAN: I've never really been able to get a handle on the belief bit to be honest. I go for the smells and bells but – It's the silence that always got me. At least with science there's always something to do, something to give you the illusion that you're heading towards something. My mother could furrow her brows for hours in holy conversation but I –

I admire people's faith, I really do. I'm not even lapsed. You have to actually believe in something and I never have. No voice in my head, no divine experiences. Rationally I can weigh up that there is something out there but – It's just not scientific.

URSULA: And there's the rub. *(Beat.)* Where were you married, Jonathan?

JONATHAN: St Matthew's, Canterbury near my wife's family. I know, I know. Smells and bells. That's what I like.

URSULA: Then does it really matter? *(Beat.)* I've never found him that big on conversation.

URSULA smiles, RICHARD smiles. URSULA exits.

(As goes.) Don't miss your big moment.

RICHARD: Have you any idea what some of these women have wrestled with participating in this? How many have prayed and struggled with what it means to give? We come into this world, in tact, whole and we hope we'll leave it that way. For every sister who's signed up, there is another who has not. I have never asked a sister to defend her reason. In turn I have never felt the reasons to defend my own. *(Beat.)* Until now. So I'll go on your daytime TV show. Maybe even do the odd broadsheet. *(Beat.)* Do I want my face on *Rolling Stone*? I'm not a rock star. I'm a scientist. Yeah, we can be as brutally ambitious as the next man – I do it because yeah, I can't deny knowledge, because it's addictive trying to unravel it all. But do I want to be on. 'Richard and…whatever'? *(Beat.)* I'll leave that to you.

JONATHAN: You know, you really must do something about this shyness. It's not useful in a scientist.

RICHARD: I always saw it as part of the job description. A certain insularity. I think that's what Laura called it amongst the other 'irreconcilable differences.'

JONATHAN: That's not what I hear.

RICHARD stops, turns around, faces JONATHAN.

Ursula must have been very touched by the dedication.

RICHARD: *(Beat.)* She's not read it yet.

JONATHAN: I'm not the best person to talk about marriage. God knows it's not been easy. But I'm still with the same wife.

RICHARD: There are advantages. /

JONATHAN: Richard.

RICHARD: I can eat whatever I like now. Leave towels all over the floor if I want to.

JONATHAN: The first time I met my wife was at a dinner party, nothing particularly eventful. No weird coincidences or stray acts of elaborate fate. I've always felt a little cheated about that. Other people have their stories but we…we just met and got married. It felt like the right thing to do. There are days when I know that my wife does not desire me. There are days when I look at her and ask myself why didn't I take a taxi alone that night? But here we are, forty years down the line. I could no more survive without her than Ursula could survive outside. She will never leave here. Like it or not, Richard, some of us are in it for life.

RICHARD hesitates, sinks down in the chair he has been carrying.

I hope you don't think I'm being too direct. It's only because I like you both so much. And one can always have friendship. In another life there are any number of women I might have married but I didn't. I married my wife.

RICHARD nods.

Sam is going to talk to you about some trials. Nothing too scary, just vitamin supplements etc. It would fund us here for the next two years. We will have been here over seven by then. Some marriages don't last that long. I'd take any offer very seriously Richard.

RICHARD: Two years. That won't even scratch the surface of what we're finding.

JONATHAN: Then we cannot support you any more Richard. *(Beat.)* We're cutting your funding.

RICHARD: I published a book Jonathan.

JONATHAN: With a final chapter that still does not give any definitive answer.

RICHARD: And you think two more years funded by Tycon will do what? – …Mean we can say their product works.

JONATHAN: Yes.

RICHARD: I will not be corrupted or pressurised by a drugs company –

JONATHAN: You are a brilliant scientist Richard, but you should know by now, it's also about being a brilliant businessman. Think about it. What else are you going to do?

JONATHAN makes to go, passing HELEN just entering.

HELEN: No one can find Miriam. Robert's taken the van. I would have gone but I am half a page from the end of 'Daniel Deronda' and the sisters are on the edge of their beds.

JONATHAN: A little bird tells me you have been reading to the sisters.

HELEN: I even crochet some visits. And when it's hot, I've been known to swim.

JONATHAN: I have yet to be converted but maybe if we come again in the summer then.

HELEN: I will hold you to it.

JONATHAN exits.

JONATHAN: *(Calling back.)* You're missing your big moment.

RICHARD: She can't have gone far.

HELEN: I just don't get it with Miriam.
For a mind to have been clearly so brilliant.

RICHARD: Brilliant minds do decay.

HELEN: I flatter myself I have an instinct.

RICHARD: A brilliant young mind may not sustain the course that's all. She's 88.

HELEN: I think it's depression. Depression is –

RICHARD: A symptom, not the cause.

HELEN: I was going to say as corrosive.

RICHARD: Between 15 and 40% of Alzheimer's patients we can track are depressed. It's chicken and egg. You wake up in the morning…you don't where you are.

HELEN: This is a woman who has kept her mind in the health of an Olympian. She should have a fighting brain.

RICHARD: So at best she's depressed.

HELEN: I just think it's sad. Aren't nuns meant to be radiant? I mean doesn't this life have a secret that we all want to hold. It's beautiful and all. You know it is terrible but I really hope it is Alzheimer's because if it's not and she is just depressed then what hope is there for anyone.

RICHARD: It's got to you.

RICHARD smiles –

This place has got to you.

HELEN: No… Yes…I like it…I like coming here. It gives me… hope.

RICHARD follows her gaze out of the window.

HELEN: But all those fields and trees and all that –

HELEN looks out.

…nothing.

RICHARD: Yes.

HELEN: I don't know if I could live with that but I want to believe that they can… That comforts me… That somewhere there is goodness…happiness. Peace…
A merry heart doeth good like a medicine but a broken spirit drieth the bones. It's from Proverbs… One of the nuns was reading it.

HELEN looks up, URSULA stands in the doorway.

HELEN: Miriam still missing?

URSULA: We normally get a phone call –

From far off the ring of a phone –

…about now. She'll be fine. 'Daniel Deronda'… Still?

HELEN: Half a page and I've hated every minute of it.

URSULA holds up a copy of RICHARD's book.

URSULA: Well, now we'll all have something new to read.

RICHARD reaches to take it.

URSULA snatches it away.

URSULA: This is hot off the press. There's a box downstairs, waiting to be signed but I thought –

URSULA searches for a pen, holding it out for RICHARD, opening the book for her to sign but something makes her stop, her gaze falling on the inscription inside.

…I'd get in first.

HELEN makes to go.

RICHARD looks to URSULA.

RICHARD: It's only –

URSULA instinctively raises her hand, to silence him as she reads until –

URSULA: 'For Ursula with love'.

URSULA closes the book, busying herself.

RICHARD: I'm sorry. I should have told you I was.

URSULA shakes her head, tears starting to fall down her cheeks.

You're crying. Why are you crying? It wasn't meant to make you cry.

RICHARD searches for a handkerchief, rifling through his pocket.

URSULA: It's the champagne. Really. There's a reason why nuns shouldn't drink.

RICHARD gives up his search, helpless.

RICHARD: I have a sleeve.

URSULA: A sleeve is… Good idea.

URSULA wipes her face with her cardigan sleeve.

RICHARD: It's just a silly inscription. I can have them take it out. The next press run –

URSULA: No. *(Beat.)* It's –

RICHARD: Really I can.

URSULA: Thank you.

URSULA and RICHARD look at one another, the silence hangs.

URSULA: I couldn't find my toothbrush this morning which of course is worrying particularly as it turned up in my sock drawer but –

RICHARD: I didn't mean.
There is a compound called CX516 that is being developed by the drugs company Tycon. Sam is working for them

now. It's not appropriate for you now but it may be an option at a later date.

URSULA: Richard –

RICHARD: There's also vitamin supplements that I think we should be thinking about.

URSULA: Miriam wouldn't talk to me this morning. I sat with her for an hour and she didn't say a word. Just stared out of the window. At least she was talking last week. I mean not much but…I don't know what to do with her. I don't know what to do if she is not coming back. *(Shrugging.)* The other night I heard Miriam in here eating breakfast, quarter to three in the morning.

RICHARD: Ursula –

URSULA: Ruth has been trying to get Miriam to take communion. She's refused it every day. Not to accept his sacrifice, that would be enough to drive me out of my mind.

RICHARD: It won't happen like that.

URSULA: Dribbling cornflakes down my chin at three in the morning…

RICHARD: It won't change the – .

URSULA: Don't.

RICHARD: …It won't change the way I –

URSULA: You're a kind man but…I can barely function as it. Anymore decline and –

RICHARD: No. I won't listen to that.

URSULA stops, overwhelmed suddenly, the silence hanging between them.

I like our walks.

And our letters?

URSULA: You're a very good… You've been a very good friend to me, Richard.

RICHARD: I live on the fourteenth floor. It's a very small apartment. I have a bedroom, a small study, the kitchen's not a lot to write home about… There's a park, it's not very big, it backs onto a car plant but… It's nice, it's pretty green – I've never lived there with anyone else… I rented it out when Laura – She didn't like the wallpaper. *(Beat.)* She said it made her want to cut her throat. It's about two blocks from a good deli and there's an Italian place I go to Sundays… I like pasta, I've always liked pasta, it's the one thing I cook OK.

URSULA: Right.

RICHARD: Is right a good sign? *(Beat.)* When it's late, and if it's a quiet night, the intersection gets buzzy in rush hour, I can hear the conversation of my neighbour, she's a singing teacher… 84… Sometimes, she sings bits of…I don't know… It's in some kind of language, it's very… I like it… *(Beat.)* Come back with me.

URSULA hesitates, laughs –

I'm serious. Look at this place –

Silence.

URSULA: They'll be waiting to talk to you. You know how excited they get.

RICHARD: Is that a yes or a no, Ursula?

RICHARD slides the book across to URSULA.

I wrote it for you. *(Beat.)* Think about it.

URSULA does not move, the proof of the book resting between them.

RICHARD: It would be something to tell the grandchildren.

RICHARD makes to go, leaving the proof of the book on the table. URSULA does not move. JONATHAN enters.

JONATHAN: Richard, please, they're close to chanting for you if you don't get down there immediately.

RICHARD picks up the last chair, exiting.

JONATHAN: Sam's here.

JONATHAN crosses the room.

URSULA: Lovely.

JONATHAN: I opened another bottle. I hopes that's alright.

URSULA: That's it I'm not letting you drive home tonight.

JONATHAN: I'm hoping to get Richard plastered.

URSULA: Good idea.

JONATHAN: He's a little sore. We've cut his funding.

URSULA hesitates –

URSULA: What?

JONATHAN: I know. But we simply can't support this project if he doesn't accept Sam's offer.

URSULA: Sam's offer?

JONATHAN: Tycon want to fund the study. He's going to have to say yes. Otherwise –

URSULA: What – ?

JONATHAN: He's a fool. He's coming up for retirement. This kind of opportunity won't come around again. Even science has its prejudices. We're all getting too old. And men like Richard, they are nothing without their work. You have to talk to him.

URSULA: Me?

JONATHAN: You can persuade him, Ursula. If anyone can you can.

URSULA: When did you tell him this?

JONATHAN: Just now.

URSULA sinks into a chair.

He's reeling a little, but he'll be fine. The most important thing is he doesn't do anything rash. He's a hopeless romantic, Richard, but truth is it's all about the pursuit with Richard never about crossing the finishing line. It's the essential tension of Richard's life. I do admire that but unfortunately the rest of the world just want a few certainties –

JONATHAN smiles at URSULA.

…in this strange and difficult world? You more than anyone must understand that. Your faith remains so central in the face of the unknown. It makes one feel better to know there are people like you, places like this in the world.

JONATHAN looks at URSULA, with a look of silent understanding…

Ursula?

URSULA: Yes.

JONATHAN: Thank you.

Silence. He exits.

The sound of someone on the approach, URSULA turns thinking –

URSULA: I –

URSULA looks up to see MIRIAM standing in the doorway with bare feet. She is in some disarray.

You've got no slippers on.

URSULA gets up, approaches her.

Your nightdress it's all…

She leads her over to a chair and sits her down, starting to rub her feet.

You know how wet the grass gets. *(Beat.)* Never mind, never mind…let's…like blocks of ice… Here…

URSULA continues to rub MIRIAM's feet. Silence.

Is that any better?

URSULA looks at MIRIAM's hand.

You've been gardening again.

MIRIAM: The bulbs –

URSULA: I'll get Robert to replant them.

MIRIAM: Give them back to me now, I'm not a fool.

URSULA: No one is saying that you are, Miriam.

MIRIAM: Back and forth, with that spade, turning over the earth, when there really is little point. Aileen was the only one who loved that garden. Someone needs to tell the poor man to give it up and we can just let it go. It's gone, Ursula. It's just all gone.

URSULA: No Miriam.

MIRIAM: Can't I see it with my own eyes? Don't I see it every day, Ursula.

URSULA goes to comfort MIRIAM. MIRIAM suddenly pushes URSULA away.

Will no one listen to me anymore? Will none of you just please?

URSULA: We're listening, Miriam. We're all listening.

MIRIAM: Then why can none of you hear what I am trying to say. That this place, that this…place is… It is time that this place…

URSULA: We just did the carpet, Miriam.

MIRIAM pauses, looking down at the carpet.

We chose it together.

MIRIAM: We did.

URSULA: Yes, red…you said that… Physicians used to drape it on the bodies of those with smallpox in the seventeenth century. The colour

MIRIAM: …drew out the blood, like meeting like

MIRIAM calms, sinks into her chair a little.

You wanted ochre but I said orange. So we settled on red.

URSULA: Yes.

MIRIAM: I hope they didn't overcharge.

URSULA: No, Miriam. They did us a very good deal. The underfelt was half price.

URSULA touches MIRIAM's forehead.

You're very hot.

MIRIAM: I'm very frightened.

URSULA drapes a blanket around MIRIAM, taken from a chair.

URSULA: It's alright. You sit for a while.

MIRIAM: Difficult. My breath.

Silence.

URSULA: Audrey's going to read the Angelus tonight. She's a good girl. The first evening I did the Angelus it was Easter and you made me learn the Regina Caeli in Latin and recite it in front of all the sisters when you knew I barely had spoken a word before then.

URSULA pulls the blanket tight around MIRIAM.

She slips in and out of consciousness.

If you want to go out, I can walk with you. Another month and we could go as far as the weir. It's still pretty iced up in parts but when it gets the sun –

Silence.

I swam only yesterday. Sometimes when I'm wading in through the reeds, and it's ten below zero even I wonder if I'm a little mad. Maybe I am. *(Beat.)* Am I mad, Miriam?

Silence.

I don't think I am. *(Beat.)* It would be nice if you said something.

Silence.

Finally I have got Audrey doing the VAT... I just thought I can't let Ruth go and muck them up again... I keep telling her, 'don't put Cherie down as a vatible expense because she may do the sisters hair lovely but we can't get money off it.' *(Beat.)* You know Ruth. Her maths is – You made me good at mine.

Silence.

You missed us on the telly, can you believe that? I could ask Audrey to read the Regina Caeli this year. What do you think?

Silence.

Maybe I will ask her. She's panned out quite well. When she puts her mind to it, she's really a very strong-willed girl.

Silence

I didn't make her stay.

Silence.

This is a difficult life. It's lonely. There is often little reward. You pray and you pray and you never know if your prayers are answered because people don't often ring back and say thanks. *(Beat.)* I did tell her, I made it clear. *(Beat.)* Because you never told me that.

Silence.

The absence is hard.

URSULA bends down, close to MIRIAM taking her hands.

The absence of nothing is hard.

URSULA squeezes tight on her hands.

Miriam?

MIRIAM's breathing is heavy.

Can you hear me?

URSULA grips tight on MIRIAM's hands looking her straight in the eyes.

Why didn't you tell me how hard it was?

URSULA grips tighter onto MIRIAM's hands, twisting them, tighter and tighter until –

(Struggling.) Remember, *O most gracious Virgin Mary, that never was it known that anyone who fled…your protection, …implored your help, or sought your…intercession was left unaided…O Virgin of virgins, my mother.*

URSULA slowly starts to cry, her hands still clenched around MIRIAM's hand, hurting her.

To you do I come, before you I stand, sinful and sorrowful. O Mother of the Word Incarnate, despise not my petitions, but in your mercy, I fly unto you…in your mercy, hear and answer me.

MIRIAM slowly looks down as URSULA sobs into MIRIAM's lap, loosening her grip.

There is no God. You didn't tell me that.

URSULA cries, MIRIAM gently, places her hands on URSULA's head until –

And I hate you for it, Miriam. I hate you, hate you, hate you.

MIRIAM's hand gently slides, her body quietly slumps, her breath growing heavy as URSULA looks up slowly realising –

RUTH: *(Calling through.)* You missed the whole thing, Ursu –

RUTH enters, freezing on seeing –

URSULA holding MIRIAM in slumped embrace.

Act Five

The Refectory.

Dawn. The next morning. Early morning light just scissored through the blinds –

JONATHAN sits smoking a cigarette and drinking coffee. RICHARD stands leant up against the window, a coffee in hand.

JONATHAN: This could be awkward. You try not to admit it to yourself, but I find myself drawn to the tiny pulse of a vein, the fleck in an iris…the beyond, but one is rarely…I have never been here. Only as I'm here – The last batch, there were concerns, they weren't as well preserved as they could have been –

RICHARD: …She's not dead yet.

JONATHAN wavers, goes to speak.

JONATHAN: Very true. *(Beat.)* Deserved. *(Long beat.)* But as I am here –

RICHARD: You're a viper.

JONATHAN: I'm a realist. And a neurologist and I have an interest. There were concerns that the formalin was out of date.

RICHARD: I have seen fourteen of the donations made from the UK convents, three were from here and they arrived fine. I have no complaints. The pathologist is very good. The funeral home very obliging. We don't need to piss them off. They know how to do their job.

JONATHAN: *(Beat.)* You don't have to stand before the board. We have the giants of the pharmaceutical companies desperate to get into bed with this. Not just Tycon. I had an interesting call from Zanden only yesterday, keen to do some anti-inflammatory trials on the sisters in –

RICHARD: You're a whore, you really are.

JONATHAN: It does no harm to flirt.

RICHARD: No you are worse. You pimp us out. You make us all into whores.

JONATHAN: Grow up, Richard. Take the money. Stay in your lab. One day you may just get some kind of a result.

RICHARD: Fuck you!

RICHARD and JONATHAN look up. SAM stands, drying his wet hair, an air of affluence to his dress. He smiles.

Silence –

JONATHAN: So she got you at last.

SAM: Ursula? No. She had me a couple of years ago. The trick is to get up early. When the mist is hanging low and it's just you and a moorhen gliding through. I needed that.

SAM holds out his hand to RICHARD.

Hello Richard. We didn't get to see you last night after –

RICHARD: I had some work to do in my room.

SAM: You sure know how to talk to the sisters. They were enraptured.

JONATHAN: And after that TV appearance.

RICHARD: Oh yes.

SAM: Your book sales will be up 20%.

RICHARD: All royalties go straight back into the convents.

SAM: I'm impressed.

RICHARD: I wrote it for the sisters. They get little funding and you've seen the state of some of the buildings.

SAM: That's one more slate on a very expensive roof.

RICHARD hesitates. JONATHAN heads out.

JONATHAN: I need some coffee.

JONATHAN exits.

SAM: It's very good. Chapter seven, particularly.

RICHARD: *(Beat.)* It needs one or two tweaks –

SAM: Yes, but, on the whole.

RICHARD: *(Beat.)* It's hardly definitive. I'd need more than two years.

SAM: So Jonathan told you – ? Are you going to accept?

RICHARD flicks his cigarette out of the window, making to go. SAM stops him.

Richard, what is the problem? The money was shit, the hours…you know the hours, they were just not conducive –

RICHARD: Science isn't like baseball, you don't get to do it just for the weekend.

SAM: This is interesting. What I do is interesting?

RICHARD: What? A drugs rep?

SAM: You're still pissed off at me.

RICHARD: No, I'm not pissed off.

SAM: You're still pissed off.

RICHARD: Trying to replace you was a headache for months. Ruth is pretty trained up now and Audrey's very good keeping it all in line if we need her – So if I am a little… short with you… We miss you, Sam… You were…you could be very good –

SAM: They made me an offer.

RICHARD: We could have made you an offer.

SAM: Have you seen my car?

RICHARD: You needed a car?… We could have got you a car.

SAM: They treat me very well. I feel I'm doing something. They give me a lot of respect.

RICHARD: I thought it was all that stuff you'd been leaking to them over the years.

SAM laughs. RICHARD laughs, shrugs, suddenly defeated.

SAM: I'm getting married.

RICHARD: My commiserations. I'm not the best person…

SAM holds out the packet of cigarettes to RICHARD. RICHARD takes one.

SAM: Come on…give me a break. *(Beat.)* We're on the same team.

RICHARD: Yours have nicer shirts.

SAM: We can be on the same team.

RICHARD: I don't like match fixing.

SAM hesitates, holds out a lighter. RICHARD takes it, lights his cigarette, hands it back to SAM.

Does Helen know?

SAM: She went back to George.

RICHARD takes a seat.

Any news?

RICHARD shakes his head.

RICHARD: The doctor's with Miriam now.

SAM sinks down in his seat.

SAM: You don't mention which convent the sister is from? *(Beat.)* Chapter seven, it's different from the rest of the book…I mean it's all insightful, it's all a very good analysis of the study but…I don't know exactly but something in the way you write that chapter… It's almost…tender. A sister, with both parents potentially carrying the APOE-4 gene? If we could get her signed up to one of the trials. The data on that could be very interesting to us.

RICHARD: No.

SAM: You won't even consider it? Fuck. Fuck. Do you know what I have done to get this deal in place with this study? Do you know the hours I have spent trying to translate to the goons at Tycon what your research means?

RICHARD: You left the study, Sam. That's as much as you get.

SAM: Tycon would make their gratitude clear. All we're interested in the effects of vitamin supplements on the sisters.

RICHARD: I won't rush this, Sam. I won't. I don't care how much it's worth to you, or Jonathan or Tycon. The last trial was disappointing. I won't endorse anything –

SAM: But if it would help Ursula.

RICHARD freezes, he hands back the proof of the book to SAM.

The sister is Ursula. I'm not stupid, Richard.

RICHARD: Helen told you. If this gets out to anyone, then that is it.

SAM: I'm saying nothing, but you've got to admit…

RICHARD: Back off, Sam.

SAM hesitates, throws his hands up, concedes.

SAM: You have to at least admit there is something pretty magical here.

RICHARD: Magical.

SAM: Sister Ambrose, Sister Loretta… That sister in Missouri…I forget her name –

RICHARD: Philomena.

SAM: All of them, their MMSEs scores going out of the roof and yet they're opened up and…the brain is a mess, they would have been lucky to string a sentence together let alone remember their name. Aren't you curious, that there is an answer in that? I mean these sisters, they have got something we want and when we find it –

RICHARD starts to laugh to himself.

RICHARD: We?

SAM: I wonder sometimes how interested you are in finding a cure for this. You deliberately block any intervention, any genuine desire to capitalise positively from the work here…I think you're scared, because the pharmaceuticals might get ahead, might just get that answer first and then you're fucked. Sure, you'll get a nice pat at the odd convention, but God help us they find some actual way of stopping Alzheimer's. It'll be the miracle pill they'll be praising, and you'll be left with nothing, just this gaping hole in your empty life, Richard, with nothing to fill it.

RICHARD: That is such crap.

SAM: You keep spitting out your tired tirade as much as you like, Tycon is a big company, there are other studies we can do without you. Because when we do find an answer –

RICHARD: It's that you might *not*, that's what worries me, you little prick. That you might *not*.

RICHARD looks up to see HELEN, holding a book and her reading glasses.

HELEN: How lovely, you two, as ever, getting along so well. *(To SAM.)* You look –

SAM: Thanks.

HELEN: …fat.

RICHARD smiles, HELEN smiles.

That was cruel. But it felt good.

SAM: How's George?

HELEN: What can I say? George got new glasses. They knock years off him.

SAM: I'm sorry.

HELEN: I missed the cat.

HELEN goes over and feels the pot, pouring the last dregs into his cup.

This coffee's shit. *(Beat.)* Did the doctor –

RICHARD nods.

RICHARD: He's been with her since four –

HELEN checks her watch.

HELEN: Ursula was very, not herself, there was such despair… Ruth thought it was the champagne. It doesn't agree with me either. Still…

URSULA enters, her reading glasses and the proof of the book in her hand.

URSULA: You're getting eggs. They could be scrambled or poached or fried, Charlottes's sneaked into the kitchen again. Audrey's been trying to ease her quietly out for the last six months, but somehow she always slips her way back in. If you don't let her, she mopes around the place like a neutered cat. Whatever, you'll get something.

HELEN: You look exhausted.

URSULA: I'm fine. I tried to get some sleep at about six but… It gave me the chance to catch up with my reading. There is the funniest scene in the kitchen. Jonathan is attempting to make his own coffee. Charlotte is grinding the bean. It's Nescafé but she's trying to convince him it's real.

HELEN: Any word on.

URSULA: No. *(Beat.)* Ruth's with her now. She wanted Ruth. *(Beat.)* It's a very strange thing watching someone die. It's a slow fade. The breath gets very shallow. I've opened the window. I'll go back in a minute but I just –

JONATHAN enters, carrying a pot of fresh coffee.

What time did you get to bed?

URSULA takes in SAM and JONATHAN, their general dishevelled attire.

No?

SAM: The sister's had us playing whist.

URSULA goes to pour herself a cup of coffee.

URSULA: If you've lost money I've no sympathy.

URSULA spills some, the cup shaking in her hand.

RICHARD: Let me do it.

RICHARD pours her a cup –

URSULA: The mist… It's hanging like a gauze over everything. *(Beat.)* This is my favourite time of the year. Aside from the fact it is my birthday, my true birthday, March is a very optimistic month, filled with signs of the resurrection.

URSULA drinks her coffee.

I've called the hospital. They'll pick her up soon after I presume it will be as it was with Aileen and the Brody sisters? *(Beat.)* …One or two of the sisters don't think you actually take anything out. There's been much heated debate over the years, but the best one put forward was by Hilary who said that you follow the hairline. *(Beat.)* I always worry you might get them mixed up.

RICHARD: We try our best.

URSULA: Because I was thinking – *(Beat.)* I don't want you to take Miriam's. *(Beat.)* I'd rather you didn't.

JONATHAN: Ursula –

RICHARD: No decision has to be made –

JONATHAN: She's signed the consent form.

URSULA: I'm unsigning it.

JONATHAN: You can't do that. Miriam's wishes are clear –

URSULA: And I'm saying no. She doesn't need to be prodded and poked any more.

JONATHAN: You've been such a supporter.

URSULA: Yes.

JONATHAN: May I ask/

URSULA: Don't keep persisting Jonathan, or I'll know you've been visiting for more than just our company.

JONATHAN hesitates.

JONATHAN: I'll have to call the office.

JONATHAN exits.

URSULA: Helen, Ruth was asking if you might read to Miriam, she might want a few minutes relief.

HELEN: Yes of course. Right.

HELEN exits.

URSULA: *(Beat.)* I can't actually do it, can I?

RICHARD: No.

URSULA: I thought not. Then I'm asking you. Please don't take her brain.

RICHARD: She's not –

URSULA: No.

RICHARD: So there's no decision to be made yet –

URSULA: *(Beat.)* How much did you lose?

SAM: A couple of… Twenty pounds… Sister Bernadette said it was for/

URSULA: It never goes in the blind box. You need to get better at cards.

RICHARD: Sam do you want to go and check on –

SAM hesitates, nods, understanding.

SAM: Sure.

SAM exits.

They sit in silence until –

RICHARD reaches out to URSULA, the cup of coffee awkward in his hand.

URSULA: You're spilling your coffee.

RICHARD curses, wiping the stain from his shirt.

It'll stain.

RICHARD: So it stains.

URSULA: Just dab it with a bit of water.

RICHARD: It's fine… Don't fuss, OK.

URSULA: Champagne…does not suit me.

RICHARD: Ursula –

URSULA: Do you know the painter Grünwald?

RICHARD hesitates –

RICHARD: You sent me those tickets, I meant to go…

URSULA: He was German. Sixteenth century. A bit of a mystery. I mean there are doubts as to whether he even existed. But a number of paintings… One painting, of Christ, The Crucifixion, has been attributed to him. It's very unusual because – You really should try some religious art.

RICHARD: I liked that picture of Mary by the cross…

URSULA: It was on a biscuit box you gave Ruth, last Christmas –

RICHARD: They were expensive cookies.

URSULA: Honestly Richard you have no shame…

While the Italians were painting altarpieces of luminous beauty, Grünwald supposedly painted it as it was. Christ is gaunt, palm strained, wounds seeping, Mary weeping at his feet, begging for him to be brought down. And all around the sky is black, apocalyptic. *(Beat.)* It terrifies me but…I used to make myself look at it, tell myself anyone who painted this must know that God exists. He must be sure that the Son of God did come down and that he died for our sins. It comforted me. Next to it Grünwald has painted the resurrected Christ. He's glowing and magical and omnipotent. He's saying… Look one has to go through such pain, such martyrdom, because there's the promise of eternal life. It's a lie…I see now it's a terrible lie… It's propaganda of the worst kind. 38 years I've lived by this lie. This place gets harder the older you get. You start with verve, you feed that verve. You read, you absorb, you learn. You set yourself challenges; you do all you can, believing that somehow it will bring you closer to him. Often I didn't. I have not believed. What saved me is that Miriam did, had the best 'fighting' brain of anyone I have ever known. She would question. She would challenge this. She would encourage me to discover more, to find an answer, but the truth is… Knowledge just takes you further away. It's the darkest place.

But that does not mean I can leave.

URSULA holds the book in her hand, holding it out to him, to give it back.

Faith must remain because it cannot be proven.

Silence.

Thank you. It is a beautiful book.

Silence.

Take the money, Richard.

RICHARD: Did Jonathan – ?

URSULA: Take the dirty, filthy, corrupt and beautiful money. It will buy you a couple more years.

RICHARD: I –

URSULA: Take it. This is what I am.

URSULA holds out the book to him once more.

It's what you are.

AUDREY: *(Calling out.)* Ursula –

RICHARD takes the book from her. AUDREY enters, a copy of the morning newspaper and a pot of coffee in hand.

AUDREY: We made the papers. *(Reading.)* 'West Coast sisters hold key in "contemplative" life.' *(To RICHARD.)* Charlotte's done you breakfast.

URSULA: I'll swim before mine.

AUDREY: Third column.

URSULA looks over AUDREY's shoulder at the paper –

And a photo.

URSULA looks up and sees RUTH –

URSULA: Has she – ?

RUTH nods.

RUTH: I'm sorry.

URSULA suddenly cries. Sudden. Shocking. Like an animal.

ALL: Hail Mary
Full of Grace
The Lord is with thee
Blessed art thou among women
And Blessed is the fruit
of they womb, Jesus.
Holy Mary
Mother of God,
Pray for us sinners now,
And at the hour of death.
Amen.

…letting the tears slowly subside until –

RUTH: Ursula –

RUTH reaches out to touch URSULA, comfort her.

I'm sorry. She didn't know what she was saying at the end.

URSULA: She called out for you. She wanted you. I'd want you too.

SAM enters eating a piece of toast.

SAM: *(As enters.)* They're talking about taking her to St Peters –

RICHARD: Shut up, Sam.

URSULA: It's fine. It's fine. Why else are you here? If you wanted to follow, Robert could take the van –

URSULA makes to go, RICHARD stops her.

Please Richard, let's not…this is why you are here. This is why you come here. To this place, to this shitty little decaying corner of nowhere, nowhere that we have tended and loved and believed in…believe in… How do we believe in… How do I believe in…now…without without…

URSULA sobs, until she is laughing, sobbing and laughing.

I'll swim first.

URSULA makes to go.

RUTH: Shall I call –

URSULA: They're standing by.

SAM: *(Beat.)* I'm sorry.

URSULA: You've butter on your cuff. Samuel. Where did you steal that suit?

SAM: My fiancée… I think… *(Reading label inside the jacket.)* Hugo Boss.

SAM absently wipes as URSULA goes over to the window, drawing back the blinds –

URSULA: That's lucky, he must be the same size as you.

A sea of snowdrops, just visible through the window. URSULA considers, exits.

AUDREY: I'll go and keep an eye out for the –

AUDREY hurriedly exits.

RUTH: *(Calling out.)* Tell Anna Maria, I've laid out her habit and veil –

AUDREY has gone.

Is there any left in that pot?

RICHARD nods, going to pour RUTH a cup.

I better go phone Miriam's family. She has a cousin in Vermont. Please don't worry about Ursula. I know you will but. She's always been more dramatic than the rest of us. Miriam called it her 'artistic' mind. But it will pass. It will come to pass.

RICHARD hands RUTH a cup of coffee. She drinks, following RICHARD's gaze out of the window.

RICHARD: She swims too far –

RUTH: *(Nods.)* Yes.

RICHARD: The reeds, she should swim closer to the –

RUTH: *(Beat.)* She will come back.

RUTH goes to clear up the coffee cups and pot as JONATHAN enters with HELEN. RUTH exits.

SAM: Is it here?

JONATHAN: Just coming up the drive. Why don't you take Helen? I can follow in my car.

RICHARD: *(To HELEN.)* You OK?

HELEN nods.

HELEN: I just read until –

RUTH exits.

You know we pick away at these women's lives and yet I never think about their dying.

JONATHAN: *(Beat.)* We should get going.

HELEN: Yeah –

JONATHAN: Richard –

RICHARD nods.

This one will be interesting…

JONATHAN finishes up his coffee and makes to go.

SAM: *(To RICHARD.)* You coming?

RICHARD remains looking out –

RICHARD: What time is it?

SAM finishes his coffee, and goes to follow.

SAM: Five past, by my watch... *(To HELEN.)* Are you coming with me?

HELEN: OK, but you keep your hands to yourself. I'm a married woman.

SAM: Yeah, yeah, yeah.

SAM makes to go, holding out his hand to RICHARD.

Richard?

RICHARD: Two years. You can have two years.

SAM smiles with surprise. RICHARD hesitantly shakes it.

SAM: We'll be in touch.

The toot of a horn outside.

HELEN: I'll push him out the door when we take a sharp bend.

RICHARD smiles. SAM exits.

I leaked the data to Tycon. *(Seeing look.)* What can I say? Love does strange things to you.

HELEN follows RICHARD's gaze through the window –

I can't see her.

RICHARD points a finger –

RICHARD: She should turn any –

RICHARD nods to himself, a sense that she has.

HELEN: Don't leave me with them too long. I don't trust those two.

HELEN kisses him on the cheek. She exits. RUTH comes in, her coat on.

RUTH: All gone? Never mind. *(Beat.)* I thought I might go with her but.

RUTH takes off her coat.

I'll be needed here. *(Beat.)* Will you be working while you're here, Richard?

RICHARD: No, I fly back tonight. We won't be back here until the fall.

RUTH: I keep threatening to go and visit our sisters in America.

RICHARD: You should come… I could do with someone to help… There's this book tour –

RUTH: Me?

RUTH smiles, surprised, makes to go, bell in hand.

RUTH: I'll go wake the sisters. Charlottes's crying into her scrambled eggs. Someone's got to eat them –

RUTH exits. RICHARD looks back, watching her.

RICHARD: *(To audience.)* In my apartment block, there is an elevator. I travel in it every day. Once in the morning, once in the evening. On occasion it gets stuck. Not for long but enough to feel the cold seep of claustrophobia. If someone is there, I front it out. Cough, adjust my tie, bend down, tie a shoelace, breathe. But if I'm alone, for a moment I lose my mind, I mean really on the edge of losing my mind and then –

That hum kicks in and we're moving again. I flirt with changing my life in that moment, turning it all on its head. In those few terrifying seconds I will be braver, I will work harder, I will live more fully. I will but then… I get out at my floor. As I do every day.

URSULA enters, dripping wet, drying her hair.

URSULA: I swear someone swallows the remote.

URSULA checks her watch, as she goes on a search for the remote control.

I promised the sisters I'd get this mended, before their quiz…

The distant ring of the bell.

When often it's just a simple case of changing the batteries.

URSULA at last finds the remote and aims it at the TV. She tries to turn it on. Nothing.

I normally nick them from Margaret's alarm clock.

URSULA fiddles with the back of the remote box.

URSULA: But today –

URSULA tries to turn on the TV with the remote. Nothing.

URSULA starts to fiddle with the remote –

RICHARD: *(Beat.)* Our study has shown at worst –

URSULA grips his hands, they look at one another.

RICHARD: *(Long beat.)* …even in some of those sisters whose pathology in death have confirmed severe damage to the brain tissue –

URSULA resumes fiddling with the remote control.

…who may have genetic links, who were less educated, whose mother never took folic acid before birth, even in some of these sisters, we have found in life so little cognitive failure that it stuns science – . *(Beat.)* It gets lonely, that doesn't mean it's not out there.

URSULA: I struggle with miracle.

RICHARD: Well for now, I'm sorry Ursula but the miracle is yours.

From outside.

AUDREY: *(Calling out.)* Ursula –

RICHARD: We'll be back in the fall. And the year after. And the year after that –

AUDREY passes by the doorway as URSULA absently rubs the batteries in her hand, pushing them back in the remote.

AUDREY: …did you remember you were going to go over the Regina Caeli with me?

URSULA: It went right out of my head.

URSULA tries the remote again. Suddenly the TV comes on, some inane morning TV quiz –

AUDREY: *(As goes.)* Even if you forget him, he won't forget you, *(Calling back.)* I'm struggling with the Latin…part.

URSULA: You'll love Latin.

AUDREY's gone. URSULA stands watching, remote in hand. The action suddenly freezes.

RICHARD: *(To audience.)* There is a gallery I visited on my honeymoon. It was raining and I remember my wife and I ran in just to get away from the damp and the misery. We stayed for over an hour. My wife was… To be frank, I am not an art lover. She wandered, cooing and smiling, delighting in every corridor. I went in search of coffee.

Standing in line at the cafeteria, there was a painting; it was just above the central door. I remember it struck me. I was drawn to it straight away. I can't even remember the artist. David something… I'm not good with names. I tried to buy a postcard. I looked on every rack. They'd run out. It was obviously a popular choice.

A monk is standing on shore looking out over a wide sea. It's not exactly stormy, but it's threatening and yet there is light. Seeping through the clouds, not in biblical proportions but enough, just feathering the darkness. The monk is tiny, a speck on the sand. I think his arms are out.

When I returned to Chicago, that was where we were living at the time, I tried to get hold of it but –

Life has drifted on, my marriage is long over, we even have a new president –

It is August, yeah August, and I have just come in from work. It's late and I've picked up a takeout. The fan on the air conditioning has broken again. It's like an oven this time of year.

On the door mat is a postcard. I recognise it straight away.

Monk on the Seashore

Casper David Friedrich 1774-1840.

'Sticking close to the bank as I can. Saw this and thought of you. He was big in the German Romantic movement. See you next year. Ursula'.

On the TV screen –

A hostess is standing before a row of letters. The action suddenly springs back into life.

URSULA: Here we go. Here we go.

Suddenly the picture shifts on the TV. URSULA goes forward and slaps it. RICHARD smiles, watching URSULA.

RICHARD: *(To audience.)* Miriam's brain was…there were signs of degeneration… It confirmed what I thought… Obvious Alzheimer's… But you don't die of it… Pneumonia, that's what killed her… Pneumonia got her in the end… Ursula never asked to know…and I never told her. The pathology of a sister is for her alone and… It's a very private affair.

Some nights, when I am sitting in the lab, holding up a slide to the light, I see the wonderment of life in a flash, the tiny plaques and tangles that carry the mysteries of *us. (Beat.)* Ursula comes to mind. It is often late, and the last technician is just checking out. Somewhere in another place –

URSULA: Psephology P.S.E.P.H.O.L.O.G.Y.
(Shouting at the TV screen.) That's easy…that's easy.
RICHARD turns to look at URSULA.

RICHARD: *(To URSULA.)* Let's get you a new TV.

URSULA: Huh?

URSULA goes back to watching the game show. RICHARD watches her.

RICHARD: *(To audience.)* It keeps my faith.

URSULA stands, remote in hand, in front of the TV.

URSULA: *(Shouting at the TV screen.)* Come on, you can do it. Ten letters, from the Greek.

From the TV screen, some inane answer.

It could be worse.

The babble of the quiz show.

Lights fade on URSULA as she stands, remote in hand.

The End.